The 20-Minute Natural Foods Cookbook

The 20-Minute Natural Foods Cookbook

by
Sharon Claessens
(Coauthor of *The Natural Healing Cookbook*)

Design:
Barbara Field

 Rodale Press, Emmaus, Pennsylvania

Library of Congress Cataloging in Publication Data

Claessens, Sharon.
    The 20-minute natural foods cookbook.

    Includes index.
    1. Cookery (Natural foods) I. Title.
II. Title: Twenty-minute natural foods cook-
book.
TX741.C58   641.5'637   81-15729
ISBN 0-87857-375-5 hardcover   AACR2

2   4   6   8   10   9   7   5   3   1   hardcover

To my husband, Mat, who endured the failures, praised the successes, and offered only encouragement in between.

Contents

Acknowledgments

I would like to express special thanks for the inspiration, valuable suggestions and assistance given to me by: Mark Bricklin, who suggested writing the book; Emrika Padus, who edited it; Anita Hirsch, Rhonda Diehl and Janice Kay of the Rodale Test Kitchen staff, who honed each recipe; Marian Wolbers, who honed the copy; Carol Matthews, who researched the book; Barbara Field, who designed it; Carol Petrakovich, Barbara Hill, Brenda Peluso and Diana Gottschall, who helped prepare the manuscript; Robert Warmkessel, who carefully copy-edited it; and Linda Stefanowicz, who helped me to organize my own kitchen more efficiently.

Foreword

Most cookbooks are about a certain cuisine or food: French, Chinese, vegetarian. There are even cookbooks wholly inspired by a machine, such as a food processor.

This is a different kind of cookbook. Its inspiration is not so much a style of cooking as it is a new lifestyle. Or better, a new kind of *person.*

Who is that person?

To me, it's the person who believes that enjoying healthful meals prepared with natural ingredients is one of the most important things he can do to enhance his total well-being. And who sometimes wonders why he's able to do that only once a week.

It's the person who yearns for a life of tranquility and the appreciation of simple, natural pleasures. And yet finds herself busier than she's ever been before—working, learning, traveling, fixing, sharing and caring.

It's the person whose bookshelves are crammed with cookbooks—the pages of which are stained with nothing but thumbprints.

The 20-Minute Natural Foods Cookbook is for the kind of person I see all around me, and the kind of person I am, too.

Never before, perhaps, have so many people wanted so much out of life—and had so little time to enjoy it. Between inflation, two-job marriages and the quest for self-improvement, the momentum of our lifestyle has us all dancing a furious reel of achieving and coping. When we aren't running down the hall to pick up the new batch of computer printouts, we're reading an article on the calming powers of meditation. When we're not taking the kids to nursery school, we're taking the babysitter home. When we aren't cleaning the house, we're caulking it. When we aren't steaming in a traffic jam, we're jogging. And when we aren't doing any of the above, we're rushing to catch the next plane to Jamaica.

Something has to give. And usually, one of the first things to go is the time spent preparing daily meals. An occasional fast meal is one thing, but millions of people today are more often than not having sandwiches, minute steaks, TV dinners or take-out pizza for dinner. *There must be a better way,* we think every night, but the solution seems forever to elude us.

Sharon Claessens's new book is, in my opinion, the "better way" we have all been seeking. It is a bridge between the reality of our frenzied lifestyle and the ideal of honest, natural foods that taste good and are good for us.

It is not a bridge of compromise—or of expensive kitchen gadgets, either—but of sound culinary art and years of experience in preparing natural foods.

Even at Rodale Press, where natural foods research and cookery have been going on for many a moon, Sharon's recipes caused considerable interest as they went through the testing process. At first, people were skeptical that good recipes using natural foods could be made in 20 minutes or less. But skepticism soon turned to excitement. Everyone involved with this project began asking when the book would be finished so they could begin using it in their own homes.

I especially like the idea that Sharon permits us to enjoy certain dishes that simply can't be made from scratch in 20 minutes by telling us how parts of the meal can be made in advance, when we have a little more time to spend in the kitchen. And how other dishes can be prepared in 20 minutes and then left to bake while we change our clothes, read the newspaper or play with the kids.

Another thing I like about *The 20-Minute Natural Foods Cookbook* is that the author doesn't give us 99 ways to broil prime ribs or saute scallops and shrimp. Sure, that's eating quickly and "well," but who can afford it as daily fare? Nor does she ask us to buy a microwave oven or any other expensive equipment that we may not even have room for in our kitchens.

But however quick, healthful and economical these recipes may be, no recipe and certainly no cookbook can be called a success unless the reader actually *enjoys* the taste. Here at Rodale Press, our cookbook chefs submit only their best recipes to our Test Kitchen staff, and each of those dishes is sampled by a panel of taste testers. Interestingly, many of the people chosen for the test panels have no particular love for natural foods. So a natural foods recipe has got to taste pretty darn good to get passing grades. No matter how good the author of the recipe may think it is, if the panel gives it a low score, it's o-u-t. So what we have in this book is not just a collection of recipes, but a collection of winners.

Publication of *The 20-Minute Natural Foods Cookbook* is not an isolated phenomenon. It is, I believe, an integral part of a broad social change I see happening all around us. Wherever I look, I see people finding new, ingenious ways to fulfill their dreams of a more natural life. Not by going back to a caveman lifestyle, or by getting hung up in fantasy, but by building their own imaginative bridges from reality to ideal.

People who dream of an active life in the fresh air but are chained to desks most of the day are finding that half an hour a day of intensive exercise can keep their bodies beautifully toned and energized. People who dream of creating beautiful objects with their hands but whose fingers fly mostly over the face of a typewriter are finding great satisfaction as home craftspeople. People who dream of living on a country estate, surrounded by emerald fields and luscious orchards, are finding that a simple solar greenhouse built onto the side of their present, affordable home is a kind of magic magnet that draws in the vital energy of the sun and turns their house into a shelter where everything natural is right at home.

This book does much the same for natural foods, opening our kitchens and our lives to their healthy magic.

Mark Bricklin
Executive Editor
Prevention® Magazine
Rodale Press

Introduction: The Book in Brief

The heart of this book is its recipes: quick, easy, nutritious and tasty. With that in mind, I'll keep my words to a minimum.

The 20-Minute Natural Foods Cookbook is arranged in three sections. The first and largest section, Make It Fast, contains recipes for dishes you can have on the table in 20 minutes or less. Soups, salads, breakfasts, eggs, main dishes and desserts: choose any of them to make, or round out, your meal.

In the second section of the book, Make It Easy, there is a good selection of recipes that can be *put together* in 20 minutes or less. The only difference here is that some baking or chilling is required. There's nothing that has to be tended, however, so you are free for other activities. Every dish here is table-ready within the hour.

If you can spare a couple of hours on a weekend or evening to prepare food for the week ahead, the third section, Make It Ahead, is for you. I've included fabulous breads, worth every minute of their making, easy stocks, brown rice and crepes. You'll learn how to cook beans in quantity with little effort so you'll always have some on hand for quick meals. I also show you how to store everything, so that when you *don't* have time, a meal is only minutes away. Finally, I offer wonderful recipes in this section which make use of the cooked beans and rice.

Now, take a few minutes to walk around your kitchen. Do you know where most of your cooking utensils are? Can you put your hands on them quickly, almost without looking? Are they convenient to your work area? If not, it's time to do a little reorganizing.

Your biggest time-saver is having things where you need them when you want them. If you are cleaning vegetables in the sink, you should be able to reach a cutting board and sharp knife without walking all over the room.

Place all your items for cleaning and preparing foods close to the sink. Saucepans, skillets and baking pans should be stored between the work area and the stove. Silverware, plates and serving dishes should be stored closest to the dining area.

Have your most frequently used items in the handiest spots, and store rarely used items out of the way. A few drawer dividers will keep similar items together so you won't waste time clawing your way through clutter.

If you like the idea, a large ceramic crock on the countertop can hold wooden spoons, spatulas, a potato masher, a pancake turner and other wares within easy reach of the work area and the stove.

Herbs and spices should be handy to your work area but within easy reach of the stove for last-minute seasoning adjustments. Do not place these directly over the stove, however, because heat destroys their flavor. If you arrange them alphabetically on shelves, or on a lazy Susan with the most frequently used ones in front, you will save time locating what you want.

And last, but not least, keep any leftovers tightly covered in your refrigerator or freezer.

Now, before you delve into the preparation of the recipes, you may wonder what they have to offer, besides being fast.

You can see from the table below that by eating foods in their most natural state, you are limiting your sodium intake. High sodium intake has been

Sodium in Natural vs. Processed Grains and Vegetables

GRAINS	Sodium (milligrams per ½ cup unless noted)	VEGETABLES	Sodium (milligrams per ½ cup unless noted)
Rice		Peas	
Brown rice, *cooked without salt*	3	**Fresh peas**	2
Crisp rice breakfast cereal	142	Frozen peas	92
White rice, *prepared per package instructions*	383	Canned peas	200
Spanish rice	387	Pea soup	450
Corn		Mushrooms	
Fresh corn	trace	**Fresh mushrooms**	6
Corn flakes	126	Cream of mushroom soup	477
Canned corn	302	Canned mushrooms	484
Corn bread *(1 serving)*	490	Potatoes	
Wheat		**Baked potato** *(1)*	6
Rolled wheat, *cooked without salt*	1	Hashed brown potatoes	223
Saltines *(4)*	123	Instant mashed potatoes, *prepared per package instructions*	246
Bread, *storebought (1 slice)*	142		
Waffle *(1)*	356		

SOURCE: Adapted from *Nutritive Value of American Foods in Common Units,* Agriculture Handbook No. 456, by Catherine Adams (Washington, D.C.: Agricultural Research Service, U.S. Department of Agriculture, 1975).

implicated in the problem of high blood pressure. It is recommended here that your intake of sodium remain below 1,200 milligrams daily.

Also, the meals have a good range of natural fiber—linked to healthier heart function and better digestion. Fruits, vegetables, beans and whole grains will provide their share of fiber.

And, I use fresh ingredients, foods with their vitamins pretty much intact—not processed out of existence. Whole grains repeat the story. I don't call for white flour and white rice, foods that have been stripped of their bran, minerals and nutrients, then "enriched" with a token few of them.

There are many reasons why I can recommend the recipes in this book. But one of the most important is this: they taste so good. Enjoy them!

Gearing Up: Equipment

My list of kitchen equipment is short. I do not depend on lots of mechanical genies in the kitchen to create quick meals. In fact, if you have access to any kitchen, no matter how small, the recipes in this book are suitable for you.

Oh, you may have to do a bit of improvising: a metal colander inside a kettle if you have no steaming basket, or a stainless steel bowl set inside a pot in place of a double boiler. Ovenproof mugs can replace custard cups for baking.

I do suggest a few items that will make your work in the kitchen faster and easier. One is a set of sharp knives, and a sharpener to keep them that way. A set of ovenproof casseroles that can also be used atop the stove, such as enameled cast iron, saves time since you can bring ingredients to a boil before placing them in a hot oven.

Because the recipes here frequently call for garlic, I suggest buying a good, and I emphasize *good,* garlic press. Some cooks think it takes too long to clean the garlic press after it has been used. Actually, you can clean out the press in seconds. Place the *unpeeled* garlic clove in the press. After the garlic has been pushed through, remove the garlic peel from the inside of the press. Most of the garlic that remains in the holes will cling to the skin and can be removed at once. Then, using a nylon fingernail brush (available at any five and dime store), poke the bristles through the holes from the outside to dislodge any remaining garlic. Rinse. Voilà! In 15 seconds, the garlic press is clean. (I have included enough time in the recipes for you to clean the press while you work so the garlic doesn't dry and stick.)

Incidentally, that fingernail brush is a very useful and inexpensive piece of kitchen equipment. In addition to cleaning garlic presses, it can be used to remove grated lemon or orange peel from the fine teeth of a grater. So be sure to keep a fingernail brush close at hand by the kitchen sink.

Here is a list of some basic items for the kitchen:

8 × 8-inch baking dish
9 × 13-inch baking dish
baking sheet
blender
8½ × 4½-inch bread pans
medium and large flameproof, ovenproof casserole dishes
cheesecloth
colander
crepe pan
cutting board
electric mixer
fingernail brush
garlic press
grater with fine, medium and large holes
large kettle
measuring spoons and cups
small, medium and large mixing bowls
nutmeg grater
9-inch pie plate
small roasting pan, for oven-cooking beans
small, medium and large saucepans
sharp knives
small, medium and large skillets
medium souffle dish
spatula
vegetable brush
wire whisk
wooden spoons

Stocking Up: Ingredients

You are probably familiar with most, if not all, of the ingredients used in this book. Included here are just a few words on some of the items, along with hints on buying and storing them.

AGAR-AGAR: This is a vegetable gelatin made from sea algae. It is available in health food stores and oriental food shops.

BAKING POWDER: Choose a brand made without aluminum compounds. There is some evidence that ingested aluminum accumulates In the brain and could, over time, cause memory loss and brain deterioration. Aluminum-free baking powder is available in health food stores and some supermarkets. This leavening agent should be stored tightly covered in a cool, dry place.

BAKING SODA: A leavening agent which depends on acid in a recipe, such as lemon juice or buttermilk, to be effective. Store in a cool, dry place.

BAKING YEAST: Purchase in bulk at a health food store if you plan to bake often. Dry yeast keeps well if stored tightly covered in a cool, dry place. One tablespoon is equal to the small packets available in supermarkets.

BRAN: I use wheat bran, the hull of the wheat berry, which is discarded in the milling of white flour. It is valuable as a source of fiber. Store in a cool, dry place.

BREWER'S YEAST: This yeast has no leavening powers, but it is valuable as a source of B vitamins and is high in protein. It is available at health food stores. If you like, you can add brewer's yeast to bread, cereals, pancakes and casseroles. Store in a cool, dry place. Some prefer yeast "flakes," which have a milder taste. Find the nutritional yeast you like best.

BUCKWHEAT FLOUR: Unlike wheat and rye, buckwheat is not a grain; it is the fruit of a plant similar to rhubarb. The whole, dark flour adds a characteristic flavor to pancakes. Store tightly wrapped in the refrigerator.

BULGUR: Parboiled, dried and cracked wheat, quick-cooking bulgur can be used in place of brown rice or potatoes as a side dish. It is available in health food stores. Bulgur should be stored tightly covered in a cool, dry place.

BUTTERMILK: Low in calories and butterfat, this cultured milk contains enough acid to interact with baking soda to leaven baked goods. Buttermilk also tenderizes the crumb of yeast breads. It should be stored in the refrigerator.

CAROB POWDER: Resembling chocolate in taste, carob is also called St. John's bread. The powder is made by grinding the carob pods. Carob is naturally sweet, high in fiber and low in fat, and it contains appreciable amounts of calcium. While chocolate contains caffeine and often sparks allergic reactions, carob, a legume, does not. Carob powder is available in health food stores and should be tightly covered and stored in a cool, dry place.

CHEESES: Only unprocessed cheeses have been included in this book. Avoid products labeled "processed cheese" or "cheese food." When choosing cottage cheese, look closely at the ingredients and stick to those without additives. Keep cheese wrapped and refrigerated.

CORNMEAL: Choose stone-ground, whole grain cornmeal, and store in the refrigerator, tightly wrapped.

CORN TORTILLAS AND TACOS: Because these are difficult to make at home without just the right kind of cornmeal and the proper equipment, I recommend they be purchased at the supermarket. Most brands are made simply from cornmeal, water and lime, with no preservatives and, many times, no salt. Tortillas are often found in the dairy case or freezer and should be refrigerated. Store the tacos, wrapped, in a dry place.

DRIED FRUITS: Fruits that are naturally dried, without preservatives or coloring agents, are best. Store in a cool, dry place.

DRIED PEAS AND BEANS: Choose legumes that are uniform in color, without the fading that would reveal they are quite old. Legumes can be balanced with whole grains, nuts, seeds or dairy products to provide complete, valuable protein for pennies a pound.

HERBS: If you are trying to cut back on salt, make friends with herbs! They will give your meals color and flavor while you look after your health. Grow your own, or purchase them fresh or dried. Always keep a bunch of fresh parsley in the refrigerator to use while cooking or as a vitamin-rich and colorful garnish. To refrigerate the parsley, wrap in a damp paper towel and place in a plastic bag, or put the stems into a glass of water.

HONEY: Although honey is used in place of white sugar in this book, honey is still a potent sweetener and should be used sparingly. Store in a covered jar in a cool, dry place. If kept in the refrigerator the honey may crystallize, which does not spoil the honey but makes it more difficult to use.

LECITHIN: This is my indispensable friend when it comes to lightly oiling bread pans and casserole dishes. A drop or two of liquid lecithin along with a little corn or sunflower oil can be spread over baking surfaces, creating a very effective nonstick coating.

MOLASSES: Medium unsulfured molasses can be substituted for honey in most recipes without changing their taste. Molasses, especially blackstrap molasses, is rich in minerals. Both can be found in health food stores and should be stored in a cool, dry place.

NUTS: Choose fresh, unsalted nuts. When unshelled, nuts can be stored in a cool, dry place. Refrigerate nuts that have been shelled.

OATS: Rolled oats are made from groats that have been hulled, then steamed and rolled flat. They are highest in protein among the cereals. Store in a cool, dry place.

OILS: Safflower, sunflower, soy or corn oils can be used interchangeably for cooking or salads. Sesame oil and olive oil have distinctive flavors, olive oil being especially nice for salads. Avoid cottonseed or coconut oils, both of which are high in saturated fat. Anything marked "vegetable oil" might contain one or both of these.

PASTA: I call for whole wheat pasta, but you may want to try spinach or artichoke pasta as well. These have a milder taste and, if you are not a whole wheat pasta fan, may taste more like what you are used to while you move toward a more natural diet.

RICE: Brown rice, with nutrients and fiber intact, is the rice to buy. It is available in either long or short grain. Supermarkets often carry long grain brown rice. Store in a cool, dry and dark place.

SEAFOOD: Once frozen fish has been defrosted, do not refreeze it. Use fresh fish within a day or two of purchase. Do not overcook fish; as soon as the translucent flesh turns opaque, it is done. When using water-packed red salmon, crush the soft bones and combine with the flaked fish for added calcium.

SEEDS: Buy seeds at the health food store, where they are available untreated and in bulk. They should be raw and unsalted for best use in recipes. Seeds can be stored tightly covered in the refrigerator if they have been hulled (such as sunflower seeds) or in a cool, dry place if they are unhulled.

SESAME TAHINI: Made of ground, hulled sesame seeds, tahini is an oily paste used in some Middle Eastern dishes. It can be used in sandwich spreads and dips. Available in health food stores and ethnic shops, tahini should be stored in a cool place or in the refrigerator if it is not used frequently.

SPROUTS: Do not sprout seeds, beans or grains that have been fumigated or treated with chemicals (as are seeds meant for planting). Instead, grow sprouts with seeds meant for human consumption; they can be purchased in quantity at health food stores.

TAMARI: I use tamari in these recipes in place of salt, but it is used sparingly because of its high sodium content. This soy sauce is a traditional oriental flavoring, made from fermented soybeans. Avoid popular commercial brands, which are produced by chemical means. Tamari, or naturally fermented soy sauce, is available in health food stores and ethnic shops. Store on the shelf.

WHEAT GERM: This is the heart of the wheat, rich in protein, B vitamins, vitamin E, iron, potassium and zinc.

WHOLE WHEAT FLOURS: Whole grain flour is used throughout this book because it is far higher in nutritive value and valuable fiber than white flour. To measure, spoon lightly into a measuring cup or sift, then measure, adding the bran that was sifted out. Whole wheat pastry flour differs from whole wheat bread flour (designated in the book as simply "whole wheat flour" and used as an all-purpose flour): pastry flour is made from soft spring wheat, while bread flour is made from hard winter wheat. Pastry flour contains little or no gluten, which gives dough its "stretchy" quality, so it cannot be used for yeast breads, but it is perfect for creating the crumbly textures required in quick breads and in cakes. Store flours in moisture-proof containers in the refrigerator.

Coming to Terms: Glossary

BAKE: To cook in an oven. It is recommended that oven temperatures for breads baked in glass be set 25°F lower than for those baked in aluminum; our recipes are based on baking in an aluminum pan. A mixture of a few drops of corn or sunflower oil and a few drops of liquid lecithin smoothed over baking surfaces guarantees stick-free baking.

BEAT: To mix vigorously with a motion that lifts the mixture over and over onto itself in order to incorporate air. Whites are most easily beaten when they are at room temperature. When using an electric mixer, start on a low speed, then work up to medium or high speed as the eggs become frothy. Utensils must be clean and dry, and there must be no speck of egg yolk mixed in with the whites. The whites should be shiny and should stand in peaks when beaten.

BOIL: To cook food in liquid at 212°F. Many bubbles of steam rise and break the surface in a boiling liquid.

BROIL: To cook with direct radiant heat.

CHOP: To cut into pieces.

CUBE: To cut into square pieces.

DICE: To cut into small, square pieces.

FOLD IN: To add an ingredient, such as beaten egg whites, gently, in order to hold the air bubbles in the mixture. A rubber spatula can be used; it is pushed through the middle of the mixture, then brought up one side of the bowl, allowing the mixture to gently fall back over onto itself.

GARNISH: To add a decoration.

GRATE: To shave off particles of food by rubbing the food over a grater.

MINCE: To cut or chop extremely fine.

PEEL: To remove the skin of a fruit or vegetable.

POACH: To cook in a liquid under the boiling point at a very gentle simmer so that the water barely moves.

XXV

ROAST: To cook with dry heat, usually in an oven.

SAUTE: To cook thinly sliced or minced foods quickly in an open pan in heated butter or oil.

SCALD: To heat to just below the boiling point, when small bubbles appear where the liquid touches the pan.

SHRED: To cut into very thin strips, such as with cabbage, or to rub over the largest holes of a grater.

SIMMER: To cook a liquid or a food in a liquid just at the temperature (about 185°F) where bubbles come gently to the surface.

STEAM: To place food above boiling water, where it is surrounded and cooked by steam.

STIR: To mix ingredients with a circular motion.

STIR-FRY: To cook small pieces of food in hot oil, usually in a wok, moving the food around as it cooks. The term is generally associated with Chinese food.

WHIP: To beat rapidly to incorporate air into an ingredient, such as cream. For whipping cream, the beaters, bowl and cream itself should be well chilled.

Make It Fast

When my editor first suggested this book, I spent about an hour expressing my views that people should become more familiar with their foods, take the time to prepare dishes lovingly, and painstakingly plan their menus. By the time I left his office, my position elaborately expressed, I found I had exactly an hour to get home, prepare dinner, eat with my husband, and get both of us off to a seminar on organic gardening. My poetic feelings about relating to raw ingredients faded fast in the flurry.

Luckily, I had cooked some beans the weekend before, and I put together a tasty tortilla dinner in 20 minutes flat! So through a baptism by fire, I became the first of the ardent supporters of this book's concept: Cook it well, and fast.

Because I was able to get our meal on the table so quickly, my husband and I had some time together at the end of a busy day. My leisure time, as little as I had on that particular occasion, was spent relaxing with him, not in the kitchen. And the meal we ate, rich in vitamins, minerals and fiber, never suffered for our cramped schedule. And that meant we had the energy to take on more that day.

In this section, the largest in the book, I'll show you how to make it fast. (Bean recipes are in the last section of the book. There's no need to have them on hand for any of the recipes here.) When you want to eat well, but *now,* flip through any of these pages. You can be savoring a soup, digging into a dip, enjoying the flavor of a frittata or simply snacking—in minutes.

Each recipe is accompanied by a stylized clock. The black band on the clock face shows how many minutes it will take to prepare the recipe.

These recipes will work *with* your busy schedule to set you free so you can spend your time as you like: enjoying your family, reading a good book or walking in the rain.

Breakfasts

Creamy Cheesy Scrambled Eggs *Makes 2 servings*

Serve with fresh fruit and whole wheat toast.

1. Melt butter in a medium skillet over low to medium heat. Pour in the eggs, and stir gently from time to time as the eggs cook.

2. When the eggs are about half done, stir in the cottage cheese and distribute evenly. Cook another minute or two, until the eggs are cooked through, but still moist, then serve.

1 tablespoon butter
3 eggs, beaten
¼ cup cottage cheese

Whole Wheat Waffles *Makes 2 servings*

Serve with applesauce or fresh fruit topping. Bring the waffle iron to the table and cook them as you eat.

1. Place the flour, baking soda and cinnamon in a medium mixing bowl. In a smaller bowl, beat the egg and add the buttermilk and oil. Heat the waffle iron.

2. Stir the egg mixture into the dry ingredients just until combined.

3. Bake the batter on a lightly oiled hot waffle iron, and serve.

Note: Waffles can also be served at dinner as a main dish, topped with *Creamed Tuna and Peas* (page 50).

1 cup whole wheat flour
1 teaspoon baking soda
½ teaspoon cinnamon
1 egg
1 cup buttermilk
2 tablespoons corn oil

3

Makes 2 servings # French Toast

2 eggs
½ cup heavy cream
½ teaspoon vanilla extract
½ teaspoon cinnamon
4 slices whole wheat bread
fresh fruit
maple syrup

1. Beat the eggs in a shallow bowl. Add the cream, vanilla and cinnamon.

2. Cut the bread slices into halves, and dip them into the egg mixture. Let the bread soak about a minute.

3. Lightly oil a large heavy-bottom skillet or griddle, and cook the bread on both sides until golden brown.

4. To serve, chop fresh fruit, in season, and scatter over the French toast. Drizzle with maple syrup.

Makes 2 servings # Buttermilk Pancakes
Light and tasty.

1 cup whole wheat flour
1 teaspoon baking powder
½ teaspoon baking soda
2 tablespoons melted butter
2 eggs, beaten
1½ cups buttermilk
maple syrup or fresh fruit

1. Mix together the dry ingredients in a medium bowl. Add the butter, eggs and buttermilk to make desired consistency.

2. Bake on a lightly oiled griddle, turning pancakes when bubbles have appeared on the unbaked surface. Serve with maple syrup or fresh fruit.

Makes 2 servings # Hearty Wheat Pancakes
A breakfast to cheer you any day.

1 cup whole wheat flour
½ cup wheat germ
2 teaspoons baking powder
1 egg
1½ cups milk
2 tablespoons safflower oil
maple syrup or fresh fruit

1. Place the flour, wheat germ and baking powder in a large bowl and stir together.

2. Beat the egg in a small bowl. Add it along with the milk and oil to the dry ingredients. Stir just until combined.

3. Heat a large, lightly oiled skillet or griddle, and make four pancakes at a time. Keep the first four warm while cooking the last four pancakes. Serve immediately with syrup or fruit topping.

Blueberry Pancakes with Blueberry Topping
Makes 2 servings

Fresh blueberries for breakfast? Who wouldn't love 'em?

1. Combine the dry ingredients in a medium bowl.

2. Stir the milk into the egg, then add the mixture to the dry ingredients, also adding ¾ cup of the blueberries. Stir with a spatula just until the ingredients are combined.

3. Pour the batter on a lightly oiled griddle, about ¼ cup of batter for each pancake. Turn when bubbles appear on the surface. When first batch of pancakes is done, keep them warm while preparing remaining pancakes.

4. To prepare topping, combine remaining blueberries with the maple syrup in a blender. Process on medium speed until combined. The topping can be heated in a small pan over low flame, if desired.

5. Serve pancakes with blueberry topping.

1 cup whole wheat flour
¼ cup wheat germ
1 teaspoon baking powder
¼ teaspoon cinnamon
1¼–1½ cups skim milk
1 egg, beaten
2 cups blueberries
2 teaspoons maple syrup

Buckwheat Pancakes
Makes 2 servings

If you enjoy the special flavor of buckwheat, you'll love digging into these!

1. Place the flours and the baking soda in a medium mixing bowl. Combine well.

2. Add the buttermilk, egg and oil. Stir together.

3. On a lightly oiled griddle, bake the pancakes, turning when bubbles appear across the surface of each. Serve with maple syrup or fresh fruit.

½ cup buckwheat flour
½ cup whole wheat flour
½ teaspoon baking soda
1½ cups buttermilk
1 egg, beaten
2 tablespoons sunflower oil
maple syrup or fresh fruit

Makes 2 servings # Fruited Maple Porridge
This is a hands-down favorite!

1½ cups water
½ cup bulgur
2 tablespoons pitted dates
2 tablespoons raisins
2 teaspoons maple syrup
milk

1. Place the water and bulgur in a small saucepan over medium heat. Chop the dates and add with the raisins and maple syrup to the water and bulgur.

2. Bring mixture to a boil, then reduce heat and simmer about 10 minutes, until the bulgur is soft. Serve hot with milk.

Makes 2 servings # Date-Molasses Porridge
A nice change for breakfast.

1½ cups water
3 tablespoons pitted dates
⅔ cup rolled oats
2 tablespoons wheat germ
1 tablespoon medium
    unsulfured molasses

1. Place the water in a medium saucepan over high heat and bring to a boil. Meanwhile, chop the dates and add to the water.

2. When the water is boiling, add the oats, wheat germ and molasses. Stir and bring to a boil, then reduce heat and simmer until thickened.

3. Remove from heat, cover, and let stand a minute or two. Serve hot.

Makes 1 serving # Ricotta Sundae
A wonderful way to treat yourself for breakfast. Or try it for lunch. Either way, you won't have to feel guilty about calories!

1 small, ripe banana
½ cup ricotta cheese
¼ cup seedless grapes, halved
1 teaspoon wheat germ
1 teaspoon bran
¼ teaspoon cinnamon
½ cup sliced strawberries
2-3 tablespoons yogurt
1 tablespoon chopped walnuts
1 whole strawberry with stem,
    garnish

1. Cut the banana in half lengthwise, and place the halves in a bowl.

2. Combine the ricotta with the grapes, wheat germ, bran and cinnamon. Form into a "scoop" and set in the middle of the banana halves.

3. Top with the sliced strawberries, then drizzle with yogurt. Sprinkle with walnuts, top with the whole strawberry and eat up!

Breakfast Cereal Mix   *Makes 4 cups*

Not only can you prepare a custom-made cereal mix in 5 minutes, but you'll have enough made up to last a week of mornings! Following this recipe are additional recipes that can be made in minutes with this mix.

1. Combine the ingredients in a large bowl.

2. Place the mix in a tightly covered container and store in the refrigerator.

Note: Serve mix as any other cereal, or toss with chopped fresh fruits instead of adding milk. There will be plenty of moisture in the fruit to complement the cereal.

Variations: Customize your mix by adding a few tablespoons of seeds, such as sesame or sunflower, or by adding chopped nuts.

2 cups rolled oats
1 cup bran
½ cup wheat germ
½ cup soy flakes
½ cup raisins
1 tablespoon brewer's yeast
   (optional)
2 teaspoons cinnamon (optional)

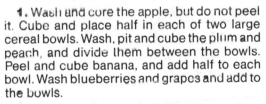

Mixed Fruit Cereal Bowl   *Makes 2 servings*

This is a special treat in late summer, when a variety of colorful fruits is available.

1. Wash and core the apple, but do not peel it. Cube and place half in each of two large cereal bowls. Wash, pit and cube the plum and peach, and divide them between the bowls. Peel and cube banana, and add half to each bowl. Wash blueberries and grapes and add to the bowls.

2. Sprinkle each of the bowls of fruit with ½ cup of the cereal mix. Top with yogurt and sprinkle with chopped walnuts.

Note: To serve four, make the same amount, but serve it with whole grain toast spread with ricotta cheese.

Variation: At other times of the year, seasonal fruits can be used: strawberries, cherries, oranges, pineapple, nectarines and pears.

1 apple
1 plum
1 peach
1 banana
¼ cup blueberries
¼ cup seedless grapes
1 cup *Breakfast Cereal Mix*
   (above)
1 cup yogurt
¼ cup chopped walnuts

Buttermilk-Raisin Pancakes with Fresh Fruit Sauce

Makes 2 servings

⅔ cup *Breakfast Cereal Mix* (page 7)
⅓ cup whole wheat flour
½ teaspoon baking soda
1 egg
1 tablespoon sunflower or soy oil
1 cup buttermilk or yogurt
1 apple, cored and chopped, or 1 banana, sliced
½ cup apple juice or other fruit juice
2 tablespoons honey

1. Combine the cereal mix and flour in a large bowl, and stir in the baking soda.

2. In a small bowl, beat the egg. Stir in the oil and buttermilk or yogurt.

3. Add the egg mixture to the dry ingredients and stir lightly until combined.

4. Pour the batter into a large, lightly oiled skillet, using about ¼ cup batter for each pancake. Turn pancakes when bubbles appear on the surface.

5. To prepare the fruit sauce, place the apple or banana in a blender with the apple juice or fruit juice and honey. Blend on medium speed until smooth.

6. Serve pancakes hot with fruit sauce on the side.

Hot Raisin Breakfast Cereal

Makes 1 serving

On cold mornings you can have a protein-rich, hot breakfast in a flash. You might want to add fresh fruit slices to the cereal after cooking.

⅔ cup *Breakfast Cereal Mix* (page 7)
1¼–1½ cups water
3 tablespoons raisins

1. Place the cereal mix, water and raisins in a medium-size saucepan. Bring to a boil, stirring, and reduce heat.

2. Simmer until creamy, about 4 to 5 minutes.

German Omelet   *Makes 2 servings*

Cousin to the crepe and the familiar pancake, this dish boasts its own unique character. Delicious plain or filled.

1. Place the eggs, milk, flour and nutmeg, if desired, in a blender. Process on low speed until smooth.

2. Melt half the butter in an omelet pan and when the butter has stopped foaming and is hot, add half the egg batter. Swirl the pan and as you do, pull the edges of the omelet toward the center of the pan, using a knife. Keep swirling to get new batter to the outside of the pan.

3. When the omelet is golden brown on the bottom and no longer runny on top, fold it and slip it onto a serving plate. Repeat with the remaining butter and egg batter, quickly remixing the remaining batter on medium speed in the blender before pouring into the pan.

Variations: Fill the omelets with sweet or savory fillings before folding. Possibilities include cooked chicken, mushrooms or other vegetables, poached fruits, applesauce or other fruit sauces.

3 eggs
⅓ cup skim milk
2 tablespoons whole wheat flour
dash of grated nutmeg (optional)
2 teaspoons butter

Appetizers & Hors d'Oeuvres

Fruit Fondue   *Makes 12 servings*

Make more or less, depending on the size of your group. This also makes a fine dessert.

1. Peel the pineapple, remove the core, and cut the pineapple into bite-size chunks. Hull the strawberries, leaving them whole. Remove stems from grapes.

2. Arrange the fruit in alternating "spokes" on a round platter.

3. With a wooden spoon, cream together the cream cheese and yogurt with the honey. Place in a small bowl in the center of the serving dish. Garnish plate generously with mint sprigs. Provide toothpicks for dipping the fruit into the yogurt mixture.

Note: Cover the entire plate with plastic wrap and chill if fruit is not being served immediately.

Variations: Use apples, cut in large cubes. Slice bananas on the diagonal and dip lightly in lemon juice to prevent browning. Try cubed melon or melon balls. Serve a side dish of chopped walnuts into which the fruit can be dipped after it is coated with the yogurt mixture.

1 pineapple
1 quart strawberries
1 pound seedless grapes
½ cup cream cheese
½ cup yogurt
2 teaspoons honey
mint sprigs, garnish

Makes 4 servings **Fresh Fruit Cocktail**

Attractively served in a hollowed-out grapefruit half, this dish can serve as an appetizer or a dessert.

2 pink grapefruit
1 large banana
½ cup seedless grapes
½ cup sliced strawberries, sliced peaches, pitted cherries or blueberries
honey (optional)
whole strawberries or other berries, garnish
mint sprigs, garnish

1. Cut each grapefruit in half across. Section each of the halves, remove the grapefruit pieces, and place them in a medium bowl. Carefully remove the membranes without tearing the grapefruit skins.

2. Slice the banana diagonally. Add it to the grapefruit pieces along with the grapes and sliced strawberries, peaches, cherries or blueberries. Add a little honey to the fruit, if desired, and toss.

3. Place the mixed fruits in the hollowed-out grapefruit halves. Top with some of the whole berries, and garnish with mint sprigs.

Makes 1 cup **Guacamole Dip**

2 medium, ripe tomatoes
1 large avocado
2 tablespoons chopped red onions or scallions
1 tablespoon fresh coriander leaves
2 tablespoons olive oil
¼ teaspoon tamari
1–2 fresh hot peppers
parsley sprigs, garnish
corn tacos

1. Place tomatoes under a broiler. Turn when the skins have charred on one side, after about 5 minutes.

2. Meanwhile, peel the avocado and save the pit. Cut up the avocado as you place it in a blender. Add the onion or scallions, coriander, oil, tamari and hot peppers (enough to make a spicy, not searing, blend).

3. When the tomatoes are slightly blackened on both sides, use an oven mitt or a terry towel to remove from broiler. Peel, then slit the tomatoes on all sides, and squeeze out the juice and seeds. Use care, as the liquid is hot.

4. Coarsely cut up the tomatoes as you add them to the blender.

5. Process the ingredients on low, then medium speed until rather smooth. Some lumps can remain. Stop the blender and scrape down the sides as necessary.

6. Place the guacamole in a serving bowl, push the pit in the center to keep the dip from turning brown, and chill before serving. To serve, remove pit, smooth top of dip, and garnish with parsley sprigs. Break up corn tacos, and place them around the bowl for dipping.

Stuffed Mushrooms with Walnuts and Cheese *Makes 4 servings*

You will want to find very large, perfect mushrooms to stuff.

1 small onion or 2 scallions
4 teaspoons olive oil
8 large mushrooms
1 tablespoon fresh parsley
2 teaspoons tamari
½ cup walnuts
1 teaspoon dried basil
1–2 ounces Cheddar cheese
4 cherry tomatoes, garnish
parsley sprigs, garnish

1. Chop the onion or scallions, and begin to cook them in a large saucepan with half of the olive oil.

2. Brush off the mushrooms, and carefully remove stems. Chop stems coarsely; set caps aside. Mince parsley and add it to the onion along with the mushroom stems and 1 teaspoon tamari. Stir together and cook over low heat about 3 to 4 minutes.

3. Meanwhile, grind the walnuts in a blender with short bursts at high speed. Stir the ground walnuts into the onion mixture, and add the basil. Remove to a side plate.

4. Add the remaining 2 teaspoons of oil, and place the mushroom caps in the pan. Stir to coat the caps with oil on all sides, then add a few spoonfuls of water and cover the pan. Steam the mushroom caps about 5 to 7 minutes.

5. Cut eight small slices of the cheese to place on the mushroom caps.

6. When the mushroom caps are finished cooking, place them upside down in a shallow ovenproof pan or dish. Fill each cap with a generous spoonful of the onion mixture, then top with a cheese slice.

7. Broil just until the cheese is well melted.

8. To serve, place two stuffed mushroom caps on each serving plate. Place a cherry tomato on each plate, and garnish with parsley.

Makes 1 cup   # Deviled Cashew Nuts

Your guests will have one devil of a good time with these!

2 teaspoons butter
1 cup raw cashew nuts
¼ teaspoon chili powder
dash of ground cumin
dash of cayenne pepper
½ teaspoon tamari
½ teaspoon lemon juice

Preheat oven to 350°F

1. Melt the butter in a small skillet or saucepan and add the nuts. Stir until the nuts are coated with butter.

2. Add the chili powder, ground cumin and cayenne. (Go light on the cayenne, or your guests will be speechless.) Stir to combine.

3. Cook the nuts over low heat about 5 minutes or until lightly toasted. Remove from the heat. Stir in the tamari and lemon juice.

4. Spread the nuts out in the bottom of a 9-inch pie plate, or on a cookie sheet or baking tray. Pop into a 350°F oven for 15 minutes, checking occasionally so they don't become too brown. Allow the nuts to cool before serving in a small bowl.

Makes 4 servings   # Avocados Eldorado

A visual delight to get any meal off to a fine start.

2 large avocados
1 lime, squeezed
½ cantaloupe or honeydew melon
¾ cup seedless grapes
honey (optional)

1. Cut the avocados in half lengthwise, and remove pit. Sprinkle cut halves with some lime juice to prevent discoloring.

2. Using a melon baller, cut out about a dozen small balls from the melon half. (Cut up remaining melon later for use in other dishes.)

3. Place a mixture of melon balls and grapes in the avocado halves. Sprinkle with lime juice, and drizzle with a little honey, if desired.

Makes ½ cup   # Goat Cheese Spread

A flavor that's purely Middle Eastern. Serve on whole wheat pita bread, cut into triangles, for an appetizing hors d'oeuvre.

¼ pound chevre (goat cheese)
¼ cup olive oil
¼ teaspoon crumbled dried
   rosemary
parsley sprig, garnish

1. Crumble the chevre into a small bowl. Add the oil and rosemary and stir together.

2. Serve immediately in a small serving dish, garnished with parsley. If chilled, allow spread to return to room temperature before serving.

Cheese and Walnut Canapés

Makes 10 servings

1. Place the walnuts in a blender and process in short bursts at high speed until ground.

2. Mix the cream cheese with the sour cream and coriander until smooth. Stir in the ground walnuts.

3. If the cucumbers were waxed, peel. If not, score the skins lengthwise with the tines of a fork. This creates an interesting pattern on the edges of the slices. Slice the cucumbers into rounds.

4. Place the cream cheese mixture in a small serving bowl and surround with the cucumber rounds. Let each person spread his or her own.

Variation: Serve spread on whole wheat crackers or on other sliced, raw vegetables in place of the cucumber rounds.

½ cup walnuts, preferably
    black walnuts
1 cup cream cheese
2 tablespoons sour cream
½ teaspoon ground coriander
2–3 cucumbers
parsley sprigs, garnish

Apple and Cheddar Slices

Makes 4 servings

New Englanders enjoy sharp cheese with apple pie. This recipe allows you to enjoy these contrasting tastes, without baking, at the beginning of a meal rather than at the end. You'll find this dish, like the old New England lifestyle, both simple and good.

1. Wash and core the apple, but do not peel it. Cut each half into eight thin wedges. Combine the lemon juice and water in a shallow bowl. Dip the wedges into the mixture to prevent browning.

2. Cut the cheese into 16 thin slices, about the size of the apple wedges. Place a piece of the cheese on each apple wedge.

3. Arrange the apple and cheese slices in a circle on a plate. Pile watercress in the center.

1 large, tart apple
1 tablespoon lemon juice
1 tablespoon water
2 ounces sharp Cheddar cheese
watercress, garnish

Makes 4 servings **Broccoli-Stuffed Eggs**

2 broccoli florets, about 3
    inches long
4 hard-cooked eggs
1 tablespoon water
1 tablespoon lemon juice
1 tablespoon cottage cheese
1 teaspoon Dijon-style mustard
1 teaspoon minced scallions
½ teaspoon dried marjoram
½ teaspoon tamari
¼ teaspoon paprika

1. Peel the thin, tough green skin from the stems of the florets. Place over boiling water, and steam until tender.

2. Meanwhile, cut the eggs in half and carefully remove the yolks. Place the yolks with the water, lemon juice, cottage cheese, mustard, scallions, marjoram, tamari and paprika in a blender.

3. When the broccoli is tender but still bright green, rinse with cold water to stop cooking. Trim off about ½ inch of the buds for use as a garnish, and chop the stems.

4. Place the stems in the blender with the other ingredients and process on low speed until smooth, scraping down the sides of the blender as necessary.

5. Stuff the egg whites with the yolk mixture, and garnish each half with some of the broccoli buds. Serve chilled.

Makes 4 servings **Cheese-Filled Pears**

Try, too, as a light luncheon dish (allowing a whole pear per person) or even as a dessert.

2 medium, ripe pears
1 teaspoon lemon juice
½ cup ricotta cheese
2 tablespoons shredded
    Cheddar cheese
2 tablespoons finely chopped
    pineapple
1 tablespoon chopped walnuts
spinach or lettuce leaves
mint or parsley sprigs, garnish

1. Cut the pears in half lengthwise and remove core, leaving a generous cavity for the filling. Sprinkle pears with lemon juice to prevent them from turning brown.

2. Combine the cheeses with the pineapple and walnuts. Divide the filling among the pear halves.

3. Serve on a bed of spinach or lettuce, garnished with mint or parsley sprigs.

Fresh Herb and Garlic Dip with Crudités *Makes 12 servings*

A dip served with raw vegetables: the fresh approach.

1. Place the cottage cheese, milk, chives, parsley, basil, curry, paprika and garlic in a blender. Process on medium speed until smooth.

2. Carefully hollow out the head of cabbage from the top. Cut a slice from the stem end so the cabbage will rest firmly on its base. Fill the hollowed-out cabbage with the dip.

3. To serve with raw vegetables, place the cabbage filled with dip in the center of a serving plate. Choose as many or as few raw vegetables as you like, but consider a range of colors and textures for a more attractive plate. Cut the vegetables into attractive shapes, such as diagonal slices or julienne strips. Cherry tomatoes, mushrooms and radishes can be left whole. Garnish with rings cut from green or red pepper and watercress or parsley sprigs.

Note: Cut the vegetables as close as possible to serving time. Cut vegetables can be stored in plastic bags in the refrigerator until ready to use.

1 cup cottage cheese
½ cup milk
2 tablespoons chopped fresh chives
2 tablespoons fresh parsley
½ teaspoon dried basil
⅛ teaspoon curry powder
⅛ teaspoon paprika
1 garlic clove
1 small red cabbage
raw vegetables: carrots, scallions, zucchini, cauliflower, broccoli, green beans, celery, cherry tomatoes, mushrooms, cucumbers, Jerusalem artichokes, radishes, fennel bulb
green pepper or sweet red pepper, garnish
watercress or parsley sprigs, garnish

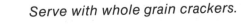

Tuna Dip *Makes 1½ cups*

Serve with whole grain crackers.

1. Place the sour cream, cottage cheese, parsley, scallion and thyme in a blender. Process on medium speed until smooth.

2. Add half the tuna, and blend again on medium speed until smooth.

3. Flake the remaining tuna and stir into the dip. Pour into a serving dish, and garnish with parsley sprigs.

⅔ cup sour cream
⅓ cup cottage cheese
1 tablespoon fresh parsley
1 scallion, cut up
¼ teaspoon dried thyme
6½ ounces water-packed tuna, drained
parsley sprigs, garnish

Makes 4 servings **Stuffed Dates**

This hors d'oeuvre is rather sweet, so serve before a light meal, such as a luncheon. Also delightful as a snack!

12–16 pitted dates
Cheddar cheese strips
almonds or toasted
   cashew nuts
fresh pineapple cubes
mint sprigs, garnish

1. Cut the dates lengthwise along one side. Stuff with an assortment of the above fillings (about four dates with each type of filling).

2. Arrange the dates on a serving plate, and garnish with mint sprigs.

Variations: In spring, garnish the serving plate with fresh, unhulled strawberries. Try soft, pitted prunes in place of dates.

Makes 8 servings **Feta Cheese Ball**

Cheese balls are a fine way to use up odds and ends of cheeses. Grate or crumble these before adding to the cream cheese.

1 cup cream cheese
¼ cup crumbled feta cheese
1 tablespoon minced scallion
3 tablespoons minced fresh
   parsley
whole grain crackers
1 pint cherry tomatoes, garnish

1. With a wooden spoon, or kneading by hand, combine the cream cheese, crumbled feta, scallion and 1 tablespoon of minced parsley. Form into a ball (or a log shape, if preferred).

2. Roll the cheese ball in the remaining minced parsley until coated.

3. Place the cheese ball on a serving plate. Attractively arrange the crackers and cherry tomatoes around the cheese ball.

Variation: Use ¼ cup or more of other strongly flavored cheeses, finely grated or crumbled, in place of feta. Cheddar, Roquefort and Romano are some examples.

Makes 1¼ cups **Herbed Feta Cheese Spread**

Serve with whole grain crackers.

¾ cup cottage cheese
½ cup crumbled feta cheese
1 tablespoon minced fresh
   parsley
½ teaspoon dried basil
½ teaspoon dried marjoram
½ garlic clove

1. Place the cheeses in a blender with the herbs and the garlic, minced or pushed through a garlic press.

2. Process on low to medium speed until smooth, stopping the blender to scrape down the sides as necessary.

3. Place in an attractive serving bowl and arrange crackers around the dish.

Variation: For a dip, thin mixture with milk.

Soups

Cream of Spinach Soup *Makes 4 servings*

A fabulous color is only one of this delicious soup's attributes!

1. Carefully wash the spinach and remove stems. Place the spinach leaves in a large saucepan or kettle over medium heat, and add the garlic, pushed through a garlic press. Add the tamari and cream. Steam spinach only until the spinach is wilted. Stir occasionally.

2. Place the wilted spinach and buttermilk in a blender and process on medium speed until very smooth. Serve immediately.

10 ounces spinach
1 garlic clove
1 tablespoon tamari
½ cup heavy cream
1 cup buttermilk

Cheddar Cheese Soup *Makes 2 servings*

A thick, hearty and quick soup—perfect after a winter's day outdoors.

1. Place the bread cubes, a few at a time, in a blender, and process with short bursts on high speed to obtain crumbs. Or, alternatively, crumble the bread cubes by hand.

2. Place the bread crumbs with the remaining ingredients in a medium saucepan, and stir over medium heat until the mixture comes to a boil. Reduce heat and continue to stir until the cheese is melted and the mixture well blended and smooth, about 5 to 6 minutes. Serve hot.

Variation: Other cheeses, such as longhorn, can be substituted for Cheddar.

1 cup whole wheat bread cubes
¾ cup cubed Cheddar cheese
1½ cups skim milk
2 teaspoons Dijon-style
    mustard
dash of cayenne pepper

Cabbage Soup Mexican-Style

Makes 4 servings

Made with ripe tomatoes and chili powder, this soup is garden fresh.

1 tablespoon corn oil
2 cups shredded cabbage
1 medium yellow onion, chopped
3 large, ripe tomatoes
3 garlic cloves
2 teaspoons tamari
1 teaspoon blackstrap molasses
1 teaspoon chili powder
½ teaspoon ground cumin
½ cup water

1. Heat a large saucepan with the oil and add the cabbage and onion. Cook over medium heat until limp and slightly browned, stirring occasionally.

2. Meanwhile, remove the tough cores from the tomatoes. Quarter two of the tomatoes, and place them in a blender with the garlic, tamari and molasses. Blend on medium speed until smooth.

3. Add the tomato mixture to the cabbage and onion and bring to a boil. Chop the remaining tomato and add it to the soup along with the chili and cumin. Add ½ cup of water, or more if the soup is too thick.

4. When soup is boiling, reduce heat and simmer until cabbage is relatively tender, about 10 minutes. Serve hot.

Note: Also delicious as a cold soup.

Corn Soup

Makes 4 servings

Excellent flavor and texture make this a good soup choice.

½ sweet red pepper, finely chopped
1 small onion, finely chopped
2 teaspoons corn oil
1 teaspoon butter
1½ cups fresh or frozen corn
½ cup light cream
2 teaspoons tamari
2 teaspoons whole wheat flour
1 cup milk
dash of grated nutmeg
parsley sprigs, garnish

1. In a large skillet or saucepan, cook the pepper and onion in the oil and butter until tender. Keep the heat low to prevent browning.

2. Meanwhile, place 1 cup of the corn, the cream and the tamari in a blender. Process on medium speed until fairly smooth.

3. When the pepper and onion are tender, stir in the flour and continue stirring over low heat for 2 to 3 minutes. Add the milk slowly, stirring each time some is added to prevent lumping.

4. Add the corn and cream mixture and the remaining corn to the soup in the skillet. Heat through and serve, topped with nutmeg and garnished with parsley sprigs.

Salmon and Tuna Chowder

Makes 4 servings

Thick and tasty.

1. In a large heavy-bottom saucepan, melt the butter. Add the onion and red pepper. Cook over low to medium heat until tender, about 10 minutes.

2. Meanwhile, put the water on the stove in a small saucepan over high heat and bring to a boil. Mince the celery leaves.

3. Remove the skin from the salmon, if desired, and crush the bones well. Flake the tuna. Add both, along with the boiling water, celery leaves and oregano, to the large saucepan.

4. Add the cream, heat through and serve. Do not boil the chowder after adding the cream, or it may curdle.

2 teaspoons butter
1 small onion, finely chopped
1 small sweet red pepper, finely chopped
2½ cups water
1 tablespoon celery leaves
7¾ ounces water-packed red salmon, drained
6½ ounces water-packed tuna, drained
¼ teaspoon dried oregano
½ cup heavy cream

Cream of Watercress Soup

Makes 4 servings

Nice color and flavor.

1. Heat the oil and butter in a large skillet. Chop the scallions and stir into the heated oil. Turn heat low to medium.

2. Coarsely chop the watercress, including stems, and add it to the pan. Stir over medium heat just until the watercress is wilted.

3. Add a dash of nutmeg and the stock. Bring to a boil, then reduce heat and simmer 8 to 10 minutes.

4. Place the cooked watercress and stock in a blender, and, holding down the blender lid with a kitchen towel to prevent an eruption of the hot liquid, process on low, then medium speed until smooth.

5. Return the soup to the pan, and add the cream. Heat (do not boil) and serve, garnished with parsley sprigs.

1 tablespoon safflower oil
1 tablespoon butter
4 scallions
1 large bunch watercress
dash of grated nutmeg
1½ cups *Stock* (pages 175–76)
1 cup light cream
parsley sprigs, garnish

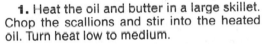

Makes 4 servings # Mushroom Soup

3 cups water
1 carrot
1 onion
2½ cups mushrooms
1 tablespoon butter
1½ tablespoons tamari
1 teaspoon blackstrap
   molasses
1 teaspoon minced fresh basil

1. Place the water in a large saucepan over medium heat. Wash and trim the carrot. Slice thin and add to the water. Peel and quarter the onion. Slice thin and add. When the water comes to a boil, turn down heat to simmer.

2. Brush clean (or, if needed, wash) mushrooms. Trim and slice thin. Place the butter in a small skillet. When it is melted, add the sliced mushrooms and cook 3 to 4 minutes, until golden. Then add the mushrooms to the carrots and onion.

3. Add the tamari, molasses and basil to the saucepan. Simmer soup until the vegetables are tender but not too soft, about 5 more minutes. Serve hot.

Makes 4 servings # Zucchini Soup

3 small zucchini
1 small green pepper
4-6 scallions
1½ tablespoons olive oil
2 cups *Stock* (pages 175–76)
1 cup milk
dash of cayenne pepper

1. Thinly slice the zucchini. Cut the pepper into short, thin slices. Slice the scallions.

2. Place the olive oil in a medium skillet and warm it, then add the zucchini, pepper and scallions. Cover and place over low to medium heat, stirring occasionally, for about 10 minutes.

3. Place half the vegetables with the stock in a blender. Process on low to medium speed until smooth. Return this mixture to the skillet.

4. Cook an additional 5 minutes. Remove from the heat. Stir in milk and a dash of cayenne. Chill the soup before serving.

Variation: For a slightly tarter soup, let the zucchini mixture cool a bit, then add 1 cup buttermilk in place of the milk.

Snappy Salmon Soup   *Makes 2 servings*

1. In a medium heavy-bottom saucepan, melt the butter. Finely chop the onion, and cook it over low heat in the butter until tender, about 5 minutes.

2. Place the milk in a small saucepan and scald.

3. Remove the skin from the salmon, if desired. Crush the bones well and add with the flaked salmon to the onion. Sprinkle with thyme, and add the scalded milk. Heat through and serve.

1 teaspoon butter
1 small onion
2 cups milk
7¾ ounces water-packed red salmon, drained
⅛ teaspoon dried thyme

Tomato Cream Soup   *Makes 2 servings*

Best with garden-ripe tomatoes, of course!

1. Peel tomato, cut in half across and squeeze out the seeds. Cut up coarsely and place in a blender.

2. Add the remaining ingredients, except mint. Process on medium speed until mixture is smooth.

3. Pour the soup into a medium saucepan and heat gently, but do not boil. Mince the mint leaves.

4. Serve hot, garnished with the mint.

1 large or 2 medium, ripe tomatoes
½ cup milk
½ cup heavy cream
1 tablespoon fresh dillweed
2 teaspoons tamari
¼ teaspoon celery seeds
fresh mint leaves, garnish

Peach Soup   *Makes 2 servings*

An excellent summertime treat. Chill the bowls in the freezer when you begin the soup.

1. Wash peaches, but do not peel. Remove the pits and any brown spots.

2. Place the peaches in a blender with the buttermilk and cardamom. Blend on medium speed until smooth. Serve in chilled bowls.

Note: The peaches must be very ripe, indeed, to provide the proper sweetness.

3 large, very ripe peaches, chilled
¼ cup buttermilk
⅛ teaspoon ground cardamom

Make-It-Snappy Fish Stew

Makes 4 servings

2 cups milk
3 medium potatoes
2 medium onions
1 pound fish fillets
1 tablespoon fresh dillweed
1 large, ripe tomato
1 scallion, chopped, garnish

1. Place the milk in a large saucepan over medium heat to scald. Meanwhile, cube the potatoes. There should be about 2 cups.

2. Place the potatoes in the scalded milk. Chop the onions, and add them to the pot. When the mixture begins to simmer, turn down the heat somewhat.

3. Rinse and cut the fish fillets into bite-size pieces. Mince the dill.

4. Peel the tomato, cut in half across and squeeze out the seeds.

5. When the potatoes and onions have boiled 10 minutes, add the fish for the next 5 minutes of cooking. Stir in the dill.

6. Add the tomato for the final 2 minutes of cooking, just long enough to heat the tomato through. Serve hot, sprinkled with chopped scallion.

Chilled Cucumber Soup

Makes 4 servings

Refrigerate the cucumber and yogurt beforehand so you can serve this soup cold as soon as it is made. You might also chill the bowls in the freezer when you start the soup.

1 medium cucumber
2 cups yogurt
2 teaspoons vinegar
2 teaspoons fresh mint leaves
1 teaspoon fresh dillweed or
    fresh rosemary or ¼
    teaspoon dried dillweed
1 teaspoon olive oil
½ garlic clove, minced
mint sprigs, garnish

1. Peel cucumber. Cut in half lengthwise. Remove seeds by running a sharp-edged teaspoon along the center of each cucumber half.

2. Place one cucumber half in a blender with ½ cup of yogurt and the remaining ingredients, except the mint. Process on medium speed until smooth.

3. Shred or finely chop the remaining cucumber half. Stir by hand into the blended mixture, along with the remaining yogurt.

4. Serve soup in chilled bowls, garnished with mint sprigs.

Lentil Soup *Makes 6 servings*

A hearty soup with a great taste.

1. Place the lentils with water in a large saucepan. Cover pan. Bring liquid to a boil, reduce heat and simmer lentils, partly covered. As water is heating, mince and add garlic, and add bay leaf.

2. Place the corn oil in a medium skillet. Quarter and thinly slice the onions, and add them to the oil over medium heat, stirring until well browned. Set aside.

3. When the lentils have simmered 15 to 18 minutes and are tender but not mushy, remove from the heat. Remove bay leaf. With a potato masher, coarsely mash the lentils in the liquid. Stir in the onion, tamari, molasses and turmeric. Serve hot.

Note: Freeze or refrigerate leftovers for later use.

1 cup dried lentils
4 cups water
3 garlic cloves
1 bay leaf
1 tablespoon corn oil
2 large onions
2 tablespoons tamari
1 teaspoon blackstrap molasses
dash of turmeric

Green Pea Soup *Makes 4 servings*

Great color and great taste—an asset to any meal.

1. Heat a large skillet with the butter. When the butter is melted, stir in the flour. Stir over medium heat for a minute or two before adding milk all at once.

2. Add the peas to the skillet and stir. Reduce heat and allow peas to simmer about 10 minutes, or just until tender.

3. Meanwhile, measure and then wash the spinach. When the peas are tender, stir the whole leaves of spinach into the soup. Fold them into the hot liquid so that they wilt.

4. Place the yogurt, tamari and nutmeg in a blender. When all of the spinach is wilted, pour the soup mixture into the blender with the yogurt. Process on medium speed until the soup is smooth. Serve hot or chilled.

2 tablespoons butter
2 tablespoons whole wheat
   flour
1½ cups skim milk
1 cup fresh peas
2 cups tightly packed spinach
½ cup yogurt
1 teaspoon tamari
dash of grated nutmeg

Makes 4 servings # Winter Apple Soup
A hit!

¼ cup dried lentils
2 cups water
1 bay leaf
1 medium sweet red pepper
2 medium apples
1 tablespoon tamari
1 teaspoon honey
¼ teaspoon ground coriander
dash of grated nutmeg

1. Place the lentils, water and bay leaf in a medium saucepan over high heat and cover. When water comes to a boil, reduce heat and simmer.

2. Finely chop the pepper; there should be about 1 cup. Add to the lentils, raising heat until soup boils, then reducing heat to simmer again.

3. Core and finely chop the unpeeled apples. Add to the soup, bring to a boil again, and simmer. Add tamari, honey, coriander and nutmeg.

4. When lentils and peppers are tender, after 15 to 18 minutes of cooking, remove bay leaf and pour about three-fourths of the mixture into a blender. Process on low speed until smooth.

5. Add the pureed mixture to the remaining soup in the saucepan. Stir over medium heat until combined. Serve hot.

Makes 4 servings # Cheddary Cheese and Tomato Soup

I discovered this soup in the wilds of western Massachusetts, then spent several days trying to duplicate it. Do use garden-ripe tomatoes!

6-7 very ripe tomatoes
2 tablespoons butter
2 garlic cloves
2 cups grated sharp Cheddar cheese
parsley sprigs, garnish

1. Peel the tomatoes and cut them in half across. Squeeze out the seeds.

2. Place the tomato pulp (there should be 3 cups) in a blender. Process on low speed until smooth.

3. Melt the butter in a medium skillet over medium-high heat. Add the blended tomato pulp and the garlic (pushed through a garlic press). Bring to a boil, then reduce heat just slightly and boil for 8 minutes.

4. When the tomatoes have boiled for 8 minutes, remove from the heat. Stir in the grated cheese until melted, then serve immediately, garnished with parsley.

Avocado Soup   *Makes 4 servings*

A creamy blend.

1. Melt the butter in a medium saucepan over low heat. Stir in the minced scallion and cook over low heat just until translucent.

2. Add the flour and continue to stir for 2 to 3 minutes. Slowly pour in 1 cup of the stock and stir until smooth. Turn heat very low and allow liquid to simmer.

3. Meanwhile, place the remaining cup of the stock in a blender with the avocado and cream. Process until thoroughly combined.

4. Pour the blended avocado mixture into the saucepan and heat through.

5. To serve, pour the hot soup into a tureen or individual serving bowls. Top with a dollop of yogurt and sprinkle with the sliced scallions.

Note: You should serve this soup at once, since avocado has a tendency to brown quickly. If any soup is refrigerated for later use, place the avocado pit with the soup and cover tightly. This will help maintain the delicate color of the avocado.

1 tablespoon butter
1 scallion, minced
2 teaspoons whole wheat flour
2 cups *Stock* (pages 175–76)
1 avocado, peeled and pitted
½ cup heavy cream
yogurt, garnish
sliced scallions, garnish

Sweet Potato Soup   *Makes 4 servings*

A blended soup with lively color and taste.

1. Coarsely chop the red peppers. You should have about 2½ cups. Cut the scallions in 2-inch lengths.

2. Place the peppers, scallions, stock and garlic (pushed through a garlic press) in a blender. Process on medium speed until smooth.

3. Place the blended soup in a medium saucepan. Bring to a boil, then reduce heat and simmer for 10 to 15 minutes. Taste soup and add tamari if needed.

4. To serve, place in a tureen or individual bowls. Sprinkle with minced parsley.

3 large sweet red peppers
7-8 scallions
2 cups *Stock* (pages 175–76)
1 garlic clove
2 teaspoons tamari (optional)
1 tablespoon minced parsley, garnish

Cream of Carrot Soup

Makes 4 servings

4 medium carrots
1 small onion
1½ cups water
2 tablespoons butter
1 teaspoon fresh tarragon or
    ½ teaspoon dried tarragon
1 teaspoon lemon juice
1 cup heavy cream
2 egg yolks
1 scallion, minced, garnish

1. Scrub the carrots and slice thin. Slice the onion.

2. Put the water in a small saucepan over medium heat to boil.

3. Melt the butter in a large saucepan, and add the carrots and onion. Stir over medium heat 1 or 2 minutes, until the onion is translucent. Add tarragon and lemon juice.

4. Add the boiling water, then cover and simmer carrots for 10 minutes.

5. Meanwhile, pour the cream into the small saucepan. Place the egg yolks in a small bowl and beat them slightly. Mince the scallion.

6. When the carrots are nearly done, scald the cream.

7. When the carrots have simmered 10 minutes, pour them into a blender, and add the scalded cream. Process on low speed until smooth.

8. Stir a little of the soup into the beaten yolks, then add the yolk mixture to the soup with the blender on low speed.

9. Serve the soup in individual bowls. Sprinkle some minced scallion over each serving.

Variation: Substitute minced fresh mint leaves for the minced scallion.

Sweet Pepper Soup

Makes 4 servings

1 onion
1 tablespoon butter
1 medium sweet potato
1½ cups boiling water
½ cup milk
1 teaspoon medium unsulfured
    molasses
¼ teaspoon ground coriander

1. Quarter the onion and slice thin. Melt the butter and cook onion over low heat.

2. Meanwhile, scrub and quarter the sweet potato. Slice the sweet potato thin and add to the onion. Add the boiling water and cover. Simmer about 5 minutes or until sweet potato is tender.

3. Pour the sweet potato, onion and water into a blender. Puree on low speed, and return the mixture to the saucepan.

4. Add the milk, molasses and coriander. Heat through before serving.

Eggs

Eggs Benedict Arnold *Makes 4 servings*

This dish turns traitor on the traditional high-fat, low-fiber offering.

1. Place the ricotta, lemon juice, yogurt and egg yolk in a blender. Process on medium speed until smooth. Add the hot water slowly, while the blender is running, if possible.

2. Place the butter in a medium saucepan, and melt it over low heat. Add the ricotta sauce, and turn heat very low to warm the sauce.

3. Place about an inch of water in a medium skillet. Bring to a boil, then lower heat to simmer. Break the eggs into a small bowl, one at a time, and quickly slip them into the simmering water. Cover and poach the eggs about 5 minutes, until the whites are firm.

4. Meanwhile, toast the bread. To assemble, drain the eggs. Place an egg on each slice of toast and spoon the sauce over top. Dust each serving with a little paprika. Serve hot.

Variation: Place a thick tomato slice on each piece of toast, then warm under a broiler before adding egg and sauce.

⅔ cup ricotta cheese
2½ tablespoons lemon juice
1 tablespoon yogurt
1 egg yolk
¼ cup hot water
1 teaspoon butter
4 eggs
4 slices whole grain bread
paprika, garnish

29

Makes 4 servings

Tuna Frittata

Serve with whole wheat bread and salad.

1 sweet red pepper
1 teaspoon corn oil
1 teaspoon butter
5 eggs
2 tablespoons milk
1 tablespoon minced fresh
   parsley
1 teaspoon minced fresh basil
   or ½ teaspoon dried basil
6½ ounces water-packed tuna,
   drained
1–2 tablespoons grated
   Parmesan cheese

1. Remove the seeds and core from the pepper. Chop. Heat the corn oil in a 9-inch skillet, then add the butter. Cook the pepper over low to medium heat until it is nearly tender, about 10 minutes.

2. Meanwhile, beat the eggs and add the milk, beating until combined.

3. Sprinkle the herbs over the soft peppers, then sprinkle the tuna evenly over the layer of peppers in the pan.

4. Pour the egg mixture over the pepper and tuna. Cook without stirring over low to medium heat until the bottom is well set.

5. Sprinkle with Parmesan, and place under a broiler until the top is set and the frittata is firm and slightly puffed, about 3 to 4 minutes. Cut the frittata into four servings and serve from the pan.

Variation: Substitute mushrooms and scallions for the pepper.

Makes 1 serving

Sweet Citron Omelet

Wonderful for a luncheon, this omelet with a twist—lemon flavor—is a taste surprise.

2 eggs
1½ teaspoons honey
½ teaspoon finely grated
   lemon rind
¼ teaspoon vanilla extract
1 teaspoon butter
lemon slice, garnish
mint sprig, garnish

1. Beat the eggs with the honey, lemon rind and vanilla in a small bowl.

2. Heat an omelet pan or medium skillet. When it is hot, add the butter, and when the butter is melted, but not browned, add the egg mixture and cook over medium heat. Pull the edges of the omelet toward the center so the uncooked egg reaches the edges of the pan. Continue pulling the eggs toward the center and swirling the pan until the eggs are cooked.

3. Fold over, then slide the omelet onto a serving plate. Garnish with a lemon slice and a sprig of mint.

Potato Frittata   *Makes 4 servings*

1. Place the water in a medium saucepan and bring to a boil over high heat. Wash but do not peel potatoes, dice them, and place them in the water. Return water to the boil.

2. Rinse and trim scallions, then chop coarsely, including green tops. Add immediately to the boiling potatoes. Reduce heat and simmer.

3. Beat the eggs in a small bowl, and add the tamari.

4. When the potatoes have boiled about 8 minutes and are nearly tender, heat a medium-size iron or other ovenproof skillet, and add the oil. When the oil is hot, add the butter. Quickly drain the vegetables. Transfer the vegetables to the hot skillet and stir briefly.

5. Sprinkle the paprika and basil over the vegetables, then pour on the beaten eggs. Do not stir.

6. Over low to medium heat, allow the eggs to cook about halfway through, then place the pan under a hot broiler for a minute or two to cook the top of the eggs. The frittata will become attractively puffed. Serve directly from the pan.

Variation: Try chopped celery or green peppers in place of scallions.

3 cups water
2–3 medium potatoes
    (about ¾ pound)
3 scallions
5 eggs
1 teaspoon tamari
½ teaspoon sunflower oil
½ teaspoon butter
½ teaspoon paprika
½ teaspoon dried basil

Makes 4 servings # Middle Eastern Omelet

If you think this might be just another omelet, let yourself in for a wonderful surprise . . .

1 medium red onion
1 large sweet red pepper
2 tablespoons corn oil
1 cup chopped, ripe tomatoes
6 eggs
¼ cup fresh parsley
½ cup crumbled feta cheese
parsley sprigs, garnish

1. Halve the onion lengthwise and cut it into thin half-circles. Halve the pepper, and remove stem and seeds. Slice into 2-inch strips.

2. Heat the oil in a large heavy-bottom ovenproof skillet. Add the onion and pepper, and cook over medium heat until the onion is translucent, stirring often.

3. Add the tomatoes, and simmer the vegetables together until they are tender.

4. Meanwhile, beat the eggs and mince the parsley. When the vegetables are tender, add the eggs and parsley, sprinkle with feta and stir everything together. Cook over low to medium heat until eggs begin to set.

5. Place the omelet under a broiler until cooked through and golden on top. Serve in the pan, garnished with parsley sprigs.

Eggs with Spinach and Feta

Makes 4 servings

For a quick and attractive luncheon dish, this is an excellent choice.

1 tablespoon olive oil
1 medium onion, chopped
10 ounces spinach
1 garlic clove
½ cup crumbled feta cheese
4 eggs
paprika, garnish

1. Heat the oil in a medium skillet. Add the onion and cook over medium heat, adding a few spoonfuls of water to prevent scorching.

2. Meanwhile, wash the spinach and remove stems. Allow water to cling to the leaves for steaming. Tear leaves into several pieces.

3. When the onion is translucent and slightly tender, push the garlic clove through a press into the skillet. Stir, then add the spinach, a little at a time. Cover skillet, and as spinach wilts, add more until all the spinach is wilted.

4. Stir in the feta. Make four "nests" in the spinach mixture, crack the eggs and place an egg in each nest, without breaking the yolks.

5. Cover the skillet and steam until eggs are cooked, or place the pan under a broiler to cook the eggs. Garnish eggs with a dusting of paprika and serve immediately.

Herbed Mushroom Omelet

Makes 1 serving

Serve with whole grain muffins or toast.

1. Trim the stem ends of the mushrooms, and wash or wipe mushrooms clean. Heat a small skillet while slicing mushrooms, then add the oil and the sliced mushrooms. Add tamari and basil and stir. Reduce heat and cook mushrooms about 4 to 5 minutes, stirring occasionally. Turn off the heat when the mushrooms are done.

2. Meanwhile, place the eggs in a small bowl and beat with a fork until light. Mince the parsley and beat into the egg. Add the nutmeg.

3. Place an omelet pan or medium skillet over medium heat, and add the butter. When the butter has melted and is turning golden, add the egg mixture and swirl the pan slightly to distribute the egg evenly. Continue to swirl the pan, pulling the cooked edges of the omelet toward the center of the pan. The uncooked egg will then run toward the outside of the pan where it will cook.

4. When the omelet is no longer runny but still soft on top, place the mushrooms on half of the omelet. Fold one-third of the omelet over the filling, then tilt the pan and roll the omelet onto a plate. Serve garnished with fresh parsley.

1 cup mushrooms
1 teaspoon sunflower oil
1 teaspoon tamari
½ teaspoon dried basil
2 eggs
1 tablespoon fresh parsley
dash of grated nutmeg
1 teaspoon butter
minced fresh parsley, garnish

Omelet Fillings

Choose any of the following, or create your own combinations for a flavorful stuffed omelet.

chopped fresh herbs: tarragon, basil, dillweed, parsley, marjoram
minced fresh leeks sauteed in butter
sliced mushrooms with herbs sauteed in butter
minced scallions sauteed in butter
tomatoes, seeded and finely chopped
shredded Cheddar, Swiss or longhorn cheese
sliced fresh strawberries
lettuce leaves, chopped and sauteed in butter
spinach, chopped and sauteed in butter
crumbled feta cheese
cottage cheese sprinkled with fresh herbs
green pepper sauteed in butter with herbs or scallions
sour cream

Makes 4 servings **Eggs Florentine**

An attractive dish for a brunch or luncheon. Serve with whole grain rolls or bread.

1 pound spinach
2 teaspoons olive or sunflower oil
1 teaspoon butter
1 garlic clove
4 eggs
¼ cup grated Cheddar or
   longhorn cheese

1. Wash the spinach, allowing water to cling to the leaves for steaming. Remove the stems and chop coarsely.

2. Heat a large ovenproof skillet over medium heat, and add the oil and butter. When the butter is melted, add the spinach and the garlic (pushed through a garlic press). Cover and steam the spinach until it is wilted. Reduce heat, stir and simmer the spinach, covered, until tender, about 5 minutes.

3. Place about an inch of water in a medium skillet. Bring to a boil, then lower heat. Break the eggs into a small dish, then quickly slip the eggs into the simmering water. Cover the skillet, and let the eggs stand in the hot water about 5 minutes, until the whites are firm.

4. Drain any liquid from the spinach. Drain the poached eggs, and place them on a bed of spinach.

5. Sprinkle with the cheese and place under a hot broiler just until the cheese is melted.

Mexican Omelet   *Makes 2 servings*

A fan of hot 'n' spicy foods? Then enjoy!

1. In an 8- or 9-inch skillet, heat the oil. Cook the pepper and scallions over low heat, adding a few drops of water and covering the pan to steam vegetables.

2. While the vegetables are steaming, beat the eggs in a small bowl, add the water and continue to beat until combined.

3. Place the cherry tomatoes, hot peppers, tamari, chili, cumin and garlic (pushed through a garlic press) in a blender. Process on medium speed until smooth.

4. When the green pepper and scallions are soft, pour the beaten eggs into the skillet. Allow the eggs to set, without stirring, over low heat.

5. Sprinkle the cheese over top of the eggs. When the bottom of the omelet has set, place the pan under a broiler until the cheese is melted and the omelet is puffy.

6. Pour the tomato sauce evenly over the top of the omelet, and spread nearly to the edges. Return omelet to the broiler until the sauce is heated through. Cut in half and serve.

1 tablespoon corn oil
½ green pepper, chopped
3 scallions, chopped
3 eggs
2 tablespoons water
1 cup cherry tomatoes
1–2 fresh hot peppers
1 teaspoon tamari
¼ teaspoon chili powder
¼ teaspoon ground cumin
1 garlic clove
¼ cup grated Cheddar
      cheese

Egg and Corn Scramble   *Makes 2 servings*

For a light supper, serve with sliced tomatoes and crusty whole wheat bread. Outstandingly delicious and colorful.

1. Heat the oil and butter in a medium skillet. Chop the scallion and place it in the skillet, and add the green pepper. Stir over low heat about 5 minutes, or until tender.

2. Stir in the corn and basil. Beat the eggs in a bowl, then add the milk and beat to combine.

3. Add the eggs to the skillet when the corn has been heated through. Stir eggs occasionally until set. Serve hot, garnished with rings of green pepper.

1 teaspoon corn oil
2 teaspoons butter
1 scallion
2 tablespoons diced green
      pepper
1 cup cooked corn
¼ teaspoon dried basil
4 eggs
2 tablespoons milk
green pepper rings, garnish

Makes 4 servings **Curried Eggs on Toast**

A quick main course for luncheon or dinner.

5 eggs
3 tablespoons butter
2 tablespoons minced onions
2½ tablespoons whole wheat flour
1 teaspoon curry powder
2 cups milk
4 slices whole wheat toast
parsley sprigs, garnish

1. Cover the eggs with water in a medium saucepan and bring to a boil over medium heat. Reduce heat and simmer for 15 minutes, until eggs are hard-cooked.

2. In the meantime, melt the butter in a large skillet and cook the onions until they are translucent. Add the flour and curry powder and stir together a minute or two. Add the milk and turn up heat until sauce begins to simmer. Turn down heat to lowest setting and simmer sauce, uncovered, stirring occasionally, until thickened.

3. When the eggs are done, run them under cold water, then peel and slice them into the curry sauce.

4. Serve curried eggs over toast. Garnish with parsley sprigs.

Vegetarian Main Dishes

Mediterranean Vegetables with Cheese
Makes 4 servings

Serve over brown rice or with whole grain pasta.

1. In a large saucepan, bring the water to a boil over high heat.

2. Meanwhile, in a large skillet, heat the oil. Thinly slice the onion and the zucchini into rounds. Add the onion to the oil, stirring occasionally over medium heat until the onions are golden.

3. Slice the eggplant into rounds about ½ inch thick, and cut these into ½-inch strips. When the water is boiling, add the eggplant. Return the water to a boil, then reduce heat and simmer until the eggplant is just tender, about 8 minutes.

4. When the onions are tender, add the zucchini to the skillet. Stir over medium heat, then cover. Cut the tomatoes in half across, and remove some of the seeds and juice. Chop coarsely.

5. When the zucchini is nearly tender, after about 5 minutes, add the tomatoes, garlic (pushed through a garlic press) and basil. Top with the drained eggplant and feta. Stir ingredients together and heat through. Serve hot.

Note: As a vegetable side dish, omit feta. Serve hot or chilled.

4 cups water
2 tablespoons olive or
   sunflower oil
1 large onion
1 medium zucchini
   (about ½ pound)
1 small eggplant (½–¾ pound)
2 large, ripe tomatoes
1 garlic clove
2 teaspoons fresh basil or
   ½ teaspoon dried basil
¾ cup crumbled feta cheese

Makes 2 servings

Cheese-Topped French Toast with Tomato

Try a lunchtime variation on a breakfast theme: French toast made slightly more elaborate with a tomato and cheese topping. Serve with a fresh green salad.

1 egg
¼ cup skim milk
4 slices whole grain bread
1 cup shredded or diced Cheddar, longhorn or Swiss cheese
dash of cayenne pepper
1 large, ripe tomato

1. Beat the egg and add half of the skim milk, beating to combine. Dip the bread into the egg mixture to coat both sides.

2. Place dipped bread on a lightly oiled baking sheet and broil, turning when the first side is golden.

3. Meanwhile, in a small pan, melt the cheese with the remaining 2 tablespoons of skim milk over very low heat. Stir in the cayenne.

4. Remove the baking sheet from the oven. Slice tomato, and place a slice on each piece of bread, then coat with the cheese sauce. Place under the broiler just until the cheese sauce begins to brown lightly. Serve immediately.

Makes 1 serving

Cheese and Vegetable Pocket Sandwich

1 whole wheat pita bread
¼ cup shredded sharp Cheddar cheese
¼ cup shredded carrots
¼ cup alfalfa sprouts
1 scallion, minced
1 tablespoon minced fresh parsley
3 cherry tomatoes, halved
1 lemon slice
Blender Mayonnaise (page 91)
parsley sprigs, garnish

1. Cut the pita bread in half and open up the "pockets."

2. In a small bowl, toss the cheese, carrots, sprouts, scallion, parsley and cherry tomatoes together. Sprinkle with juice from the lemon slice and toss with a little mayonnaise to moisten.

3. Fill the pita bread halves with the cheese and vegetable mixture. Place on a serving plate and decorate with parsley sprigs.

Spaghetti Feta-Style   *Makes 2 servings*

Friends delight in pasta with cheese; you'll delight in the cooking—with ease!

1. Bring a large kettle of water to a boil over high heat. When the water is boiling, stir in the spaghetti and return water to a boil. Turn heat to medium and boil spaghetti uncovered.

⅓ pound thin whole wheat spaghetti
1 egg
1 cup crumbled feta cheese

2. Break the egg in the serving bowl and beat until light. Finely crumble the feta, and add it to the bowl.

3. When the spaghetti is cooked just until firm-tender, about 9 to 10 minutes, drain and immediately toss with the egg and cheese while the spaghetti is hot. Toss until the spaghetti is well coated. Serve immediately.

Note: The success of this dish depends upon the flavor of the cheese. Try to find an Italian or Greek food shop where feta is sold in bulk.

Variations: Add 1 cup of peas to the pasta as it cooks. Sprinkle the dish with minced fresh basil or dried basil.

Pita Pizzas   *Makes 2 servings*
Amazingly good!

1. Chop the onion and green pepper. Heat a medium skillet with the oil, and cook the onion and pepper until firm-tender, stirring occasionally. Push the garlic clove through a garlic press into the onion and pepper just before removing them from heat, and stir.

1 medium onion
½ green pepper
2 teaspoons olive oil
1 garlic clove
2 whole wheat pita breads
3 tablespoons tomato paste
½ teaspoon dried basil
½ teaspoon dried oregano
mozzarella, fontina or Gruyère cheese

2. Meanwhile, place the pita breads under a broiler and toast one side. Remove from broiler and spread tomato paste over the untoasted sides.

3. Sprinkle with basil and oregano. Top with the cooked onion and pepper mixture.

4. Place thin slices of cheese over the pizzas. Broil until the cheese is melted. Serve immediately.

Variations: Try sauteed mushrooms, sweet red peppers or scallions in place of onion. Try chopped fresh parsley or flaked tuna as garnishes.

Makes 2 servings # Presto Pesto and Pasta

Based on the Italian "Pesto alla Genovese," with fresh basil and garlic.

⅓ pound whole wheat spaghetti
1 cup peas
½ cup walnuts
⅔ cup olive oil
2 large garlic cloves, minced
½ cup grated Parmesan cheese
2 teaspoons dried basil
1 cup packed fresh basil leaves

1. Bring a large kettle of water to a boil over high heat. Place the spaghetti in the boiling water, stir, and allow to cook, uncovered, until firm-tender, about 9 minutes. About 4 to 5 minutes before the spaghetti is done, add the peas and allow to return to a boil.

2. Meanwhile, place the walnuts, oil and garlic in a blender. Process on medium speed until smooth. Add the Parmesan, dried basil and 2 tablespoons of boiling water from the spaghetti pot. Blend on medium speed until combined.

3. Mince the basil leaves fine, by hand, and place in a medium to large serving bowl. Add the walnut mixture and stir to combine.

4. Drain the spaghetti and peas and toss immediately with the pesto sauce. Serve hot.

Broiled Mushrooms and Cheese on Toast

Makes 2 servings

1 teaspoon corn oil
1 teaspoon butter
2 cups sliced mushrooms
½ teaspoon dried basil
2 teaspoons tamari
2 slices whole wheat bread
⅓ cup grated Swiss, Cheddar or longhorn cheese
parsley sprigs, garnish

1. In a medium skillet, heat the oil and butter, then add the mushrooms. Stir over medium heat until they are cooked through, then add the basil and tamari.

2. While the mushrooms are cooking, toast the bread. Place toast in a small, shallow ovenproof pan or plate.

3. Top the bread with the mushrooms and sprinkle with cheese. Broil until the cheese is melted. Serve hot, garnished with parsley sprigs.

Fettucini with Ricotta and Basil
Makes 4 servings

This recipe's golden sauce flecked with basil makes any pasta attractive.

1. Bring a large pot of water to a boil. Add the fettucini and boil, uncovered, just until firm-tender.

2. Meanwhile, place the egg yolks and lemon juice in a blender. Process on low speed just until combined.

3. Add the ricotta. Process on low to medium speed, stopping to scrape down the sides as necessary, until the sauce is smooth.

4. Coarsely chop the basil leaves, then add them to the ingredients in the blender. Stir the basil into the sauce with the spatula. Process on medium speed just a few seconds to chop the basil more finely and incorporate it into the sauce.

5. Place the ricotta sauce in the bottom of the serving bowl. When the fettucini is done cooking, drain quickly, then add the hot pasta immediately to the sauce in the bowl. Toss to coat the fettucini evenly. Add Parmesan; toss again. Serve hot.

½ pound whole grain fettucini
2 egg yolks
3 tablespoons lemon juice
¾ cup ricotta cheese
⅓ cup packed fresh basil leaves
grated Parmesan cheese

Fruited-Cheese Cantaloupe Cup

Makes 2 servings

Fruity, light and pretty, too—a lunch in its own disposable "dish," which might be packed for a picnic.

1 cantaloupe
1 cup cottage or ricotta cheese
½ large, ripe banana
½ cup strawberries
½ cup yogurt
dash of cinnamon
mint sprigs, garnish

1. Cut the cantaloupe in half and remove seeds. Set aside.

2. Place the cottage or ricotta cheese in a medium bowl. Dice the banana and strawberries and stir them into the cheese along with the yogurt.

3. Stuff the cheese mixture into the cantaloupe halves. Dust with cinnamon, and garnish with mint sprigs. Serve chilled.

Oriental Broccoli

Makes 4 servings

Serve over cooked brown rice for a main dish with a taste of the Orient.

6 cups broccoli spears
   (2 bunches)
4 scallions
¼ cup sunflower oil
¼ cup sesame seeds
4 teaspoons vinegar
4 teaspoons tamari
1 tablespoon honey
3 garlic cloves
2 teaspoons minced fresh
   ginger root
1 cup cubed tofu

1. Place a large kettle with an inch or two of water over high heat. Cut the broccoli stems into ¾-inch pieces and separate florets. Cut the scallions into ½-inch pieces.

2. When the water boils, put the broccoli and scallions in a steamer or metal colander and place in the kettle. Cover and steam about 10 minutes.

3. Meanwhile, place the oil, sesame seeds, vinegar, tamari, honey and garlic (pushed through a garlic press) in a blender. Add the ginger. Process on medium speed until ingredients are well combined. Place sauce in a small pan over low heat to warm through.

4. When the broccoli is nearly tender, after about 8 minutes of steaming, add the tofu, and steam for the remaining 2 minutes. Remove broccoli and tofu to a large serving bowl.

5. Toss with the sesame sauce.

Variation: To serve as a salad, omit the tofu, and chill.

Sunrise Sandwich *Makes 1 serving*

A novel twist for peanut butter lovers.

1. Toast the slice of bread. Mix the peanut butter with the scallions.

2. Spread the toast with the peanut butter mixture. Cover with tomato slices. Broil until the tomatoes are heated through.

3. Serve topped with alfalfa sprouts.

1 slice rye bread
¼ cup peanut butter
1–2 teaspoons chopped
    scallions
thick slices of ripe tomato
¼ cup alfalfa sprouts

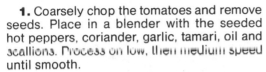

Guacamole Tacos *Makes 4 servings*

Farmer cheese is similar to the cheese used in some Mexican dishes. Although it is not traditionally served with guacamole, it offers extra protein in these vegetarian tacos.

1. Coarsely chop the tomatoes and remove seeds. Place in a blender with the seeded hot peppers, coriander, garlic, tamari, oil and scallions. Process on low, then medium speed until smooth.

2. Pour half of the blended mixture into a small serving dish. Peel and remove the pit from the avocado. Add the avocado, farmer cheese and lemon juice to the tomato mixture remaining in the blender. Process on low, then medium speed until smooth.

3. Chop the onion and place in a small serving dish. Place the sprouts and lettuce in other dishes.

4. To serve, heat the taco shells briefly in a hot oven or under a broiler. (Watch them carefully so they don't burn.) Place some of the guacamole mixture in the bottom of each taco, then garnish with chopped onion, sprouts and lettuce. Add a little of the tomato sauce on top. Provide plenty of napkins for this casual finger food.

2 large, ripe tomatoes
3–4 fresh hot peppers
1 tablespoon fresh coriander
    leaves
2 garlic cloves
1 tablespoon tamari
1 tablespoon corn oil
3 scallions
1 large, ripe avocado
1 cup farmer cheese
2 tablespoons lemon juice
1 small onion
2 cups alfalfa sprouts
1 cup chopped lettuce
12 taco shells

Makes 4 servings # Welsh Rarebit

Served over whole wheat toast, a satisfying main dish.

1 tablespoon butter
1¼ cups milk
1 egg, beaten
2½ cups shredded sharp Cheddar
   or Swiss cheese
½ teaspoon dry mustard
1 teaspoon tamari
¼ teaspoon curry powder
dash of cayenne pepper
4 slices whole wheat toast

1. Place the butter, milk, cheese and seasonings in the top of a double boiler set over boiling water or in a heavy-bottom pan over very low heat. Stir together until the mixture is slightly thickened and the cheese is melted.

2. Serve immediately over whole wheat toast.

Fish

Perch Fillets with Walnut Sauce   *Makes 4 servings*

The unique blend of feta cheese and walnuts harmonizes beautifully with fish.

1. Place the perch fillets in a large skillet with sufficient water to nearly cover them. Cook over medium heat until the water simmers, then cover the pan, turn down heat and poach the fish until opaque throughout (about 8 minutes).

2. Place the walnuts in a blender. Grind into powder with short bursts at high speed.

3. Add the feta and cream to the walnuts. Process on low to medium speed until well blended, stopping the blender and using a spatula to incorporate all the nuts from the bottom of the blender.

4. Place the walnut sauce in a small saucepan and heat gently over low heat.

5. To serve, arrange the fish fillets on a serving platter and spoon the sauce over them. Garnish with parsley sprigs.

Note: For a finer sauce, strain through a layer of cheesecloth or a strainer before spooning the sauce over fish fillets.

Variations: Substitute cod, haddock or flounder for the perch.

1½ pounds perch fillets
½ cup chopped walnut meats
½ cup crumbled feta cheese
¾ cup heavy cream
parsley sprigs, garnish

Makes 2 servings # Haddock with Vegetables

An excellent combination that earns high ratings.

3 medium, ripe tomatoes, chopped
4 scallions, finely chopped
¼ cup minced fresh parsley
2 tablespoons water
2 tablespoons lemon juice
1 garlic clove, crushed
1 tablespoon olive oil
1 tablespoon tamari
½ teaspoon dried thyme or basil
¾ pound haddock fillets

1. Place all of the ingredients except the haddock in a medium skillet over high heat. Stir together and bring to a boil.

2. Reduce heat, place the haddock over top of the vegetable mixture, and cover the skillet. Steam the fish over the simmering mixture about 10 minutes, or until the fish is opaque throughout, but not cooked dry.

3. Carefully remove the haddock and keep it warm on a serving platter.

4. Boil down the vegetable mixture in the skillet over high heat for 3 to 4 minutes, until it is thick. Pour over the haddock and serve.

Spaghetti with Tuna and Garden Vegetables

Makes 4 servings

A rare treat—fresh vegetables and pasta!

¼ teaspoon hot red pepper flakes
¾ pound whole wheat spaghetti
2 scallions
1 medium or 2 small zucchini
2 medium, ripe tomatoes
¼ cup olive oil
2 teaspoons dried basil
6½ ounces water-packed tuna, drained
2 tablespoons grated Parmesan cheese (optional)

1. Place a large kettle half filled with water over high heat. Add the pepper flakes. Cover and bring to a boil, then add the spaghetti. Boil the spaghetti, uncovered, until firm-tender; then drain.

2. Meanwhile, chop the scallions and dice the zucchini. Cut the tomatoes in half across and squeeze out the seeds and juice. Chop the tomatoes.

3. Heat the olive oil in a large skillet, and add the scallions. When they have wilted, add the zucchini. Stir over low to medium heat for 2 to 3 minutes before adding the tomatoes. Sprinkle with basil and cover the skillet.

4. After another 3 to 4 minutes of cooking, when the zucchini is firm-tender, stir in the tuna. Cover and heat through, then turn off heat.

5. Toss the tuna mixture with the drained spaghetti. Serve immediately, with Parmesan, if desired.

Salmon Steaks with Mustard-Dill Sauce
Makes 4 servings

1. Place the water in a large, shallow pan or skillet and set over high heat. Coarsely chop the onion, and scrub and slice the carrot and celery. Add the vegetables to the water with the vinegar.

2. When the water comes to a boil, carefully add the salmon steaks. Return to the boil, then reduce heat and poach steaks until cooked throughout, about 15 minutes.

3. Meanwhile, beat the egg yolk in a small bowl with a wire whisk. First whisk in the mustard, then the lemon juice, dill and honey. Gradually add the oil, a few drops at a time at first, and whisk thoroughly after each addition.

4. When the fish is cooked, carefully remove the salmon steaks from the poaching liquid. Discard vegetables. Place steaks on a serving platter, and spoon on the sauce. Serve garnished with lemon wedges and parsley sprigs.

4 cups water
1 small onion
1 small carrot
½ stalk celery
2 tablespoons mild vinegar
4 salmon steaks, about
　　½ pound each
1 egg yolk
2 teaspoons Dijon-style mustard
2 teaspoons lemon juice
2 teaspoons minced fresh
　　dillweed
¼ teaspoon honey
2 tablespoons sunflower oil
lemon wedges, garnish
parsley sprigs, garnish

Haddock with Ginger Glaze
Makes 2 servings

Beautiful to look at; delicious, too! Who cares if this special dish is also low in fat and high in healthful goodness? I hope you do.

1. In a medium skillet, bring ¼ cup of water to a boil. Add haddock and lower heat. Poach on one side about 2 to 3 minutes, then turn and poach until the fish is opaque throughout. Add additional water, if necessary.

2. While the fish is poaching, grate the ginger root and mince the garlic. Dissolve the cornstarch in the cold water.

3. Remove the haddock gently to a warm serving platter. Pour off any water remaining in the skillet.

4. Place the ginger, garlic, cornstarch mixture, tamari, vinegar and honey in the skillet. Over medium heat, stir until slightly thickened and reduced by almost a third.

5. Pour the ginger sauce over the warm fish fillets. Top with the scallion, and serve immediately.

¼–½ cup water
　¾ pound haddock fillets
　1 teaspoon grated fresh
　　　ginger root
　1 garlic clove
　1 teaspoon cornstarch
　¼ cup cold water
　2 teaspoons tamari
1½ teaspoons cider vinegar
1½ teaspoons honey
　1 scallion, thinly sliced

Spaghetti with Garlic Salmon Sauce

Makes 4 servings

Exotic enough for company with its mild garlic flavor, quick enough for anytime! The cooking tames the garlic's pungency.

¼ cup olive, sunflower
    or soy oil
10 garlic cloves
¾ pound thin whole wheat
    spaghetti
1 egg
15½ ounces water-packed red
    salmon, drained
3 tablespoons minced
    fresh parsley

1. Place a large kettle half filled with water over high heat and bring to a boil.

2. Place the oil in a medium skillet. Place skillet over low heat and add garlic cloves, halved or quartered. (Pieces should be large; minced or crushed garlic is much stronger in flavor.) Stir. Cook just until slightly tender, about 2 or 3 minutes, then turn off heat.

3. When water is boiling in kettle, add spaghetti and return water to a boil. Turn heat to medium and boil spaghetti uncovered.

4. Break the egg into the bottom of the serving bowl. Beat the egg until light.

5. Flake the salmon, crush the bones and add to the garlic. Add parsley and heat through.

6. When the spaghetti is cooked just until firm-tender, about 9 to 10 minutes, drain and immediately toss with the egg. Add the garlic and salmon, and toss again until they are evenly distributed throughout the spaghetti. Serve hot.

Tuna-Stuffed Avocados

Makes 6 servings

As a light luncheon dish, this offers elegance and a fine taste.

1 tablespoon corn oil
½ cup finely chopped celery
2 tablespoons finely chopped
    green onion
2 tablespoons finely chopped
    sweet red pepper
½ cup peas
3 large avocados
6½ ounces water-packed tuna,
    drained
2 tablespoons *Creamy Herbed
    Garlic Dressing* (page 90)
½ cup shredded Cheddar
    cheese

1. Place the oil in a medium skillet, and in it cook the celery, green onion and red pepper for about 5 minutes, or until nearly tender. Add the peas and stir occasionally for another 2 or 3 minutes.

2. Cut the avocados in half lengthwise and remove the pits while the peas are cooking.

3. Add the tuna and dressing to the skillet and heat through. Stuff the avocado halves and sprinkle with the cheese.

4. Broil stuffed avocado halves for about 2 minutes, or until the cheese melts. Serve at once.

Middle Eastern Fish Fillets   Makes 2 servings

"A very nice flavor; good sauce!" said the taste testers.

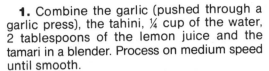

1. Combine the garlic (pushed through a garlic press), the tahini, ¼ cup of the water, 2 tablespoons of the lemon juice and the tamari in a blender. Process on medium speed until smooth.

2. Place the remaining ½ cup of water, the rest of the lemon juice, the thyme and the crushed coriander seeds (a mortar and pestle is best for crushing the seeds) in a medium skillet. Bring to a boil over medium heat.

3. Place the haddock in the skillet. Poach for 2 to 3 minutes on one side, then turn. Continue to poach until fish is opaque throughout.

4. When the fish is nearly done, gently drain any water from the skillet. Spoon garlic sauce over the fish. Cover skillet and heat through. Serve immediately, garnished with lemon slices and mint sprigs.

Note: You might substitute cod or flounder for the haddock fillets.

1 small garlic clove
¼ cup sesame tahini
¾ cup water
3 tablespoons lemon juice
¼ teaspoon tamari
½ teaspoon dried thyme
¼ teaspoon crushed coriander seeds
¾ pound haddock fillets
lemon slices, garnish
mint sprigs, garnish

Milk-Poached Flounder Fillets   Makes 2 servings

A supremely flavorful, low-fat approach to cooking fish.

1. Heat the oil in a pan that will be large enough to accommodate the fish fillets in one layer. Add the scallions and stir. Then add the water and cover. Allow the scallions to steam until softened slightly.

2. Remove the lid from the pan. Place the flounder over the scallions, and add the milk. Cover pan and poach over low heat just until the fillets are opaque clear through.

3. When the fillets are done, place on serving plate, spoon on milk sauce and garnish with the parsley.

2 teaspoons corn oil
2 scallions, chopped
2 tablespoons water
2 flounder fillets
½ cup milk
2 tablespoons minced fresh parsley, garnish

Makes 4 servings **Haddock au Gratin**

The sauce adds vegetable fiber plus taste to poached fish.

2 small potatoes
4–5 garlic cloves
2 teaspoons fresh basil or
　1 teaspoon dried basil
1½ pounds haddock fillets
½ cup yogurt, at room
　temperature
½ cup grated Cheddar cheese
parsley sprigs, garnish

1. Wash but do not peel potatoes. Dice the potatoes and place them in a small saucepan with water to cover. Bring to a boil, then reduce heat and simmer.

2. Meanwhile, peel and mince garlic cloves to obtain 1 tablespoon minced garlic. Chop basil, if fresh.

3. In a large, shallow ovenproof skillet, place enough water to cover the bottom by about ½ inch. Bring to a boil, then add fish. Reduce heat until water is just moving, and poach haddock about 5 to 7 minutes, until opaque throughout. Turn off heat, pour off liquid, and cover to keep fish warm.

4. After cooking potatoes about 8 minutes, add garlic and basil and cook 2 minutes longer, until potatoes are tender. Drain through a small sieve. Place the potatoes, garlic and basil in a bowl and mash with the yogurt until smooth. Or, place potatoes and herbs in a blender and process on medium speed until smooth.

5. Pour the sauce over the haddock, and sprinkle with cheese. Place under a broiler until the sauce and cheese are browned. Serve immediately, garnished with parsley sprigs.

Makes 2 servings **Creamed Tuna and Peas**

This is such a reliable standby on busy days at my house that it can almost be created on "automatic pilot."

2 tablespoons butter
2 tablespoons whole wheat
　flour
1½ cups milk
1 cup peas
6½ ounces water-packed tuna,
　drained
2–4 slices whole grain bread,
　toasted

1. Heat a large skillet and add the butter. When the butter is melted, stir in the flour. Add the milk all at once, and stir until combined.

2. Add the peas and bring to a boil. Reduce the heat and simmer about 10 minutes, until the peas are tender.

3. Stir in the tuna, heat through, and serve over toast.

Note: *Creamed Tuna and Peas* can also be served over *Whole Wheat Waffles* (page 3) or pasta.

Main Dish Tossed Salad
with Tuna *Makes 4 servings*

Add any fresh vegetable you have on hand for your own creation, or follow my lead for a delicious, hearty salad.

1. Wash and dry the spinach and lettuce leaves.

2. Combine the leaves in a large serving bowl with the carrot, sprouts, chopped pepper, zucchini, tuna and cheese.

3. Toss with *Vinaigrette Dressing.* Top individual servings with croutons, if desired.

4 cups loosely packed spinach
2 cups loosely packed lettuce
1 carrot, thinly sliced
½ cup alfalfa sprouts
½ green or sweet red pepper, chopped
½ medium zucchini, chopped
6½ ounces water-packed tuna, drained
¼ cup crumbled feta cheese
Vinaigrette Dressing
   (page 89)
Whole Wheat Croutons
   (page 97), garnish
   (optional)

Haddock with Basil
and Lime *Makes 2 servings*

With this dish, complete with vegetable, you need only add a fresh sliced tomato salad and a whole grain roll for a meal in no time flat!

1. Wash zucchini and trim ends. Cut in half lengthwise, then cut in thin slices crosswise. Squeeze 2 tablespoons of lime juice. Mince basil.

2. Heat a medium skillet and add the olive oil. When the oil is heated, add the butter. Place the zucchini slices in the skillet and cook about 3 to 4 minutes, just until limp.

3. Place the haddock in the skillet. Turn after 2 to 3 minutes, then sprinkle with the lime juice and basil. Cover the skillet and steam another 3 minutes or so, just until the fish turns opaque. This will depend upon the thickness of the fillets. Serve hot with any pan juices.

1 small zucchini
1 lime
2 tablespoons fresh basil
2 teaspoons olive oil
1 teaspoon butter
¾ pound haddock fillets

Makes 8 servings **Tuna Tomatoes**

Some crusty whole grain bread will complement this dish nicely.

8 medium, ripe tomatoes, chilled
6½ ounces water-packed tuna, drained
½ cup cottage cheese
2 stalks celery
1 scallion
2 tablespoons *Tofu Mayonnaise* (page 91)
1 tablespoon minced fresh basil
parsley sprigs, garnish

1. Wash the tomatoes; cut out stem end. Hollow out the tomatoes, reserving the pulp for making stock or adding to soups.

2. In a medium bowl, combine the tuna with the cottage cheese; finely chop the celery and scallion and add. Toss the ingredients with the mayonnaise and basil.

3. Stuff the tomatoes with the tuna mixture. Serve garnished with fresh parsley.

Creamed Salmon with Whole Wheat Noodles

Makes 4 servings

1 red pepper
1 tablespoon corn or sunflower oil
1 tablespoon butter
½ pound whole wheat noodles
3 tablespoons whole wheat flour
1½ cups milk
15½ ounces water-packed red salmon
2 tablespoons minced fresh parsley

1. Place a large pot of water over high heat.

2. Remove seeds and core from pepper and chop. Heat a medium skillet and add the oil and butter. When the butter is melted, cook the pepper until tender, about 10 minutes.

3. When the water in the pot is boiling, add the whole wheat noodles. Return water to a boil, reduce heat and simmer until the noodles are tender, about 10 minutes.

4. When the pepper is tender, stir the flour into the skillet. Stir over low heat a minute or two, then add the milk all at once. Raise the heat to high, and stir occasionally until the mixture begins to bubble and thicken.

5. Meanwhile, remove the skin from the salmon, saving the liquid and the bones. Crush the bones with a fork and mix with the salmon and liquid. Stir salmon into the skillet with the cream sauce. Add parsley and stir.

6. When the noodles are firm-tender, drain. Serve immediately with the salmon sauce.

Poached Fish Fillets with Broth

Makes 4 servings

Light, delicate.

1. Place all of the ingredients except the fish and the lemon wedges in a large skillet, and bring to a boil. Lower heat and simmer about 5 minutes. Remove bay leaf.

2. Place the fish fillets in the broth, cover and steam in the simmering liquid about 10 minutes, or just until the fish is tender, but not dry.

3. Remove the fish to a serving platter, keep warm, and boil down the broth for a minute or two over high heat. Pour the broth over the fish and serve hot, garnished with lemon wedges.

2 cups water
4 scallions, finely chopped
1 tablespoon minced fresh
   parsley
1 tablespoon olive oil
1 tablespoon lemon juice
1 bay leaf
1½ pounds fish fillets
  lemon wedges, garnish

Macaroni and Tuna Skillet Dinner

Makes 4 servings

1. Place a large saucepan filled halfway with water over high heat, and bring it to a boil. Then add the macaroni

2. Meanwhile, saute the onion and red pepper in the oil in a large skillet. Turn down the heat and add the ¼ cup water so that the vegetables will steam.

3. Slice the mushrooms. Add them to the onion and pepper, and when these vegetables are almost soft, after about 10 minutes of cooking, push the garlic through a garlic press into the skillet.

4. Mince the parsley and add with the basil, marjoram, oregano and tuna. Stir to heat through.

5. When the macaroni is cooked, drain and toss with the tuna mixture. Serve immediately.

1 cup whole grain macaroni
1 medium onion, chopped
½ sweet red pepper, chopped
2 tablespoons safflower oil
¼ cup water
1½ cups mushrooms
1 garlic clove
1 tablespoon fresh parsley
1 teaspoon dried basil
1 teaspoon dried marjoram
½ teaspoon dried oregano
6½ ounces water-packed tuna,
   drained

Poultry & Liver

Chicken with Cashews and Snow Peas   *Makes 2 servings*

This Chinese-style dish scores high on flavor, appearance and nutrition. Best served over cooked brown rice.

1. Cut the chicken into small, bite-size pieces. In a small bowl, combine the garlic (pushed through a garlic press), ginger, sesame oil and tamari. Stir the chicken into this marinade, and set aside.

2. Break the stem ends off the snow peas. Rinse the peas, and set them aside to dry on a kitchen towel.

3. Place the safflower oil in a wok or large skillet, and, when it is hot, stir in the cashews. Cook just for a couple of minutes, until the nuts are golden. Remove with a slotted spoon, and set them aside in a serving dish.

4. Stir-fry the snow peas in the oil about 2 minutes, just until they have turned bright green. Add to the cashews in the serving dish.

5. Stir-fry the marinated chicken in the oil just until it is opaque throughout, about 5 minutes. Mix the cooked chicken with the cashews and snow peas, and serve.

2 chicken breast halves, boneless and skinless
1-2 garlic cloves
1-2 teaspoons minced fresh ginger root
1 tablespoon sesame oil
1 tablespoon tamari
½ pound snow peas
3 tablespoons safflower oil
½ cup raw cashew nuts

Makes 4 servings # Chicken Parmesan

Everyone seems to like this combination! Side dishes of steamed broccoli and sliced tomatoes can be colorful companions.

4 chicken breast halves,
    boneless and skinless
¼ cup grated Parmesan cheese
¼ cup minced fresh parsley
1 tablespoon olive oil
1 teaspoon butter

1. Place the chicken breast halves between two sheets of wax paper, and pound the chicken with a rubber hammer or wooden mallet until it is about ¼ inch in thickness.

2. Combine the Parmesan and parsley on another sheet of wax paper, and dredge the chicken in the mixture.

3. Heat a large skillet with the oil, then add the butter. Cook the chicken breasts in one layer, about 3 or 4 minutes on a side.

4. Add a few spoonfuls of water to the skillet and cover, steaming the chicken an additional minute or two, just until cooked throughout. Serve hot.

Makes 2 servings # Chicken Breasts Asparagus

Looks and tastes so special, without any special effort.

2 chicken breast halves,
    boneless and skinless
6–8 spears asparagus
2 teaspoons corn oil
1 teaspoon butter
2 slices mozzarella cheese

1. Place each of the chicken breast halves between two layers of wax paper. Pound with a rubber mallet or other heavy implement until flattened evenly.

2. Heat about an inch of water in a pan with a steamer basket. Trim the tough bottom ends from the asparagus. Peel a thin layer of the tough green skin from the stalks. Steam about 5 minutes until crisp-tender, and remove from heat.

3. Meanwhile, place oil in a medium ovenproof skillet, large enough to hold the chicken in one layer on the bottom. Add the butter to the pan, and when it has melted, add the chicken breasts.

4. Cook the chicken breasts about 3 minutes on each side, or until the chicken is just cooked throughout. Do not cover the pan, and do not overcook.

5. When the chicken is done, place half of the asparagus spears on each piece. Top with a slice of mozzarella, and place under a broiler until the cheese is well melted.

Pineapple Chicken Mozambique   *Makes 2 servings*

Fragrant with spices, this easy-to-prepare chicken dish has an exotic flavor. Serve with brown rice or whole wheat noodles.

1. Cut the chicken breast into bite-size pieces. Chop the onion.

2. Heat a medium skillet and add 1 teaspoon oil. Add the butter, then the onion. Stir over medium heat, adding the cinnamon and turmeric. While the onion is cooking, peel the pineapple section and remove tough inner-core fibers. Cube. Yield should be about 1 cup of pineapple cubes.

3. When the onion is translucent and slightly tender, remove from the skillet and set aside. Add the remaining oil. Heat the skillet until quite hot, but not smoking, and quickly add the chicken. Stir to brown all sides of the chicken.

4. When the chicken is just nearly cooked throughout, after about 3 to 4 minutes, add the onion, pineapple cubes, raisins, parsley, tamari and lime juice. Heat through and serve.

2 chicken breast halves,
    boneless and skinless
1 medium onion
2 teaspoons corn oil
1 teaspoon butter
¼ teaspoon cinnamon
⅛ teaspoon turmeric
¼ small, ripe pineapple
2 tablespoons raisins
1 tablespoon minced fresh
    parsley
2 teaspoons tamari
2 tablespoons lime juice

Chicken with Plum Sauce   *Makes 4 servings*

Try over cooked brown rice or whole wheat pasta.

1. Melt 1 tablespoon of butter in a medium skillet. Chop the onion and add to the melted butter. Stir over medium heat until translucent, then stir in flour.

2. When the onion has begun cooking, place the tomato paste, stock or water, garlic, honey, vinegar and paprika in a blender.

3. Wash the plums and cut into thin slices.

4. Cut the chicken into bite-size pieces.

5. Add the cooked onion and flour mixture to the ingredients in the blender, and process on high speed until smooth. Return the sauce to the medium skillet, add the plum slices, and heat over a low flame.

6. Heat a large skillet with the remaining tablespoon of butter and the oil. Cook the chicken pieces about 5 minutes, until they are opaque. Place on a serving dish, cover with the hot plum sauce, and serve.

2 tablespoons butter
1 large yellow onion
1 tablespoon whole wheat flour
2 tablespoons tomato paste
¾ cup *Stock* (pages 175–76) or
    water
1 garlic clove, crushed
1 tablespoon honey
1 tablespoon mild vinegar
¼ teaspoon paprika
3 firm plums
4 chicken breast halves,
    boneless and skinless
1 tablespoon corn or
    sunflower oil

Garlic Chicken with Pasta Shells

Makes 2 servings

2 chicken breast halves, boneless and skinless
6 ounces whole wheat pasta shells
4 teaspoons olive oil
2 garlic cloves
¾ cup water
1 tablespoon tomato paste
2 teaspoons tamari
1 teaspoon lemon juice
2 tablespoons minced fresh parsley
parsley sprigs, garnish

1. Place a large saucepan of water over high heat.

2. While the water is heating, cut the chicken breasts into small, bite-size pieces.

3. When the water is boiling, add pasta, stir and cook uncovered over medium heat.

4. Warm the oil in a large skillet, and press the garlic cloves through a garlic press into the oil. (The oil should not be too hot, for the garlic becomes bitter when browned.) Add the chicken pieces immediately, and stir over medium heat to coat with the garlic and oil.

5. Add ¾ cup water, tomato paste, tamari and lemon juice, and cover the pan. Simmer over low heat about 5 minutes, stirring once or twice, just until the chicken is cooked through.

6. Drain the pasta when it is tender, but still firm to the bite. Add the parsley to the chicken. Toss the chicken with the shells in a serving bowl. Garnish with parsley sprigs, and serve immediately.

Bulgur Pilaf with Chicken Livers

Makes 4 servings

1 teaspoon corn oil
2 teaspoons butter
1 medium onion, finely chopped
1 cup bulgur
1¾ cups *Stock* (pages 175–76) or water
2 teaspoons tamari
1 pound chicken livers

1. Place the oil and half of the butter in a medium skillet over medium heat. When the butter is melted, add the onion. Stir occasionally until the onion is translucent.

2. Stir the bulgur into the skillet with the onion until some of the oil is absorbed. Add the stock or water and the tamari. Bring to a boil, cover, reduce heat and simmer about 15 minutes, until the liquid is absorbed.

3. While the bulgur is simmering, clean and quarter the chicken livers. Melt the remaining butter in a medium skillet, and briefly saute the livers, just until cooked through but still pink.

4. Place the cooked bulgur in a serving dish, and top with the chicken livers. Serve hot.

Liver with
Mixed Vegetables *Makes 2 servings*

A very attractive dish, with flavor to match.

1. Cut the liver into long, thin strips. Combine the flour and basil on wax paper, and dredge the liver slices in the mixture.

2. Heat the oil in a medium skillet, and cook the liver over low to moderate heat. The inside of each strip should remain pink. Do not overcook.

3. While the liver is cooking, chop the scallions. Cut the zucchini in half crosswise, then lengthwise. Cut each section into long, thin strips. Halve the cherry tomatoes.

4. When the liver is cooked, remove to a serving plate and keep warm. Add the scallions to the pan, add a few spoonfuls of water to prevent sticking and stir. When the scallions wilt, add the zucchini.

5. When the onions and zucchini are softened, add the cherry tomatoes and tamari, and stir to combine. Place a lid on the skillet, and allow the vegetables to steam until tender, about 10 minutes, stirring occasionally.

6. To serve, arrange the vegetables around the liver. Serve hot.

¾ pound calves' liver
3 tablespoons whole wheat flour
2 teaspoons dried basil
1 tablespoon corn oil
2 scallions
1 small zucchini
10 cherry tomatoes
2 teaspoons tamari

Liver Pâté Patties *Makes 4 servings*

Serve with Vegetarian Gravy *(page 93) or a tomato sauce.*

1. Place the onion, liver, oats, lemon juice and basil in a blender. Process on medium to high speed until combined, stopping the blender and scraping down the sides of the container with a spatula when necessary.

2. Place the blended mixture in a medium bowl, and fold in the soft bread crumbs. Form into eight patties.

3. Heat a large, lightly oiled skillet and cook the patties, turning when one side is browned. Do not overcook. Serve hot.

1 medium onion, chopped
½ pound calves' liver
1 cup rolled oats
2 tablespoons lemon juice
1 tablespoon dried basil
2 cups soft whole wheat
    bread crumbs

Side Dishes

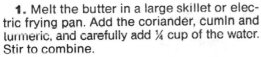

Golden Cauliflower and Peas
Makes 4 servings

Mildly spicy, this vegetable combination is a favorite in India.

1. Melt the butter in a large skillet or electric frying pan. Add the coriander, cumin and turmeric, and carefully add ¼ cup of the water. Stir to combine.

2. While the spices are simmering over low heat, quickly separate the cauliflower into florets. Add immediately to the skillet. Add the remaining water and cover the cauliflower, turning the heat to medium.

3. Chop the onion and add to the skillet along with the bay leaf. Cover the skillet, and when the mixture boils, reduce heat to simmer.

4. After the cauliflower has simmered about 10 minutes and is beginning to soften, add the peas and tamari. Cover the skillet and cook an additional 5 minutes, until the cauliflower is crisp-tender and the peas are cooked through. Serve hot.

Variation: If you like hot dishes, you might add a little cayenne pepper.

2 tablespoons butter
1 tablespoon ground coriander
1 teaspoon ground cumin
1 teaspoon turmeric
1¼ cups water
1 medium head cauliflower
1 small onion
1 bay leaf
1 cup peas
1 tablespoon tamari

Makes 4 servings

Vegetables Riviera

With a taste as good as gold.

3 small zucchini
1 medium, ripe tomato
1 tablespoon olive oil
1 garlic clove
1½ teaspoons dried basil or dried
    marjoram
grated Parmesan cheese
    (optional)

1. Cut the zucchini into round slices or 2-inch strips. Cut the tomato in half across and squeeze out seeds. Chop.

2. Place oil in a medium skillet over medium heat. Add zucchini and tomato. Push the garlic through a press, and add it along with the basil or marjoram to the skillet.

3. Cook, stirring occasionally, until the vegetables are tender, about 10 minutes. Serve hot, sprinkled with Parmesan, if desired, or serve cold.

Makes 4 servings

Carrots, Cauliflower and Pumpkin Seeds

A colorful and nutrition-rich vegetable dish with a nice combination of flavors.

1 tablespoon corn oil
1 medium onion, sliced into thin
    rings
2 cups cauliflower florets
2 medium carrots, sliced
    diagonally
1 tablespoon minced fresh
    parsley
¼ cup pumpkin seeds

1. In a large skillet, warm the corn oil, then add the onion rings. Cook over medium heat for a minute or two.

2. Break the cauliflower florets into bite-size pieces and add them to the skillet along with the carrots. Stir with the onions, then cover, adding a few spoonfuls of water so that the vegetables will steam.

3. Stir the vegetables occasionally, adding a little more water, if needed, and steam until tender, about 15 minutes.

4. Toss the vegetables with the parsley and pumpkin seeds. Serve hot.

Makes 4 servings

Carrot Relish

This unusual side dish adds a fresh note to any meal.

4 small carrots
1 tablespoon chopped fresh
    mint leaves
1 teaspoon honey
1 lime

1. Shred the carrots, which should be garden fresh if possible. Toss with the mint leaves.

2. Drizzle with the honey, and squeeze lime juice over all. Toss again and serve.

Curried Carrots *Makes 4 servings*

A wonderful treatment of carrots, and versatile, too. If there are leftovers, just refrigerate, toss with a little yogurt, and serve as a cold side dish.

1. Cut the carrots into julienne strips about 3 inches long. Place them in a large skillet with the oil, and stir over medium heat. Add ¼ cup of the water, then cover and steam carrots about 10 minutes.

2. While the carrots are steaming, mince the ginger root. Place the ginger in a small bowl, and add the poppy and sesame seeds, coriander, turmeric, cumin and chili into the bowl. Push the garlic through a garlic press and add.

3. When the carrots have steamed, add the ginger mixture and stir together. Add the butter and the remaining water. Cover and steam for 2 or more minutes, until the carrots are just firm-tender. They should not be soft. Serve hot.

4 large carrots
2 teaspoons sunflower oil
½ cup water
1½ teaspoons minced fresh
    ginger root
1 teaspoon poppy seeds
1 teaspoon sesame seeds
½ teaspoon ground coriander
¼ teaspoon turmeric
½ teaspoon ground cumin
¼ teaspoon chili powder
2 garlic cloves
2 teaspoons butter

Seasoned Broiled Tomatoes *Makes 4 servings*

1. Wash the tomatoes and cut in half crosswise. Place them on a baking sheet with cut sides down, and heat them under a broiler.

2. Place the sunflower and sesame seeds in a blender, and grind them with short bursts at high speed. Add the bread crumbs, Parmesan, brewer's yeast, herbs and spices, and blend again at high speed until mixed.

3. After 5 minutes, turn the tomatoes and return to broiler until heated through.

4. Heat a small skillet and place the butter in it. Stir in the bread crumb mixture and heat through.

5. Top the tomato halves with the bread crumbs, and return to the broiler until they are slightly browned. Serve hot.

4 large, ripe tomatoes
2 tablespoons sunflower seeds
1 tablespoon sesame seeds
¼ cup dry whole wheat bread
    crumbs
2 tablespoons grated Parmesan
    cheese
1 teaspoon brewer's yeast
1 teaspoon dried marjoram
1 teaspoon dried basil
½ teaspoon dried thyme
½ teaspoon dried oregano
½ teaspoon paprika
dash of cayenne pepper
1 tablespoon butter

Makes 4 servings # Honey-Glazed Carrots
Attractive!

4 carrots
¼ cup water
1 tablespoon butter
1 tablespoon honey
½ teaspoon lemon juice
½ teaspoon tamari
dash of grated nutmeg

1. Cut the carrots into thin sticks about 2 to 3 inches long.

2. Place the carrot sticks with the remaining ingredients in a medium saucepan, and cover. Bring ingredients to a boil, reduce heat and simmer.

3. When the carrots are crisp-tender, after about 10 to 12 minutes, remove the lid. Turn heat to high, quickly boiling off the remaining water, for about 2 to 3 minutes, tossing the carrots to coat with the glaze. Serve hot.

Sauteed Spinach with Garlic
Makes 4 servings

1 pound spinach
2 teaspoons butter
1 garlic clove
1 teaspoon tamari

1. Remove tough stalks of spinach and rinse thoroughly. Allow water to cling to leaves for steaming. Tear leaves in half.

2. In a large skillet, melt the butter. Push the garlic through a press and add to the skillet, stirring until coated with the butter.

3. Immediately add the spinach and tamari. Stir until the spinach is wilted and cooked through. Serve hot.

Makes 4 servings # Bulgur Pilaf

1 medium onion
2 tablespoons corn oil
2 tablespoons minced fresh
    parsley
1 teaspoon dried marjoram or
    basil
1 cup bulgur
2 tablespoons split red lentils
2 cups hot *Stock* (pages 175–76)
    or hot water
2 teaspoons tamari

1. Chop onion fine. Place oil in a medium saucepan and heat. Add onion and stir.

2. Mince the parsley while onion cooks. Add the parsley along with the marjoram or basil to the onion and stir.

3. When onion is translucent, stir in bulgur, then red lentils. When these are coated with the oil, add the stock or water and tamari.

4. Cook over low flame until liquid is absorbed, about 10 minutes. Cover and let rest about 5 minutes before serving.

Bulgur with Carrots   *Makes 4 servings*

1. Place the butter in a heavy-bottom skillet or saucepan. Melt over medium heat. Chop the onion and add to the butter. Stir occasionally over low heat.

2. Meanwhile, dice the carrots.

3. Add the carrots to the onion when the onion is translucent and beginning to soften. Stir the carrots and onion over medium heat for 1 or 2 minutes.

4. Add the bulgur, stirring until it is mixed with the vegetables. Add the stock or water and tamari. Bring to a boil, cover, reduce heat and simmer about 15 minutes, until the bulgur is tender and the water is absorbed. Serve hot.

Note: If water is not completely absorbed by the end of the cooking period, remove lid, raise heat and stir until the moisture evaporates.

2 teaspoons butter
1 small onion
2 medium carrots
1 cup bulgur
1¾ cups *Stock* (pages 175–76) or water
2 teaspoons tamari

Bulgur with Scallions   *Makes 4 servings*

This is a nice side dish to complement beans or lentils.

1. Heat the oil in a medium saucepan, and add the chopped scallions. Stir until the scallions wilt and begin to become translucent. Add parsley and basil.

2. Stir in the bulgur until it is mixed with the scallions. Then add the water and tamari.

3. Simmer, covered, for about 15 minutes or until the water is absorbed. Serve hot.

1 tablespoon corn oil
2 scallions, chopped
1 tablespoon minced fresh parsley
1 teaspoon dried basil
1 cup bulgur
2 cups water
1 tablespoon tamari

Quick-as-a-Whiz
Applesauce

Makes 3 cups

Red apples give a rosy glow to this good sauce.

4 cups coarsely chopped apples
1 cup water
2 teaspoons lemon juice
2 teaspoons honey
cinnamon

1. Place half of the chopped, unpeeled apples and ½ cup of water in a blender, and process on medium speed until quite smooth. Place the blended apple mixture in a medium saucepan and repeat with the remaining apples and water.

2. Add the lemon juice, honey and cinnamon to taste, and bring the apples to a boil over medium heat. Reduce heat, cover and simmer for about 10 to 15 minutes.

3. Serve hot, or chill. Store leftovers in the refrigerator.

Note: A tart apple, such as Stayman Winesap, is best. Do not use a watery apple, such as McIntosh.

Rainbow Vegetables

Makes 4 servings

Don't limit yourself to one vegetable at a time when steaming. Choose two or three for color and variety.

2 large stalks broccoli
1 sweet red pepper
1 medium onion
2 tablespoons butter
½ teaspoon dried basil

1. Place about an inch of water in a large kettle with a metal colander to steam the vegetables or in a large saucepan with a steaming basket inserted. Heat water over medium flame.

2. Remove the tough green skin from the thick broccoli stalks. Cut stalks on a diagonal and separate florets.

3. Remove the seeds from the pepper, and cut the pepper into thin strips. Slice the onion lengthwise into thin strips.

4. When the water is boiling, place the vegetables in the colander or steaming basket. Cover and steam for 15 minutes, until vegetables are crisp-tender.

5. Melt butter in a small skillet and add basil. Serve vegetables hot, drizzled with the herbed butter.

Variations: Try cauliflower, green peppers, scallions, thinly sliced sweet potatoes, leeks or other vegetable combinations.

Curried Lemon Broccoli

Makes 4 servings

1. Trim the stem ends of the broccoli, and peel a thin layer of the tough green skin from the stalks. Cut the broccoli in thirds crosswise.

2. Separate the florets and cut the stem sections into strips about the size of the florets. Steam the broccoli until tender, about 10 minutes.

3. Meanwhile, finely grate the lemon rind. Juice the lemon.

4. Place the lemon juice with the grated lemon rind, 2 tablespoons of water, honey, sesame seeds and curry powder in a small saucepan. Bring to a boil and simmer about 1 minute.

5. When the broccoli is just tender but still a little firm, remove it from the heat. Place it in a serving dish, and sprinkle it with the curry mixture. Serve hot.

Note: This dish is also good when chilled.

1 large bunch broccoli
1 lemon
2 tablespoons water
1 tablespoon honey
1 tablespoon sesame seeds
1 teaspoon curry powder
parsley sprigs, garnish

Potato Pancakes

Makes 2 servings

Try these with applesauce.

1. Place the tofu, scallion, oil and tamari in a blender. Process until smooth on medium speed.

2. Add half the potatoes and process again on medium speed until smooth. Add remaining potatoes, flour and baking powder, and process until smooth. If the batter seems too thin for pancakes, add a touch more flour.

3. On a hot, lightly oiled griddle, form pancakes by pouring a few tablespoons of batter onto the cooking surface and spreading it out slightly with the back of a wooden spoon.

4. Cook pancakes slowly on one side until well browned, then turn and brown other side. Serve hot.

¼ cup crumbled tofu
1 scallion, sliced
1 tablespoon corn oil
1 teaspoon tamari
2 small potatoes, cubed
1½ tablespoons whole wheat flour
¼ teaspoon baking powder

Makes 4 servings **Zucchini Pancakes**

These pancakes also make a terrific accompaniment for fish. Serve them plain or with a bit of tomato sauce spooned over top.

2 small or 1 medium zucchini,
    about ½ pound
2 eggs
2 tablespoons water
2 tablespoons chopped fresh
    chives
½ cup whole wheat flour
olive oil
parsley sprigs, garnish

1. Chop the zucchini coarsely, and place it in a blender with the eggs, water and chives. Process on low, then medium speed until smooth, stopping the blender and scraping down the sides as necessary.

2. Add the flour slowly, while the blender is running, if possible. (Some blenders have a removable piece in the lid for this purpose.) Continue to process on medium speed until very smooth.

3. Heat a large skillet and add enough of the oil to coat the bottom lightly. Pour out batter for four small pancakes.

4. Turn the pancakes when they are browned on one side. Finish cooking, remove and keep warm, then pour out the remaining batter for four more pancakes. Cook in the same way. Serve hot.

Makes 4 servings **Herbed Baked Tomatoes**

Best when gardens are bursting with red, ripe tomatoes.

4 scallions, minced
3 tablespoons minced fresh
    parsley
½ teaspoon dried oregano
2 tablespoons olive oil
2 tablespoons grated Parmesan
    cheese
1 garlic clove
4 large, ripe tomatoes

1. Combine the scallions, parsley, oregano, oil, Parmesan and the garlic (pushed through a garlic press or minced) in a small bowl.

2. Cut the tomatoes in half and place, cut side up, in a shallow baking dish. Spoon the herbed mixture over the tomato halves and spread across cut surface.

3. Place tomatoes in a preheated 400°F oven for 10 minutes, until the tomatoes are heated through. Place the dish under a broiler briefly to brown the tops lightly. Serve hot or at room temperature.

Spaghetti with Parsley
Makes 4 servings

Serve with poached fish.

1. Bring a large pot of water to a boil over high heat.

2. Meanwhile, heat a medium skillet. First add the oil to the skillet, then the chopped onion. Saute, stirring occasionally. Mince the parsley until fine.

3. When the water is boiling, add the spaghetti, stir, and return to a boil. Then lower heat and cook until tender, about 10 minutes.

4. When the onion is translucent, stir in the parsley. Mince or crush the garlic cloves and add them when the parsley is wilted. Turn off heat, then stir in the tamari and nutmeg.

5. When the spaghetti is done, drain and toss with the parsley sauce. Sprinkle with Parmesan and serve.

¼ cup olive oil
1 medium onion, finely chopped
1 cup fresh parsley
½ pound whole wheat spaghetti
3 garlic cloves
2 teaspoons tamari
¼ teaspoon grated nutmeg
¼ cup grated Parmesan cheese

Sauteed Cherry Tomatoes
Makes 4 servings

A wonderful side dish to make when you think you haven't time for anything . . .

1. Wash and remove stems from cherry tomatoes.

2. Melt the butter in a medium skillet. Mince the parsley and add it to the skillet.

3. Add the tomatoes, then the garlic, pushed through a garlic press.

4. Stir the tomatoes just until they are heated through (if cooked much longer, they will burst). You can turn off the heat and keep the pan covered until serving.

Variation: Eliminate the parsley and garlic, and add ½ teaspoon of honey to the melted butter before sauteing tomatoes. These honey-glazed tomatoes are gorgeous served along with a green vegetable such as asparagus or broccoli.

1 pint cherry tomatoes
1 tablespoon butter
1 tablespoon fresh parsley
1 garlic clove

Makes 4 servings **Summer String Beans**

Add zesty flavor to green beans.

1 pound green beans
1 small onion, finely chopped
1 tablespoon olive oil
¼ cup minced fresh parsley
1 garlic clove
1 teaspoon lemon juice

1. Steam the green beans until firm-tender, about 5 minutes. Remove from the heat and refresh with cold running water until the beans are cool. Set aside.

2. Meanwhile, place the onion in the oil in a medium skillet. Stir until the onion is translucent, about 5 minutes.

3. Stir in the minced parsley and the garlic (pushed through a garlic press or minced). When the parsley is wilted, stir in the green beans and lemon juice.

4. Heat the beans through, stirring over medium heat. Serve hot.

Makes 4 servings **Gingered Snow Peas**

This is an attractive accompaniment to poached or broiled fish.

1 large, firm pear
2 tablespoons safflower oil
1 tablespoon minced fresh
   ginger root
2 tablespoons chopped walnuts
2 cups snow peas

1. Core the pear and cut into long, thin slices.

2. Heat the oil in a wok or electric skillet. When it is hot, but not smoking, add the ginger root and stir quickly over medium to high heat, about 1 minute.

3. Add the pear slices and cook for an additional minute, then add the walnuts and snow peas. Stir together until the peas are bright green and still crisp-tender, just a minute or two. Serve hot.

Makes 4 servings **Fried Bananas**

A delicious accompaniment for curried dishes.

2 large bananas
2 teaspoons butter

1. Cut the bananas in half across, then quarter them lengthwise.

2. Melt the butter in a medium skillet, then place the bananas in the skillet. Cook just until heated through. Serve immediately.

Sweet Lime Carrots *Makes 4 servings*

1. Cut the carrots into long, thin fingers. Place in a medium saucepan with the corn oil and stir over medium heat for 2 to 3 minutes.

2. Add the lime juice and water. Press the garlic through a garlic press into the carrots. Stir in the honey.

3. Cover the pan and steam over low heat until the carrots are firm-tender, about 10 to 15 minutes.

3 large carrots
1 tablespoon corn oil
1 tablespoon lime juice
2 tablespoons water
1 garlic clove
½ teaspoon honey

Tabbouleh Salad *Makes 4 servings*

One of the nicest ways to eat vitamin-rich parsley that you're likely to find.

1. Place the bulgur and water in a small bowl and set it aside to soak.

2. Meanwhile, mince the parsley. Cut tomato in half across, and squeeze out the juice and seeds. Chop the tomato fine. Mince or crush the garlic clove. Finely grate ⅛ teaspoon lemon rind, and squeeze 2 tablespoons of lemon juice. If using fresh mint and tarragon, mince.

3. After the bulgur has absorbed most of the water, in about 15 minutes, drain by pouring the bulgur into a sieve and squeezing excess moisture out by hand or by pressing with the back of a spoon.

4. Place drained bulgur in the serving bowl, and add remaining ingredients, pouring lemon juice and oil over all. Toss until combined. The salad can be chilled, if desired, before serving.

Note: You can double the recipe and chill leftovers. Flavors will mingle and be enhanced.

Variation: Add 6½ ounces of drained, water-packed tuna for a light, main-dish salad, *Tuna Tabbouleh.*

⅓ cup bulgur
1 cup water
½ cup tightly packed fresh parsley
1 large, ripe tomato
1 garlic clove
1 lemon
½ teaspoon fresh mint or ¼ teaspoon dried mint
½ teaspoon fresh tarragon or ¼ teaspoon dried tarragon
3 tablespoons olive or sunflower oil

Makes 4 servings # Salmon and Pasta Salad

"Great for summer," the taste testers said. I think you'll enjoy the refreshing taste.

1¼ cups sesame pasta spirals or whole wheat pasta shells
½ green pepper
½ small zucchini
2 large scallions
1 tablespoon fresh dillweed
1 tablespoon fresh parsley
7¾ ounces water-packed red salmon, drained
2 tablespoons lemon juice
1 tablespoon olive oil
1 tablespoon *Tofu Mayonnaise* (page 91)
8 cherry tomatoes, garnish

1. Place a large saucepan three-quarters filled with water over high heat and cover. When the water boils, remove cover, add pasta and return to the boil. Turn down heat and boil pasta about 6 to 8 minutes, until firm-tender.

2. Meanwhile, chop the green pepper and dice the zucchini. Chop the scallions, including green tops. Mince the dill and parsley. Place all in a serving bowl.

3. Remove the skin from the salmon, if desired. Crush the bones and add with the flaked meat to the serving bowl.

4. When the pasta is cooked, drain and rinse with cold water until cooled. Drain thoroughly, then add to serving bowl.

5. Drizzle the lemon juice and oil over the salad and add the mayonnaise. Toss to combine. Serve immediately or chill. Garnish with cherry tomatoes.

Makes 4 servings # Hot Macaroni Salad

Delicious served with corn on the cob.

3 cups water
1 cup whole wheat macaroni
3 tablespoons corn oil
1 tablespoon cider vinegar
1 teaspoon celery seeds
1 teaspoon dry mustard
6½ ounces water-packed tuna, drained
½ cup chopped celery
½ cup chopped green pepper
3 tablespoons *Tofu Mayonnaise* (page 91)

1. Bring the water to a boil in a large saucepan. Add the macaroni, cook until firm-tender, then drain.

2. Meanwhile, bring the oil, vinegar, celery seeds and mustard to a boil in a small saucepan.

3. When macaroni is done, toss with the oil and vinegar mixture, tuna, celery, pepper and mayonnaise. Serve immediately.

Note: This salad can also be served cold.

Spinach and Mushroom Salad
Makes 4 servings

1. Place the egg in a small saucepan, and cover it with cold water. Place over medium heat, and when the water boils, turn to low heat. Simmer 10 to 15 minutes until hard cooked. The egg will take longer to cook if still cold from refrigeration. Drain, and immediately add cold water to the pan to stop the cooking of the egg. Set aside.

2. While the egg is simmering, wash the spinach and blot dry with a clean kitchen towel. Arrange on a large, flat serving plate or in a salad bowl.

3. Clean the mushrooms and slice. Place over the spinach leaves.

4. Place the sesame seeds in a small heavy-bottom pan over medium heat. Stir until slightly toasted and golden. Sprinkle over the salad.

5. Finely chop the hard-cooked egg and sprinkle over the salad. Top with salad dressing and serve.

1 egg
2 quarts unpacked spinach
1 cup mushrooms
2 teaspoons sesame seeds
Creamy Herbed Garlic Dressing
    (page 90) or *Vinaigrette
    Dressing* (page 89)

Tossed Salad with Feta Cheese
Makes 4 servings

Satisfying enough for a luncheon main dish when served with whole wheat rolls.

1. Tear the lettuce leaves into large pieces. Combine with the remaining ingredients, except dressing, in a large serving bowl.

2. Toss with *Vinaigrette Dressing* just before serving.

1 small head red leaf or romaine
    lettuce
1 cup cherry tomatoes, halved
½ cup crumbled feta cheese
½ cup thinly sliced red cabbage
½ cup broccoli florets, separated
¼ cup alfalfa sprouts
1 thin slice red onion, separated
    into rings
1 small carrot, thinly sliced
1 radish, thinly sliced
2 tablespoons chopped fresh
    dillweed
2 tablespoons minced fresh
    parsley
Vinaigrette Dressing
    (page 89)

Makes 4 servings   # Orange Cup Fruit Salad

Use the orange shell, resting in a small glass dessert bowl, as an attractive serving container. Try serving a grapefruit salad the same way.

2 large navel oranges
2 peaches
½ cup grapes
2 tablespoons yogurt
dash of grated nutmeg
2 tablespoons finely chopped
    walnuts, garnish

1. Cut the oranges in half across. Run the knife along the perimeter of the sections, then carefully remove the orange from the shell. Do this over a small mixing bowl in order to catch the juices. Chop the orange sections and place in another bowl.

2. Cube unpeeled peaches. Seed the grapes, if necessary, and cut in half. Add both to orange sections.

3. With a slotted spoon, stir the fruit, then pack into the orange shells. Place halves in small glass bowls, stemware or baking ramekins to hold them steady for serving.

4. Mix the yogurt with the fruit juice remaining in the mixing bowl. Add the nutmeg, stir to combine, then drizzle over the fruit salad. Garnish with walnuts. Serve chilled, if desired.

Variation: In winter, substitute apples and dried fruits for the peaches and grapes.

Makes 4 servings   # Papaya Salad Boats

As delicious as it is beautiful; a salad with a hint of the tropics.

2 papayas
1 small banana
½ cup red grapes, seeded and
    halved
¼ cup chopped walnuts
2 tablespoons olive oil
1½ tablespoons lime juice
2 teaspoons honey
2 teaspoons chopped fresh
    basil or mint or ½ teaspoon
    dried basil or mint
mint sprigs, garnish

1. Cut the papayas in half and remove the seeds.

2. Cube the banana and combine in a small bowl with the grapes and walnuts.

3. Add the oil, lime juice, honey and basil or mint to the banana mixture and toss until well mixed.

4. Divide the fruit mixture, and place it in the centers of the papaya halves. Garnish with mint sprigs and serve.

Oriental Tuna Salad *Makes 2 servings*
So pretty.

1. Toss the cabbage with the pineapple, carrot, tuna, mayonnaise, mustard and sesame seeds until combined.

2. Serve on a bed of lettuce leaves, garnished with parsley.

Variation: Substitute leftover cooked chicken for the tuna.

1 cup shredded Chinese cabbage
½ cup chopped fresh pineapple
1 carrot, shredded
6½ ounces water-packed tuna, drained
2 tablespoons *Mini-Calorie Mayonnaise* (page 90)
1 teaspoon Dijon-style mustard
1 teaspoon sesame seeds
lettuce leaves
parsley sprigs, garnish

Fruited Cabbage Salad with Sour Cream Dressing *Makes 4 servings*
Good color, texture and flavor combination.

1. Place the cabbage in a serving bowl. Cut banana on the diagonal into ¼-inch slices. Cut the strawberries into thick slices.

2. In a small bowl, place the sour cream, oil, lime juice and honey. Stir together well.

3. Add the sour cream dressing to the salad and toss gently. Garnish with mint sprigs.

2 cups shredded cabbage
1 large banana
1½ cups strawberries
¼ cup sour cream
2 tablespoons olive oil
1 tablespoon lime juice
1 teaspoon honey
mint sprigs, garnish

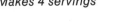
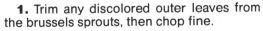

Brussels Sprout Salad Deluxe *Makes 4 servings*

1. Trim any discolored outer leaves from the brussels sprouts, then chop fine.

2. Toss the brussels sprouts with the celery, apple, raisins and sprouts. Add dressing to moisten well, and toss again before serving.

Variations: Substitute red or white cabbage for the brussels sprouts. Or substitute chopped dates for the raisins. You can also substitute 1 cup of peas (steamed until firm-tender, then refreshed in cold water) for the celery and eliminate the raisins.

2 cups brussels sprouts
1 stalk celery, chopped
1 tart, red apple, diced
¼ cup raisins
¼ cup alfalfa sprouts
Vinaigrette Dressing (page 89)

Walnuts and Sprouts Cole Slaw

Makes 6 servings

A salad that will keep for a few days under refrigeration to be used when you need it.

¼ small head cabbage
1 large carrot
½ cup alfalfa sprouts
¼ cup raisins
¼ cup chopped walnuts
⅛ teaspoon celery seeds
Mini-Calorie Mayonnaise
    (page 90)

1. Thinly slice the cabbage and place it in a serving bowl. Shred the carrot and add it to the cabbage.

2. Add the sprouts, raisins, walnuts and celery seeds. Toss with enough mayonnaise to moisten. Serve chilled.

Tomatoes with Avocado Dressing

Makes 4 servings

One of those salads that really dresses up a meal!

4 medium, ripe tomatoes
1 large bunch watercress
1 avocado
3 scallions
1 tablespoon lime or lemon juice
¼ cup *Mini-Calorie Mayonnaise*
    (page 90)
¼ cup alfalfa sprouts

1. Cut the tomatoes into thick slices. Arrange 2 or 3 slices for each serving on a bed of watercress, placed on individual plates.

2. For the dressing, peel and pit the avocado. Cut up 1 scallion and place it with the avocado in a blender. Add the lime or lemon juice and the mayonnaise. Process on medium speed until smooth.

3. Mince the remaining 2 scallions.

4. Spoon some of the dressing attractively over the tomato slices. Sprinkle with the scallion and top with the alfalfa sprouts in the center. Serve immediately.

Note: If there is any leftover dressing, store tightly covered in the refrigerator. Placing the avocado pit with the dressing will prevent the dressing from darkening.

Tomato and
Mozzarella Salad   *Makes 4 servings*

A salad ring that will star in any table setting.

1. Trim the stem ends and bottoms from the tomatoes, and cut each into four slices.

2. Trim the mozzarella slices into rounds about the size of the tomato slices.

3. On a serving plate, arrange alternate layers of tomato and cheese around the perimeter. Heap the sprouts in the center of the plate, and garnish with parsley.

4. Sprinkle with dressing and serve.

2 large, ripe tomatoes
8 thin slices mozzarella cheese
1 cup alfalfa sprouts
1 tablespoon minced fresh
    parsley, garnish
Vinaigrette Dressing (page 89)

Jerusalem Artichoke Salad   *Makes 4 servings*

"Sophisticated" describes it best.

1. Remove some of the small knobs and partially peel the Jerusalem artichokes to make them easier to handle. Slice the artichokes thin lengthwise, then cut them into matchstick strips.

2. Finely dice the red pepper. Mince the watercress.

3. Toss the artichoke strips, pepper and watercress in a medium bowl with enough dressing to moisten well. Serve on a bed of red leaf lettuce.

Variations: Substitute *Creamy Herbed Garlic Dressing* (page 90) for the vinaigrette. Serve on spinach leaves.

6 large Jerusalem artichokes
½ small sweet red pepper
¼ cup watercress
Vinaigrette Dressing
    (page 89)
red leaf lettuce

Fennel and Apple Salad   *Makes 4 servings*

A unique variation of Waldorf salad that pleases the taste buds.

1. Remove the tough outer ribs of the fennel bulb and trim off the tops. Cut fennel heart lengthwise into thin slices.

2. Chop apples, leaving peel on. Combine with the fennel and walnuts in a serving bowl.

3. In a cup, mix together the oil, lemon juice and parsley. Pour over the salad, toss and serve.

1 large fennel bulb
2 tart, red apples
½ cup chopped walnuts
2 tablespoons olive oil
2 tablespoons lemon juice
1 tablespoon minced fresh
    parsley

Pineapple, Bulgur and Almond Salad

Makes 2 servings

¼ cup bulgur
⅔ cup water
¼ teaspoon ground coriander
2 tablespoons blanched
   almonds
1 sweet red pepper
2 tablespoons minced fresh
   parsley
¼ cup chopped fresh pineapple
2 teaspoons olive oil
2 teaspoons lime juice
4 romaine lettuce leaves

1. Place the bulgur, water and coriander in a medium saucepan, uncovered, over a medium flame. When the water boils, turn down heat and simmer just until the water is absorbed, about 5 minutes.

2. While the bulgur is cooking, carefully chop the almonds with a sharp knife.

3. When the bulgur is finished cooking, place in a medium bowl, spreading out the bulgur so that it will cool quickly.

4. Meanwhile, cut the top from the red pepper, and slice off two rings to be used as a garnish.

5. Add the almonds, parsley, pineapple, oil and lime juice to the cooled bulgur and toss.

6. To serve, place two lettuce leaves on each serving plate, top with salad and garnish with a red pepper ring.

Cottage Cheese Fruit Salad

Makes 4 servings

A good diet lunch, handsomely disguised.

3 tart, red apples
1 small pear
1 cup cottage cheese
2 tablespoons chopped dates
2 tablespoons chopped walnuts
lemon juice
mint sprigs, garnish

1. Chop one of the apples and the pear, and combine them with the cottage cheese, dates and nuts.

2. Cut the remaining apples into eight wedges each. Sprinkle with lemon juice.

3. Arrange four wedges in a circle on each serving plate, and place a portion of the cottage cheese mixture in the center. Garnish with mint sprigs.

Melon and Avocado Salad *Makes 4 servings*

Colorful, healthful, delicious! Could you ask for anything more?

1. Halve the avocado and remove (but save) the pit. Using a small melon baller, scoop out the melon and the avocado.

2. Arrange the melon and avocado balls on the spinach leaves on individual serving plates. Drizzle with *Vinaigrette Dressing,* and garnish with alfalfa sprouts.

Note: Peel and chop the remaining melon to add to fruit salad; the remaining avocado can be mashed and mixed with *Tofu Mayonnaise* (page 91) for a delicious sandwich spread. Store leftover avocado with the pit to prevent discoloration.

1 avocado
¼ small Cranshaw melon or 1 small cantaloupe, chilled
spinach leaves
Vinaigrette Dressing (page 89)
alfalfa sprouts, garnish

Greek Vegetable Salad *Makes 4 servings*

1. Steam the green beans just until crisp-tender.

2. Combine the cabbage and feta in a serving bowl.

3. Mix together the oil, vinegar and thyme in a small bowl.

4. When the green beans are done, refresh them in cold water until thoroughly cooled. Add to cabbage mixture and toss with dressing.

1 cup sliced green beans
4 cups shredded cabbage
⅓ cup crumbled feta cheese
3 tablespoons olive oil
1 tablespoon vinegar
½ teaspoon dried thyme

Gingered Carrot and Pineapple Salad *Makes 4 servings*

1. Combine the carrots, pineapple, raisins and ginger, then toss with enough yogurt to moisten.

2. Serve on romaine lettuce leaves, garnished with mint sprigs.

1 cup shredded carrots
1 cup finely chopped fresh pineapple
2 tablespoons raisins
¼ teaspoon grated fresh ginger root
1–2 tablespoons yogurt
romaine lettuce leaves
mint sprigs, garnish

Avocado and Grapefruit Salad

Makes 4 servings

Pretty and refreshing; a combination that's a pleasant surprise.

1 medium avocado
1 large grapefruit
1 teaspoon olive oil
1 teaspoon honey
½ cup alfalfa sprouts

1. Cut the avocado in half and remove pit. Peel carefully. Slice each half lengthwise into six sections.

2. Peel the grapefruit, removing all of the white membrane. Using a sharp knife and a bowl underneath to catch the juice, separate the grapefruit sections from the membrane, slicing down toward the center of the fruit. When the grapefruit sections have been removed, squeeze the remaining juice from the membranes into the bowl by hand.

3. Place the avocado slices on a luncheon-size plate, arranging them like spokes on a wheel. Place a grapefruit section between each avocado slice.

4. In a small jar, measure 2 tablespoons of the grapefruit juice, and add the oil and honey. Cover and shake until combined.

5. Pile the sprouts in the center of the avocado and grapefruit ring, and pour dressing over all. Serve immediately.

Variation: Substitute lime juice for grapefruit juice in the dressing.

Herb-Garlic Potato Salad

Makes 6 servings

High in protein, low in calories, and tasty.

4 cups cubed potatoes
3 cups water
½ cup yogurt
¼ cup cottage cheese
2 tablespoons sunflower or
    corn oil
2 teaspoons fresh basil or
    1 teaspoon dried basil
½ teaspoon fresh mint or
    ¼ teaspoon dried mint
½ garlic clove, crushed
1 teaspoon Dijon-style mustard

1. While washing and cubing the potatoes (do not peel), place the water in a medium pan over high heat. Place the potatoes in the heated water when they are cubed. Bring to a boil, reduce heat and simmer until tender, about 10 minutes.

2. Meanwhile, combine the yogurt, cottage cheese, oil, herbs and mustard in a blender. Process on medium speed until smooth.

3. When the potatoes are tender, drain and place in a serving bowl. Toss with the cheese and yogurt mixture, gently so the potatoes are not broken up. Serve warm, or chill.

Cauliflower Salad — *Makes 6 to 8 servings*

1. Separate the cauliflower head into small, bite-size florets. Cut the carrot into slices. Place both over boiling water and steam about 3 to 4 minutes so that the vegetables are still quite firm.

2. Meanwhile, peel the cucumber (unless you know it personally and are quite sure it is not coated with wax). Cut in half lengthwise, then cut into slices. Place in a large serving bowl.

3. After steaming the cauliflower and carrot, run cold tap water over them until thoroughly cooled. Drain well.

4. Toss the cauliflower and carrot with the cucumber and enough dressing to moisten well. Chill.

Note: This salad is designed to retain its freshness without wilting when stored under refrigeration—it's ready to serve anytime.

1 small head cauliflower
1 large carrot
1 medium cucumber
choice of salad dressing

Herb and Avocado Salad — *Makes 4 servings*

Everyone likes the fresh herbs!

1. Rinse lettuce and remove excess moisture. Tear leaves into large pieces, and place them in a serving bowl.

2. Peel avocado half and dice. Finely chop the herbs. Arrange over lettuce leaves.

3. Add *Vinaigrette Dressing* and toss.

Note: Refrigerate remaining avocado half with the pit to prevent the avocado from darkening.

1 small head romaine lettuce
½ avocado
1 tablespoon fresh parsley
2 teaspoons fresh basil
¼ teaspoon fresh thyme
Vinaigrette Dressing (page 89)

Makes 4 servings **Pasta Primavera Salad**

8 ounces whole wheat
   spaghetti
1 sweet red pepper
1 small zucchini
2 cups broccoli florets
1 cup peas
2 tablespoons mild vinegar
2 tablespoons grated Parmesan
   cheese
¼ teaspoon dry mustard powder
⅔ cup olive oil
2 tablespoons minced fresh
   parsley
1 tablespoon minced fresh
   basil or ½ teaspoon dried
   basil

1. Bring a large kettle of water, half filled with water, to a boil over high heat. Break the spaghetti into 2-inch pieces and, when the water boils, stir in the spaghetti. When the water returns to a boil, turn down heat slightly and let the spaghetti cook until firm-tender.

2. Cut the red pepper and zucchini into long, thin slices, and combine with the broccoli and the peas in a steaming basket. Steam the vegetables until crisp-tender, about 8 to 10 minutes.

3. Combine remaining ingredients in a small bowl for dressing.

4. When the spaghetti is done cooking, remove from the heat and run it under cold water until cooled.

5. When the vegetables are steamed, run them under cold water, also until cooled.

6. Toss the spaghetti and vegetables with the dressing. Serve immediately or chill.

Variation: Add ½ cup crumbled feta cheese to the salad for a heartier dish.

Makes 6 servings **Carousel Cabbage Salad**

All the colors of a carousel meet in a crunchy blend. Leftovers can marinate in the refrigerator.

2 cups shredded red cabbage
2 cups shredded green cabbage
1 sweet red pepper, finely
   chopped
1 celery stalk, thinly sliced
3 scallions, thinly sliced
1 carrot, thinly sliced
2 tablespoons minced fresh
   parsley
¼ teaspoon celery seeds
Creamy Herbed Garlic Dressing
   (page 90)

1. Toss the cabbage, pepper, celery, scallions, carrot, parsley and celery seeds together in a large serving bowl.

2. Toss with enough dressing to moisten the salad.

Variations: Add cherry tomatoes to the blend. Add a tablespoon of fresh herbs, such as dill, basil or tarragon.

Stardust Salad Bowl *Makes 4 servings*

A unique and delicious combination sprinkled liberally with a healthful array of vitamins, minerals and fiber.

1. Place washed and dried spinach leaves in a serving bowl. Quarter and core the apples, then chop and add to the bowl. Toss to combine.

2. Cut onion rings and arrange over top of the salad. Sprinkle with tarragon and sesame seeds.

3. Either drizzle salad with dressing or serve dressing separately.

4 cups packed spinach leaves
2 tart red apples
½ small red onion
2 teaspoons fresh tarragon
1 teaspoon toasted sesame seeds
Creamy Herbed Garlic Dressing (page 90)

Sweet Potato Salad *Makes 6 servings*

1. Place the sweet potatoes in a large saucepan with enough water to cover. Bring to a boil over high heat. Reduce heat and simmer until tender, about 8 to 10 minutes.

2. Meanwhile, thinly slice the celery and chop the apple. Toss in a salad bowl with the walnuts and parsley.

3. When the sweet potatoes are done, drain. Add to the celery mixture and toss with enough dressing to coat. Serve at room temperature or chill.

Variations: Substitute roasted cashew pieces for chopped walnuts. Omit celery and use 2 tart apples.

4 cups cubed sweet potatoes
2 celery stalks
1 tart apple
¼ cup chopped walnuts
2 tablespoons minced fresh parsley
Creamy Herbed Garlic Dressing (page 90) or *Blender Mayonnaise* (page 91)

Rainbow Vegetable Salad *Makes 6 servings*

This makes a highly attractive salad for table or picnic and will dress up a cold buffet.

1. Cut the carrots and pepper into long, thin strips, about the size of the beans. Keep the beans whole.

2. Place the vegetables in a steamer, and steam just until crisp-tender, about 10 minutes.

3. Refresh the vegetables under cold running water until they are cool. Add parsley and oregano to vegetables in a serving dish.

4. Toss with enough dressing to moisten well. Chill before serving.

2 small carrots
1 large green or sweet red pepper
½ pound yellow wax beans
½ pound green beans
1 tablespoon minced fresh parsley
½ teaspoon dried oregano
Creamy Herbed Garlic Dressing (page 90)

Makes 4 servings **Cabbage Salad with Kale**

"A delicate flavor, and a nice change," the taste testers said.

2 cups shredded white cabbage
1 cup finely chopped kale
1 scallion, minced
2 tablespoons fresh mint or 2
   teaspoons dried mint leaves
1 garlic clove
2 teaspoons yogurt
1 teaspoon mild vinegar
2 tablespoons olive oil

1. Place the cabbage, kale and scallion in a serving bowl.

2. Combine the mint, garlic, yogurt, vinegar and oil in a blender. Process on high speed until smooth.

3. Pour dressing over cabbage and greens. Toss.

Makes 2 servings **Orange-Pear Salad**

Quick and colorful, this refreshing fruit salad spans the seasons.

2 oranges, chilled
1 pear, chilled
2 tablespoons *Mini-Calorie
   Mayonnaise* (page 90)
dash of grated nutmeg

1. Peel and slice oranges crosswise, removing seeds.

2. Wash and halve pear. Remove core but do not peel. Cut into slices.

3. Arrange the orange and pear slices alternately on a small serving plate.

4. Drizzle with *Mini-Calorie Mayonnaise* and dust with nutmeg. Serve chilled.

Makes 4 servings **Garden and Fruit Salad**

An unusual, tasty mix of vegetables and fruits to tempt any salad lover.

2 cups garden greens (lettuce,
   spinach or kale)
1 tablespoon sunflower oil
1 orange or tangerine
1 cup red grapes
1 tart, red apple
2 teaspoons lemon juice
1 teaspoon fresh tarragon, basil,
   mint or marjoram
mint or parsley sprigs, garnish

1. Tear the greens into large pieces and place in a serving bowl. Toss with the oil until coated.

2. Section the orange or tangerine and remove most of the membranes. Halve the grapes and remove seeds, if necessary. Dice the apple.

3. Add all the fruit to the salad bowl. Add lemon juice and the tarragon, basil, mint or marjoram and toss. Garnish with mint or parsley sprigs.

Mixed Potato Salad *Makes 4 servings*

1. Place the water and potatoes in a large saucepan and set over high heat.

2. Bring water to a boil, then reduce heat and cover. Simmer for 7 to 8 minutes.

3. Meanwhile, chop the onions, slice the celery thin and shred the carrot. When the potatoes have simmered and are slightly tender, add the remaining vegetables.

4. Turn up heat until the water returns to a boil, then reduce heat and simmer another minute or two.

5. Drain the vegetables and run under cold water for a minute to cool slightly. Toss with the minced parsley and enough mayonnaise to moisten. Serve at room temperature or chilled.

Note: Reserve the cooking water for stock.

1 quart water
3 large potatoes, cubed
1 large sweet potato
2 medium onions
1 celery stalk
1 carrot
1 tablespoon minced fresh
   parsley
Blender Mayonnaise (page 91)

Green Beans with Dill and Walnut Sauce *Makes 6 servings*

Give green beans a gourmet touch . . .

1. Leave the green beans whole. Steam just until firm-tender, about 5 minutes.

2. While the beans are steaming, place the walnuts, oil, vinegar, dillweed and mustard in a blender. Process on low to medium speed until relatively smooth, stopping to scrape down the sides of the blender frequently.

3. When the green beans are done, toss with the dillweed and walnut sauce and the pepper. Serve hot or chill.

Note: Take along chilled beans as a lavish addition to a picnic meal!

1 pound green beans
½ cup walnuts
3 tablespoons olive oil
3 tablespoons mild vinegar
1 tablespoon packed fresh
   dillweed
¼ teaspoon Dijon-style mustard
1 tablespoon minced sweet red
   pepper

Makes 4 servings **Gazpacho Salad**

Makes 4 servings **Gazpacho Salad**

The ingredients are similar to those in the Spanish soup.

2 large, ripe tomatoes
4 scallions
½ sweet red pepper
1 small cucumber
1 celery stalk
2 tablespoons lemon juice
1 tablespoon olive oil
romaine lettuce leaves
parsley sprigs, garnish

1. Cut the tomatoes in half across and squeeze out the seeds. Chop.

2. Mince the scallions and dice the pepper and cucumber. (Peel the cucumber, unless you are certain it is not coated with wax.) Slice the celery very thin.

3. Place the vegetables in a medium bowl and toss with the lemon juice and olive oil. Chill, if desired. Serve on lettuce leaves, garnished with parsley.

Makes 4 servings **Zucchini Salad**

Fresh and pretty.

2 medium zucchini
4 scallions
1 sweet red pepper
2 tablespoons olive oil
2 tablespoons mild vinegar
1 teaspoon honey
1 teaspoon dried marjoram
¼ teaspoon dry mustard powder

1. Slice zucchini on the diagonal. Thinly slice the scallions and cut the red pepper into long, thin strips. Place in a serving bowl.

2. In a small bowl, combine the oil, vinegar, honey, marjoram and mustard powder. Stir well until thoroughly combined.

3. Pour the dressing over the salad. Serve immediately or chill.

Dressings, Sauces & Miscellaneous

Vinaigrette Dressing *Makes 1 cup*

Double the amount and store tightly covered in the refrigerator for use on many salads.

1. Combine the vinegar and mustard in a blender, and process on medium speed until smooth.

2. Add the oil very slowly with the blender on low speed.

Variations: For *Garlic Vinaigrette Dressing*, add 1 garlic clove to the vinegar and mustard and process until smooth, then add oil. Add 1 cup yogurt for a creamy, lower-calorie dressing. Add 1 tablespoon fresh basil or parsley or 1 teaspoon of fresh tarragon or thyme for *Herbed Vinaigrette Dressing*.

¼ cup cider vinegar or white
    vinegar
1 teaspoon Dijon-style mustard
⅔ cup sunflower oil

Poppy Seed Dressing *Makes ¾ cup*

Try it on spinach leaves tossed with toasted cashew nuts or sesame seeds. It's sweet and mild.

1. Place the vinegar, honey, parsley and mustard in a blender. Push the garlic half through a press into the blender. Process on medium speed until the parsley is chopped fine.

2. Add the oil in three parts, blending well after each addition. Add the poppy seeds and blend just until they are distributed throughout the dressing.

3 tablespoons mild vinegar,
    preferably *Tarragon Vinegar*
    (page 92)
1 tablespoon honey
1 teaspoon fresh parsley
½ teaspoon dry mustard
½ garlic clove
½ cup olive oil
½ teaspoon poppy seeds

Creamy Herbed Garlic Dressing

Makes 1½ cups

"Love this dressing!" extolled one enthusiast. I think you will, too.

1 egg
½ teaspoon dry mustard
1 cup olive or corn oil
1 garlic clove, crushed
2 tablespoons lemon juice
2 tablespoons mild vinegar
1 tablespoon chopped scallion
    tops or chives
1 tablespoon chopped fresh
    basil or parsley

1. Place the egg and mustard in a blender. Process on low speed until the egg is thoroughly beaten.

2. Very slowly add the oil while the blender is running on low speed. Begin with a few drops of oil at a time, then continue to add in a slow stream until the oil is thoroughly incorporated.

3. Add the remaining ingredients and process on low speed until blended. Chill.

Note: Serve with green salads or on cooked, chilled vegetables.

French-Style Dressing with Garlic

Makes ¾ cup

This is a very good dressing with a nice consistency. Double the recipe if you like, and store covered in the refrigerator.

½ cup corn or olive oil
2 tablespoons cider vinegar
2 tablespoons tomato paste
1 tablespoon honey
1 garlic clove, crushed
¼ teaspoon paprika
dash of cayenne pepper

1. Place ingredients in a blender. Process on high speed until smooth. Scrape down the sides of the container, if necessary, with a rubber spatula. Serve with tossed salads or over raw, sliced vegetables. Shake before using.

Mini-Calorie Mayonnaise

Makes ¾ cup

If you want to cut back on fats, this homemade version of mayonnaise is a tasty step in the right direction.

½ cup ricotta cheese
1 egg
1 tablespoon lemon juice
1 teaspoon sunflower oil
1 teaspoon Dijon-style mustard
dash of cayenne pepper

1. Place the ingredients in a blender. Process on medium speed until smooth.

2. Store unused portion of mayonnaise in a tightly covered container in the refrigerator.

Variation: For *Mild Garlic Mayonnaise*, follow the above recipe, adding ½ garlic clove to the blender with the ingredients. Obtain stronger garlic taste by adding a whole garlic clove.

Blender Mayonnaise *Makes 1 cup*

The real thing, made in minutes with a blender!

1. Place the egg, mustard and cayenne (just a whisper!) in a blender, and process on high speed until egg is thick and fluffy, about 30 seconds.

2. Add the lemon juice and blend a few more seconds, just until combined.

3. Now comes the time for patience. Partly uncover the blender (many have a removable portion in the lid for this purpose), and while the mixture is being processed on high speed, begin adding the oil drop by drop. Slowly increase the flow until you have a steady little stream of droplets. Continue until about half of the oil has been added. Now the remainder of the oil can be added in a very slow stream. Store covered in the refrigerator.

Variations: Use ½ cup sunflower or safflower oil and ½ cup olive oil, or use sunflower oil entirely.

1 egg
¼ teaspoon dry mustard
dash of cayenne pepper
4 teaspoons lemon juice
1 cup olive oil

Tofu Mayonnaise *Makes 1 cup*

1. Combine the first four ingredients in a blender. Process on low speed until smooth.

2. When the tofu mixture is creamy, add the oil slowly and continue blending until oil is thoroughly combined.

Note: Refrigerate tightly covered.

6 ounces tofu
2 tablespoons cider vinegar
1 teaspoon Dijon-style mustard
1 teaspoon tamari
1 tablespoon sunflower oil

Garlic Vinegar *Makes 2 cups*

You might choose this as a quick gift idea, bottled and labeled attractively.

1. Place the vinegar in a medium saucepan over medium heat. When vinegar is just below boiling point, remove from heat and add the halved garlic clove and bay leaf.

2. Allow vinegar to cool, then place in a covered jar. Remove the garlic and bay leaf after one week.

2 cups white vinegar
1 garlic clove, halved
1 bay leaf

Makes 2 cups   **Tarragon Vinegar**

Tarragon is easily grown in a garden; it is also available at certain produce markets in season. This vinegar gives an added lift to any salad dressing.

2 cups white vinegar
3-inch sprig of fresh tarragon
1 garlic clove, halved

1. Place the ingredients in a small saucepan and heat just to the boiling point. Remove from heat, and take out garlic clove halves.

2. Place the tarragon sprig in a bottle (the one in which you purchased the vinegar is fine). Pour the vinegar over the tarragon. Cap and store at room temperature.

Makes 1 cup   **Whole Wheat White Sauce**

An all-purpose sauce. It's perfect for creaming vegetables or fish.

2 tablespoons butter
3 tablespoons whole wheat
    flour
1¼ cups milk

1. Place butter in a medium saucepan over medium heat. Add flour and stir for 2 to 3 minutes.

2. Add the milk all at once, stirring to remove lumps from the sauce. When the sauce thickens, remove from heat.

Makes 2½ cups   **Quick Tomato Sauce**

A sauce with a good flavor and a nice texture. Try it over pasta, fish or vegetables.

2 large, ripe tomatoes
⅔ cup tomato paste
1 scallion, quartered
1 cup water
1 tablespoon fresh parsley
2 teaspoons dried basil
1 teaspoon dried oregano
½ teaspoon dried marjoram
1 garlic clove (optional)

1. Quarter the tomatoes and squeeze out seeds. Place the tomatoes in a blender.

2. Add the tomato paste, scallion and remaining ingredients.

3. Process on medium speed until smooth.

4. Place the sauce in a medium pan over medium heat and cover. Bring to a boil, then reduce heat and simmer, stirring occasionally, for 15 minutes.

Cheddar Cheese Sauce   *Makes 2 cups*

Add this very tasty sauce to casseroles, or serve it over vegetables, noodles, rice, omelets or crepes.

1. Melt the butter in a medium saucepan. Stir in the flour and cook over low heat for 2 to 3 minutes.

2. Add the milk slowly, stirring, to make a smooth sauce. Stir over low to medium heat until the sauce begins to thicken.

3. Add the cheese and continue to stir until it melts.

3 tablespoons butter
2 tablespoons whole wheat flour
2 cups milk
1 cup shredded Cheddar cheese

Hot Taco Sauce   *Makes 3 cups*

Serve with tacos or tortillas. A sauce that will also give a fiery lift to any South-of-the-Border dish.

1. Heat the oil in a medium skillet, and add the hot peppers and onion. Cook about 5 minutes.

2. Add the tomatoes and juice and cook over medium heat, stirring occasionally, about 5 to 10 minutes.

Note: Always use rubber gloves when working with hot peppers, and *don't* rub your eyes. The oils are quite hot and can remain on your fingers for hours, even if you wash your hands.

1 tablespoon corn oil
1½ cups chopped fresh hot peppers
1 onion, finely chopped
2 cups chopped tomatoes with juice

Vegetarian Gravy   *Makes 1 cup*

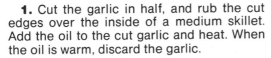

Delicious on mashed potatoes, calves' liver or baked chicken.

1. Cut the garlic in half, and rub the cut edges over the inside of a medium skillet. Add the oil to the cut garlic and heat. When the oil is warm, discard the garlic.

2. Add the flour and brewer's yeast to the oil and stir for 2 or 3 minutes over low heat.

3. Add the water slowly, stirring all the while so the gravy does not become lumpy. Add the tamari and molasses, and continue stirring over medium heat until the gravy thickens slightly.

4. Stir in the milk. Heat through and serve.

1 garlic clove
2 tablespoons olive oil
2 tablespoons whole wheat flour
1 teaspoon brewer's yeast
1 cup water
1 tablespoon tamari
½ teaspoon blackstrap molasses
¼ cup milk

Makes 1 cup **Blueberry Sauce**

1¼ cups blueberries
1–2 teaspoons maple syrup

1. Place the ingredients in a blender, and process on medium speed until combined. Serve over pancakes or desserts.

Makes 1⅔ cups **Fresh Peach Sauce**

An excellent, fresh taste; serve on pancakes and waffles, or use as a dessert topping.

2 large, ripe peaches
2 tablespoons apple cider
2 tablespoons maple syrup

1. Remove the peach pits, but do not peel the peaches.

2. Place 1 peach, coarsely chopped, in a blender with the cider and syrup. Process on medium speed until smooth.

3. Dice the remaining peach, and stir it into the blended mixture by hand.

4. To serve hot, place in a saucepan and heat, but do not boil.

Maple-Applesauce Topping

Makes 1 cup

A super topper for pancakes and desserts.

2 large, tart apples, chopped
¼ cup apple cider
2 tablespoons maple syrup

1. Place the ingredients in a blender.

2. Process on medium speed until smooth, scraping down sides of the blender as necessary.

Strawberry-Applesauce Topping

Makes 2 cups

Try on pancakes or as a substitute for jams on whole grain breads and muffins. Delicious and attractive!

1 cup strawberries
2 tart apples, quartered
¼ cup apple cider

1. Place the ingredients in a blender, and process on medium speed until smooth.

2. Store leftovers in refrigerator, tightly covered.

Walnut Sauce *Makes 1 cup*

A dessert sauce to be used with a light hand.

1. Place the honey in a small saucepan and bring to a boil over medium heat. Turn down heat and keep at a slow boil for about 2 to 3 minutes.

2. Remove from the heat. Stir in the nuts and vanilla. Serve warm over cake slices, waffles or filled dessert crepes.

¾ cup honey
½ cup chopped walnuts
¼ teaspoon vanilla extract

Banana Sauce *Makes 1½ cups*

A delicious dessert sauce. Or for a real change of pace, omit the honey and vanilla and serve over broiled fish fillets.

1. Place the milk and butter in a small saucepan over medium heat. When the milk is scalded and the butter has melted, place the milk mixture with the bananas and the remaining ingredients in a blender.

2. Process on low speed until sauce is smooth.

3. Return to the saucepan and heat through before serving.

¾ cup milk
1 teaspoon butter
2 very ripe bananas, peeled
    and halved
1 teaspoon honey
¼ teaspoon vanilla extract

Makes 1 cup **Carob Syrup**

Use carob syrup to flavor hot or cold milk drinks. Try it, too, to coat fresh fruit chunks for a fondue-style dessert.

1 cup water
½ cup carob powder
2 tablespoons honey
½ teaspoon vanilla extract

1. Place ¼ cup of the water in a medium saucepan, and stir in the carob powder to form a paste. Add the remaining water and the honey.

2. Stir over medium heat, bringing to a boil. Reduce heat and simmer 2 to 3 minutes. Remove from heat and stir in vanilla. Cool and store, refrigerated, in a covered container.

Makes ¼ cup **Saltless Seasoning**

Sprinkle over salads, or serve on other foods for added flavor — without salt.

2 tablespoons sunflower seeds
2 tablespoons sesame seeds
½ teaspoon dill seeds
1 tablespoon wheat germ
2 teaspoons dried basil
1 teaspoon brewer's yeast
½ teaspoon dried thyme
½ teaspoon paprika
½ teaspoon kelp powder
dash of cayenne pepper

1. In a blender, combine the sunflower, sesame and dill seeds. Grind in short bursts at high speed.

2. Add the remaining ingredients and combine in short bursts at high speed. Place seasoning in a small, tightly covered jar. Store in the refrigerator.

Makes 2 tablespoons **Curry Powder**

There are endless variations if you care to make your own; here is one sample. Experiment with the spices you favor!

1 teaspoon chili powder
1 teaspoon dry mustard
1 teaspoon ground cardamom
1 teaspoon ground coriander
1 teaspoon ground cumin
¼ teaspoon cinnamon
⅛ teaspoon ground cloves
⅛ teaspoon turmeric

1. Combine the ingredients in a small mixing bowl, then place in small, covered container.

Note: Double or triple recipe, if desired.

Whole Wheat Croutons *Makes 1 cup*

Serve on salads or with soups.

1. Cut the bread into cubes; there should be about 1 cup.

2. Heat the oil in a medium to large skillet, and saute the halved garlic clove briefly to flavor oil. Remove garlic. Add the bread cubes and stir to coat the bread quickly with the oil.

3. Continue stirring the bread cubes over medium heat until they are toasted brown and crisp.

4. Remove from heat, then toss croutons with Parmesan.

1–2 slices stale whole wheat
    bread
2 tablespoons olive oil
1 garlic clove
1 tablespoon grated
    Parmesan cheese

Whole Wheat
Bread Stuffing *Makes 4½ cups*

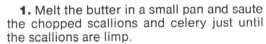

This can be used with fish fillets or to stuff mushroom caps.

1. Melt the butter in a small pan and saute the chopped scallions and celery just until the scallions are limp.

2. Grind the nuts in a blender with short bursts at high speed.

3. Combine the sauteed scallions and celery with the nuts, bread crumbs, parsley, tarragon or basil and cayenne in a medium bowl. Moisten stuffing with a little stock. Use immediately, or freeze.

Variations: To stuff fish fillets, either wrap a fillet around the filling, or place filling between two fish fillets for a "sandwich" effect. Bake at 350°F until fish is cooked throughout.

For mushroom caps, simmer the caps briefly in a small amount of stock, then stuff, sprinkle with a little grated Parmesan cheese, and run under a broiler until top is slightly browned.

3 tablespoons butter
½ cup chopped scallions
¼ cup minced celery
2 tablespoons ground walnuts
4 cups fresh whole wheat bread
    crumbs
½ cup minced fresh parsley
2 teaspoons fresh tarragon or
    basil
dash of cayenne pepper
Stock (pages 175–76)

Makes ⅔ cup **Mustard Sauce**

Serve over cooked fish, chicken or vegetables. A little goes a long way.

2 egg yolks
½ teaspoon dry mustard
1½ teaspoons honey
6 tablespoons cider vinegar
2 tablespoons milk
1 tablespoon Dijon-style mustard
1 tablespoon lemon juice

1. Place the egg yolks, dry mustard and honey in the top of a double boiler over boiling water. Add the cider vinegar and stir until the mixture has thickened.

2. Add the milk and continue to stir over the boiling water for 4 to 5 minutes. Remove from heat and stir in the prepared mustard and lemon juice.

Note: Refrigerate unused portion, tightly covered.

Makes 1¼ cups **Sesame Salad Dressing**

A more nutritious salad dressing you'll never find. Try it over shredded cabbage with some minced sweet red pepper and parsley added for color.

¼ cup sesame seeds
2-4 scallions, quartered
½ cup sliced carrots
½ sweet red pepper, chopped
¾ cup olive or sunflower oil
¼ cup lemon juice

1. Place the sesame seeds in a blender and grind them with short bursts at high speed.

2. Add the remaining ingredients and process on medium or high speed until smooth, about 1 minute.

Variation: Add ¼ cup sliced white radish (daikon) before blending.

Sunflower-Peanut Butter *Makes 1 cup*

A high-protein, high-energy spread for sandwiches.

1. Place the peanuts and sunflower seeds in a blender, and add the oil.

2. Process on medium to high speed, scraping down the sides of the container as necessary. Blend until smooth. Store tightly covered in a cool place.

Variations: Substitute all peanuts, toasted cashew nuts or walnuts for the peanut and sunflower mixture. Add 1 or 2 teaspoons of honey, if desired.

¾ cup roasted peanuts
¼ cup sunflower seeds
4 teaspoons corn oil

Crunchy Peanut Spread *Makes 1½ cups*

A crunchy, moist, delicious spread!

1. Mash the banana with a fork in a small bowl. Sprinkle with the lemon juice, and stir to combine.

2. Add the peanut butter, and stir the mixture together with a fork until combined. Fold in the celery.

Note: This makes enough spread for 4 to 6 sandwiches.

1 medium, very ripe banana
1 teaspoon lemon juice
½ cup peanut butter
½ cup finely chopped celery

Spiced Walnut-Pear Spread *Makes 1 cup*

A no-cook substitute for jams and jellies—exotically tasty.

1. Combine ingredients in a blender. Process on medium speed until smooth, scraping down sides of the blender as necessary.

2. Store any leftovers in the refrigerator, tightly covered.

2 pears, chopped
½ cup chopped fresh pineapple
¼ cup walnuts
¼ cup pitted dates
¼ teaspoon cinnamon
⅛ teaspoon ground ginger
dash of ground cloves

Beverages

Fresh Pineapple Frappé *Makes 2 servings*

A frothy, cooling pineapple drink takes the wilt out of summer.

1. Peel the pineapple and cut into chunks. Place in a blender with 2 ice cubes and process on medium speed until smooth, stirring down the sides as necessary.

2. Place the blended pineapple in a colander over a large bowl, and stir down with a wooden spoon, until the larger pieces of fiber are squeezed dry.

3. Serve the pineapple juice over ice with lime slices as garnish.

½ medium, ripe pineapple
2 ice cubes
lime slices, garnish

Strawberry Yogurt Punch *Makes 2 servings*

A little tart, a little sweet, and very satisfying.

1. Place the first seven ingredients in a blender. Process on medium, then high speed, until smooth.

2. Pour the drink into two short glasses. To garnish, choose two attractive berries with leaves. Cut about halfway up each berry from the tip, and place one on the edge of each glass. Add mint sprigs next to the berries. Serve immediately.

½ cup yogurt
½ cup milk
½ cup sliced strawberries
2 teaspoons honey
1 teaspoon fresh mint leaves
¼ teaspoon vanilla extract
4 ice cubes
2 whole strawberries, garnish
mint sprigs, garnish

Makes 4 servings   # Orange Spritzer
So refreshing!

1½ cups sparkling mineral water
1 cup orange juice
1 cup apple juice
1 teaspoon honey (optional)
mint sprigs, garnish
lemon slices, garnish

1. Combine the mineral water and juices. Add a little honey, if desired.

2. Serve over ice with a sprig of mint in each glass and lemon slices on the glass rims.

Makes 2 servings   # Citrus Medley
An oasis when hot weather gets you down.

1½ cups orange juice
1 tablespoon lemon juice
1 tablespoon lime juice
1 teaspoon honey
4 ice cubes
mint sprigs, garnish

1. Place the juices, honey and ice in a blender and process on medium speed until smooth.

2. Serve over ice, garnished with mint.

Makes 1 serving   # Tomato Juice Cocktail
A delicious low-calorie option for late summer when you are overrun with ripe tomatoes.

3 large, ripe tomatoes
¼ cup water
1 tablespoon chopped onion or
     1 scallion, chopped
1 tablespoon fresh parsley
1 tablespoon celery leaves
dash of paprika
dash of cayenne pepper
2 ice cubes
1 small stalk celery with leaves,
     garnish
lemon slice, garnish

1. Coarsely chop the tomatoes, and place them in a medium saucepan with the water. Turn heat to medium and bring to a boil.

2. Add chopped onion or scallion to the tomatoes along with the parsley, celery leaves, paprika and cayenne. Turn down heat to simmer.

3. Simmer the tomato mixture, covered, for 12 minutes. Place the tomatoes and ice cubes in a blender, and process on medium speed for 30 seconds, until smooth.

4. Put the mixture through a large strainer, pressing out the juice with the back of a wooden spoon. Serve over ice in a glass, garnished with a celery stalk and a lemon slice.

Cucumber Float   *Makes 2 servings*

Want to be cool as one? Try this when the weather turns sultry.

1. Place the yogurt, cucumber (cut up into a few pieces), mint leaves and ice in a blender. Process on medium speed until combined. Add a little water, if desired, for a thinner consistency.

2. To serve, pour into tall glasses and garnish with mint sprigs.

1 cup yogurt
1 small cucumber, peeled and seeded
1 tablespoon fresh mint leaves
4 ice cubes
water (optional)
mint sprigs, garnish

Banana Yogurt Shake   *Makes 2 servings*

A refreshing and filling picker-upper that tastes great.

1. Break up the peeled banana into pieces, and place it in a blender.

2. Add the remaining ingredients and process on medium speed until the ice cubes are crushed. Serve immediately.

1 large, ripe banana
1 egg
¼ cup yogurt
5 ice cubes
2 teaspoons honey

Hot Mulled Cranberry Juice   *Makes 4 servings*

What a delicious welcome when friends come into your home at holiday time!

1. Place the cranberries and the water in a large saucepan, and bring to a boil. Reduce heat and simmer 5 minutes, until most of the cranberries have burst.

2. Line a colander with cheesecloth, set the colander in a large bowl, and pour the cranberries and water through. Grab the edges of the cheesecloth to form a bag. Squeeze the remaining juice from the cranberries by pressing the bag with a wooden spoon.

3. Return the cranberry juice to the saucepan. Add the honey and lemon slices. Heat the cranberry juice well, but do not boil. Stir, and press lemon slices to release juice. Sprinkle with nutmeg.

4. Serve hot in punch cups or in small mugs, with cinnamon sticks as garnish.

2 cups cranberries
2 cups water
3 tablespoons honey
4 lemon slices
dash of grated nutmeg
4 cinnamon sticks, garnish

Makes 2 servings # Carob Eggnog Shake

1 ripe banana
1 cup milk
1 egg
2 tablespoons carob powder
1 teaspoon honey
¼ teaspoon vanilla extract
3–4 ice cubes

1. Cut up the banana and place it in a blender with the milk and the egg. Sprinkle the carob powder over the mixture, and add the honey, vanilla and ice.

2. Process on medium, then high speed until frothy. Serve in tall glasses.

Variation: For a plain *Carob Shake*, omit the egg.

Makes 2 servings # Banana Milkshake

1 cup milk
1 ripe banana
2 ice cubes
½ teaspoon vanilla extract
⅛ teaspoon cinnamon
dash of grated nutmeg

1. Place the ingredients in a blender and process on medium speed until smooth. Serve immediately.

Makes 2 servings # Watermelon Cooler

A summer favorite in a new form!

2 cups chilled watermelon
    chunks, seeds removed
3 ice cubes
dash of grated nutmeg

1. Place the ingredients in a blender and process on medium speed until smooth. Serve immediately.

Makes 2 servings # Strawberry-Citrus Cooler

½ cup milk
½ cup orange juice
½ cup strawberries
3 ice cubes
drop of vanilla extract

1. Place the ingredients in a blender and process on medium speed until smooth. Serve immediately over additional ice.

Strawberry-Orange Eggnog *Makes 2 servings*

Whip sweet, ripe strawberries into a summer refresher.

1. Place the orange juice, halved strawberries, egg, lemon juice, honey and ice in a blender. Process on medium, then high speed, until smooth and frothy.

2. Serve in tall glasses. To garnish, choose attractive strawberries with leaves. Cut halfway up the berry from the tip, and slip the berry onto the edge of the glass.

1 cup orange juice
1 cup halved strawberries
1 egg
1 tablespoon lemon juice
1 teaspoon honey
4 ice cubes
4 whole strawberries, garnish

Peanut Butter Lovers' Nightcap *Makes 1 serving*

Very different; surprisingly good.

1. Place the peanut butter and honey in a small saucepan with a few spoonfuls of the milk. Stir together over low heat until smooth.

2. Add the remaining milk and the vanilla, and stir over low to medium heat until hot, but not boiling.

3. Pour through a tea strainer or sieve into a cup, and serve immediately.

1 tablespoon peanut butter
1½ teaspoons honey
1 cup milk
¼ teaspoon vanilla extract

Orange Glorious *Makes 2 servings*

Creamy.

1. Place the ingredients in a blender. Whip on high speed until smooth and foamy.

¾ cup orange juice
½ cup milk
1 egg white
½ teaspoon honey
drop of vanilla extract
3 ice cubes

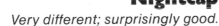

Desserts & Snacks

Raisin Nut Bars   *Makes I dozen*

Mix a delicious snack in 5 minutes, then bake!

1. Beat the egg in a medium mixing bowl and add the raisins, honey and vanilla.

2. Add the remaining ingredients and then stir together all at once. Lightly oil an 8 × 8-inch baking dish. Smooth the batter over the bottom of the dish.

3. Bake 15 minutes in a 375°F oven. Allow to cool before cutting into bars.

1 egg
¼ cup raisins
½ cup honey
1 teaspoon vanilla extract
1 cup *Breakfast Cereal Mix* (page 7)
⅓ cup chopped walnuts
½ cup whole wheat flour
½ teaspoon baking powder
½ teaspoon cinnamon

Preheat oven to 375°F

Oatmeal Raisin Chews   *Makes 2 dozen*

Mix these up in 10 minutes and bake for 10 more. . .could you find a quicker delight?

1. Stir together the tahini, molasses and raisins. Add the oats, and stir again until well blended.

2. Drop batter by spoonfuls onto a lightly oiled baking sheet. Bake at 350°F about 10 minutes, until golden.

¼ cup sesame tahini
⅓ cup medium unsulfured molasses
½ cup raisins
1 cup rolled oats

Preheat oven to 350°F

Wheat Germ and Oatmeal Cookies

Makes 2½ dozen

1 cup rolled oats
¾ cup wheat germ
½ cup whole wheat pastry flour
½ cup chopped walnuts
¼ cup raisins
½ teaspoon cinnamon
¼ cup corn oil
¼ cup honey
1 egg, beaten
1 teaspoon vanilla extract

Preheat oven to 350°F

1. Combine the rolled oats, wheat germ, flour, walnuts, raisins and cinnamon in a medium mixing bowl.

2. In a small bowl, combine the oil, honey, egg and vanilla, and beat well. Add to the dry ingredients and stir well until thoroughly combined.

3. Drop batter by spoonfuls onto baking sheet, and flatten with spoon. Bake at 350°F for about 10 minutes.

Honeyed Ginger Bananas

Makes 2 servings

A lightning-quick dessert made with fresh fruit that's especially nice in winter. It's a favorite!

1 teaspoon butter
½-inch cube fresh ginger root
1 teaspoon honey
¼ cup orange juice
2 ripe bananas
dash of cinnamon
orange slices, garnish

1. Melt butter in a medium skillet over low heat, stirring with the ginger cube. Add honey and stir.

2. Add the orange juice. Cut the bananas in half, then slice each half in two, lengthwise. Place banana quarters in the skillet, cut side down. Sprinkle with cinnamon.

3. Turn the bananas occasionally, until they are heated through and glazed. Remove the ginger and serve hot with any of the glaze remaining in the skillet. Garnish with orange slices.

Sesame Fruit and Nut Drops
Makes 1 dozen

Take the favorite dried fruits from the Middle East—figs and dates—then add the taste of peanuts and roll in sesame seeds. A perfect confection!

1. Place all ingredients except the sesame seeds in a blender. Process on medium speed, stopping the blender when necessary to scrape down the sides of the container.

2. When the ingredients are combined and rather finely chopped, remove from the blender and knead into a ball by hand.

3. Break off bite-size pieces and roll in sesame seeds. Chilling firms the texture of the confection.

¼ cup coarsely chopped dried figs
¼ cup coarsely chopped pitted dates
¼ cup peanut butter
½ teaspoon brewer's yeast
½ teaspoon blackstrap molasses
¼ teaspoon cinnamon
2 tablespoons sesame seeds

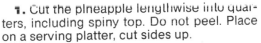

Fast and Fancy Dessert
Makes 4 servings

A beautiful, tasty combination. You won't find a quicker, more attractive dessert!

1. Cut the pineapple lengthwise into quarters, including spiny top. Do not peel. Place on a serving platter, cut sides up.

2. Slice limes longthwise into sections, and place among the pineapple quarters. Garnish with mint.

3. Serve with a knife and fork. Lime should be squeezed over pineapple as it is eaten.

Note: If you will not be serving the pineapple immediately after cutting, squeeze a little lime juice over the pineapple to prevent discoloring.

1 small, ripe pineapple
2 limes
mint sprigs, garnish

Prebaked Granola Pie Shell

Makes 1 9-inch pie shell

1 cup rolled oats
½ cup whole wheat flour
¼ cup walnuts
¼ cup sunflower oil
3 tablespoons honey

Preheat oven to 350°F

1. Combine the rolled oats and flour in a 9-inch pie plate. Grind the walnuts in a blender with short bursts at high speed. Then combine the walnuts with the oats and flour.

2. Add the oil and honey. Toss the ingredients with a fork until well blended, then press into the bottom and up the sides of the pie plate.

3. Bake in a 350°F oven for 12 minutes. Cool before filling with fresh fruit or other fillings that need no baking.

Blueberry-Peach Pie

Makes 6 servings

Make the filling while the pie shell is baking: a quick-as-a-few-minutes dessert!

4 cups sliced peaches
½ cup water
¼ cup honey
½ teaspoon vanilla extract
3 tablespoons agar-agar flakes
¾ cup blueberries
1 *Prebaked Granola Pie Shell* (page 110)

1. Place the peach slices (unpeeled), water, honey and vanilla in a medium saucepan. Bring to a boil, sprinkle with the agar, stir, and simmer ingredients together about 8 minutes, stirring occasionally.

2. Remove the peaches from the heat. Stir in the blueberries. Cool slightly, then pour into the prebaked pie shell. Cool, then chill before serving, if desired, or serve warm. The agar will set at room temperature.

Blue Gingham Yogurt Delight

Makes 2 servings

A colorful, delicious, easier-than-pie dessert or refreshing snack.

1 cup yogurt
1 cup blueberries
1 ripe banana
1 teaspoon honey
¼ teaspoon vanilla extract
dash of grated nutmeg

1. Place chilled yogurt in a serving bowl. Wash and add blueberries.

2. Quarter banana lengthwise, then slice into bowl. Pieces should be similar in size to blueberries.

3. Add honey and vanilla and stir to combine. Dust with a little nutmeg and serve.

Strawberry Pie

Makes 6 servings

A jeweled delight with fresh berries.

1. Set aside six large strawberries with caps for garnish. Hull the remaining berries and arrange them attractively in the pie shell. Place in the freezer to chill while preparing glaze.

2. Place the apple juice, lemon juice, agar and honey in a small saucepan. Bring to a boil over medium heat, then lower heat and simmer for 5 minutes, until the agar is completely dissolved.

3. Remove the glaze from the heat, and stir in the vanilla. Allow the glaze to cool for a few minutes. (If it cools too much and becomes stiff, it can be reheated.)

4. Spoon the glaze over the chilled berries in the pie shell. Chill.

5. To serve, top with mounds of *Whipped Dessert Topping,* and place a large strawberry in the center of each mound.

Variation: Substitute 4 cups of red or black raspberries for the strawberries.

4 cups strawberries
1 *Prebaked Granola Pie Shell* (page 110)
1 cup apple juice
2 teaspoons lemon juice
1 tablespoon agar-agar flakes
2 teaspoons honey
½ teaspoon vanilla extract
Whipped Dessert Topping (page 112)

Dessert Continental

Makes any number of servings

To follow a meal—especially nice to serve as conversation continues into late evening.

1. Arrange the fruits, cheeses and nuts in appropriate serving bowls, providing knives and nutcrackers and a container for discarding shells. Let your guests serve themselves.

Note: Cheese tastes best at room temperature. Remove from the refrigerator at least 30 minutes before serving.

seedless grapes
Anjou pears
assorted cheeses, including Brie, Camembert or others
unshelled nuts

Sweetened Whipped Cream

Makes 2 cups

1 cup heavy cream
1 teaspoon honey
¼ teaspoon vanilla extract

1. Place the beaters and a medium mixing bowl in the freezer section of your refrigerator for 5 minutes.

2. Combine cream, honey and vanilla in the chilled bowl. (In very warm weather, whip the cream with the bowl set over a larger bowl of ice.)

3. With an electric beater, whip on medium or medium-high speed just until the cream begins to thicken. Turn speed to low and beat just until cream forms soft peaks. Do not overbeat.

Whipped Dessert Topping

Makes 1 cup

This luscious topping adds a finishing touch to many desserts—along with extra protein and calcium.

1 cup ricotta cheese
1 tablespoon honey
¼ teaspoon vanilla extract

1. Place the ricotta in a blender with the honey and vanilla. Process on low speed until the mixture is smooth and has the consistency of heavy whipped cream. Chill.

Note: Ricotta can vary in consistency. If yours is too thick to whip, add a few tablespoons of milk.

Apple Cinnamon Slices

Makes 1 serving

Enjoy a tart and tasty treat!

1 apple
½ lime or lemon
cinnamon

1. Cut the apple in quarters, removing stems and core. Do not peel.

2. Cut into thin slices and arrange in a circle on a small plate.

3. Squeeze the lime or lemon and drizzle some of the juice over the slices. Sprinkle slices with cinnamon.

Fruit and Nut Snack   *Makes 1 cup*

This is a high-energy (meaning plenty of calories) combination that's wonderful for the hiker or other sports activist. Go easy if you get your sports thrills by radio . . .

1. Combine ingredients. Keep mixture in a closed plastic bag or jar, and refrigerate if the sunflower seeds are raw.

⅓ cup raisins
⅓ cup sunflower seeds
⅓ cup chopped walnuts

Variations: Try chopped pitted dates or prunes in place of raisins. Substitute almonds for walnuts. Add some pumpkin or sesame seeds.

Powerhouse Popcorn   *Makes 4 servings*

Boost popped corn with B vitamins, minerals and surprisingly good taste.

1. Place oil and popcorn in a heavy-bottom pan. Cover, and shake over medium heat.

2 teaspoons corn oil
3 tablespoons popcorn
2 teaspoons brewer's yeast

2. When most of the kernels have popped, remove pan from heat, pour popcorn into serving bowl, and dust with brewer's yeast.

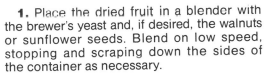

Fruit Chews   *Makes 1 dozen*

A candylike confection, with nary an empty calorie . . .

1. Place the dried fruit in a blender with the brewer's yeast and, if desired, the walnuts or sunflower seeds. Blend on low speed, stopping and scraping down the sides of the container as necessary.

¼ cup pitted dates
¼ cup raisins
¼ cup pitted prunes
¼ cup dried apricots
½ teaspoon brewer's yeast
2 tablespoons walnuts or sun-
      flower seeds (optional)
wheat germ, carob powder,
      chopped nuts, sunflower or
      sesame seeds, garnish

2. When the fruits are chopped and combined, form into small balls, about the size of a teaspoon. Roll in desired garnish. Chill, if desired, before serving.

Makes 2 dozen

Butter Almond Cookies

Delicate and delightful.

½ cup butter, at room temperature
½ cup honey
1 egg, beaten
½ cup blanched almonds
1 teaspoon vanilla extract
1 cup whole wheat flour

Preheat oven to 375°F

1. Beat together the butter and honey. Beat in the egg.

2. Place the almonds in a blender and process with short bursts on high speed until ground. Stir into the batter with the vanilla extract.

3. Add the whole wheat flour and stir in just until the batter is smooth.

4. Drop the batter from a tablespoon onto two lightly oiled cookie sheets. Bake in a preheated 375°F oven for 8 to 10 minutes, until the edges of the cookies are brown.

Cinnamon Walnut Drop Cookies

Makes 2½ dozen

1½ cups whole wheat flour
½ cup chopped walnuts
¼ cup wheat germ
1 tablespoon cinnamon
½ teaspoon baking powder
1 egg
½ cup sunflower oil
⅓ cup honey
1 teaspoon vanilla extract

Preheat oven to 350°F

1. Combine the dry ingredients in a small bowl.

2. Beat the egg in a medium bowl and add the oil, honey and vanilla. Beat until smooth.

3. Add the dry ingredients, stirring just until combined.

4. Drop batter from a soup spoon onto a lightly oiled cookie sheet. The cookies can be placed close together.

5. Bake in a preheated 350°F oven for about 10 minutes, until the cookies just begin to brown on the bottom.

Peaches in Sour Cream   *Makes 4 servings*

I remember this as one of my first dessert discoveries as a child. With fresh peaches, it is delightful.

1. Peel peaches and slice thin. Place in a serving bowl and toss with the sour cream. Sprinkle with a little nutmeg.

2. Garnish with mint sprigs. Chill, if desired, before serving.

4 large, ripe peaches
⅓ cup sour cream
dash of grated nutmeg
mint sprigs, garnish

Peaches with Almond Sauce   *Makes 4 servings*

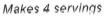

1. Halve the peaches and remove the skins and pits. Place the milk and cinnamon stick in a large skillet with the peach halves.

2. Cover the skillet and place over medium heat. When the milk boils, reduce heat and simmer 5 minutes.

3. Place the almonds in a blender and process with short bursts at high speed until they are finely ground. Stir the cream and honey into the ground nuts in the blender, then process mixture on low speed until smooth.

4. Remove the peaches to a serving bowl, arranging them cut side down. Place the blended nut mixture in the skillet with any remaining milk.

5. When the sauce is hot, but not boiling, beat a small amount into the egg yolk. Add the egg yolk mixture to the pan, stirring briskly, and remove from the heat as soon as sauce begins to thicken. It should not boil.

6. Stir in the vanilla, then pour the hot sauce over the peaches and serve.

Note: Use stainless steel, enameled cast-iron or flameproof glass pan to avoid discoloring the sauce.

4 large, ripe peaches
⅓ cup milk
1 cinnamon stick
⅓ cup slivered blanched almonds
½ cup heavy cream
1 tablespoon honey
1 egg yolk
drop of vanilla extract

Makes 2 servings

Pineapple Ambrosia

A very quick, very taste-satisfying dessert.

½ ripe pineapple
¼ cup chopped walnuts
¼ cup sour cream
dash of ground cardamom
   (optional)

1. Peel, core and cube the pineapple half. Drain.

2. In a serving dish, toss with the chopped walnuts and sour cream. Add a dash of cardamom, if desired. Serve immediately.

Make It Easy

There is no need to forgo delicious breads, muffins, pies, quiches and casseroles for lack of time. A hectic schedule in the evening need not mean going without a nutritious dinner.

The selections in this section are all put together within 20 minutes—many in less time than that—and are on the table within an hour. For example, if a recipe takes a full 20 minutes to prepare, it will bake no longer than 40 minutes. A dish with a 10-minute preparation time might require 50 minutes of baking. But many of the dishes can be put together, baked and served in 45 minutes or less!

The clock face accompanying each recipe tells the story at a glance: the black band indicates preparation time; the gray band shows how long the dish will bake.

I'll show you how to mix up a batter in minutes, leaving you free to do other things until the moment that the finished product is ready to be taken piping hot from the oven.

I've selected many of your favorites: cakes, sweet breads, muffins and quiches. While they are nearly as quick as a mix, you can make them yourself with whole wheat flour and other wholesome (and *whole*) ingredients. You'll find their hearty taste worth the few minutes you spend preparing them.

In terms of nutrition, these recipes are standouts! I've exercised a light hand with the sweeteners (honey, maple syrup and medium unsulfured molasses exclusively) and the oils. And you will find that the recipes do not contain salt.

In addition to the make-and-bake recipes in this section, there are a few that are make-and-chill. These range from appetizers, soups and salads to luscious, creamy desserts.

You can make your cake (and your pudding, too) and treat your family and guests to homemade flavor and wholesome nutrition with just a few well-spent minutes in the kitchen!

118

Appetizers &
Hors d'Oeuvres

Chicken Liver Pâté   *Makes 12 servings*

"Great texture and wonderful taste," was the verdict of a panel of taste testers.

1. Place a large saucepan half filled with water over high heat. Place a small saucepan, with the eggs and enough cold water to cover, over medium to high heat. Bring both to a boil.

2. Meanwhile, rinse the chicken livers and trim off the fat. Add the garlic, bay leaf and basil, along with the chicken livers, to the boiling water in the large saucepan.

3. When the livers come to a boil, reduce heat and simmer 5 minutes, then turn off the heat and cover the pan. When the eggs boil, turn down heat and simmer 7 to 10 minutes.

4. Cut up the onion and place it in a blender along with the parsley, tamari and butter. Drain the chicken livers and place half of them in the blender. Peel the eggs and add. Process the blender contents on low, then medium speed until smooth. Stop the blender and scrape down the sides as necessary.

5. Chop the remaining chicken livers and stir with a spatula into the blended mixture.

6. Divide the pâté among four small serving dishes. Garnish with parsley sprigs. Chill for at least 40 minutes before serving with whole grain crackers or bread slices.

2 eggs
1 pound chicken livers
1 garlic clove
1 bay leaf
1 teaspoon dried basil
1 large yellow onion
2 tablespoons fresh parsley
2 tablespoons tamari
2 tablespoons butter
parsley sprigs, garnish
whole grain crackers or bread
    slices

119

Makes 3 to 4 dozen # Bite-Size Cheese Puffs

Serve as a tasty hors d'oeuvre.

1 cup water
½ cup butter
½ cup whole wheat flour
½ cup grated Parmesan cheese
dash of cayenne pepper
dash of grated nutmeg
2 eggs

Preheat oven to 375°F

1. Place the water over high heat in a small pan. As it comes to a boil, measure out the butter, set aside, and place flour and Parmesan in a small bowl. Sprinkle the cayenne and nutmeg over the flour.

2. When the water is boiling, stir in the butter with a wooden spoon. When the butter is melted, add the flour and cheese mixture all at once, then beat together well.

3. Continue beating the mixture until it pulls together and leaves the sides of the pan, about 1½ minutes. Remove from the heat.

4. While the mixture cools, lightly oil two baking sheets.

5. When the mixture has cooled slightly, beat the eggs into the mixture one at a time. Drop the batter by the spoonful onto the baking sheets, leaving enough room for each to spread slightly. (You can also use a pastry bag.)

6. Bake in a 375°F oven for 25 minutes, or until puffed and golden brown.

Carrots and Zucchini
a la Grecque

Makes 4 servings

Another quick salad to serve anytime—it can marinate for a week!

1 cup water
¼ cup olive oil
1 carrot
3 small zucchini
2 tablespoons lemon juice
1 tablespoon fresh parsley
1 teaspoon dried tarragon
1 bay leaf
1 garlic clove
¼ teaspoon ground coriander
pinch of dried thyme

1. Place the water and oil in a small saucepan over medium heat.

2. If the carrot is thick, halve or quarter it, then cut into ¼-inch slices. Place in the saucepan, and when water boils, reduce heat to simmer.

3. Halve or quarter the zucchini, then cut into ¼-inch slices. Add these to the saucepan and turn heat up until mixture boils, then reduce heat again to simmer.

4. Add the remaining ingredients, pushing the garlic clove through a garlic press.

5. Simmer the ingredients about 8 to 10 minutes, until the vegetables are firm-tender. They should not be soft.

6. Serve at room temperature, or chill.

Cheese Tart *Makes 12 servings*

Serve very small wedges as an appetizer.

1. Melt the butter in a medium skillet, and add the onion. Cook over very low heat, stirring occasionally.

2. Chop the mushrooms and prepare the cheese. Mince the parsley. When the onions are translucent, add the mushrooms and parsley to the skillet. Stir together, cover the skillet and turn off the heat.

3. In a medium bowl, beat the eggs and add the cream and nutmeg.

4. Place the flour, oil and buttermilk in a 9-inch pie plate. Toss together with a fork to combine, then press the dough in the bottom and sides of the pie plate.

5. Place the onion and mushroom mixture in the pie plate, and sprinkle the cheese evenly across the bottom. Carefully pour in the egg mixture.

6. Bake in a 350°F oven for 35 to 40 minutes, or until puffed and golden.

Note: This makes 6 servings for lunch as a main dish.

1 tablespoon butter
1 medium onion, finely chopped
¾ cup mushrooms
½ cup shredded Gruyère or Swiss cheese
1 tablespoon fresh parsley
4 eggs
1½ cups light cream
⅛ teaspoon grated nutmeg
1 cup whole wheat pastry flour
¼ cup corn oil
2 tablespoons buttermilk

Preheat oven to 350°F

Marinated Brussels Sprouts *Makes 2 cups*

You might also substitute these for marinated artichoke hearts in salads.

1. Place a large saucepan with about an inch or two of water in the bottom over a high flame.

2. Cut the brussels sprouts in half lengthwise. When the water is boiling, place the sprouts in a colander or steaming basket over the boiling water, and cover the pan. Steam for 6 to 8 minutes, just until they are firm-tender.

3. While hot, toss with enough dressing to coat well, then cool and chill before serving.

Variations: Substitute green beans, Jerusalem artichokes or another favorite vegetable for the brussels sprouts. Use your favorite salad dressing in place of the vinaigrette.

1 pint brussels sprouts
Vinaigrette Dressing (page 89)

Makes about 2 cups **Mushroom-Almond Pâté**

Try it on rye crackers for an interesting start to dinner.

¾ cup slivered blanched almonds
1 small onion, minced
1 tablespoon olive oil
1 pound mushrooms, finely
    chopped
2 teaspoons tamari
1 teaspoon fresh tarragon or
    ½ teaspoon dried tarragon
1 garlic clove
1 egg
parsley sprigs, garnish

1. Place the almonds in a medium iron skillet. Set over low to medium heat and stir frequently until they are toasted golden brown.

2. Process the almonds in a blender with short bursts on high speed until they are ground.

3. Place the onion in the skillet with the olive oil and set over medium heat. Stir until translucent.

4. Add the mushrooms to the onion, along with the tamari and tarragon. When the mushrooms have released most of their moisture and have begun to cook dry, press the garlic into the pan through a garlic press. Stir for another minute or two, until all of the liquid has evaporated from the pan.

5. Stir the mushrooms into the ground almonds in the blender, then stir in the egg. Blend, scraping down the sides as necessary, on low to medium speed until all the ingredients are combined, but the mixture is still a little coarse.

6. Pack the pâté into small, decorative serving dishes. Garnish with parsley sprigs and chill for 40 minutes before serving.

Soups

Lentil and Watercress Soup   *Makes 8 servings*

This soup has a unique flavor and satisfying goodness. Served with whole grain bread and a green salad, it's a meal!

1. Place the stock in a medium saucepan over medium heat.

2. In a very large flameproof and ovenproof casserole dish, melt the butter and add the onions and carrots. Cook this, stirring often, over medium heat until the onion is translucent and begins to soften.

3. Add the lentils, the hot stock and the water. Turn the heat to high until the soup comes to a boil.

4. Meanwhile, chop the watercress, including stems. The yield should be about 3 cups. Stir into the soup, along with the tamari.

5. When the soup is boiling, cover the casserole dish and place in a preheated 375°F oven for 40 minutes, until the lentils and vegetables are tender.

Variations: For a thicker soup, puree 3 cups of the cooked soup in a blender and stir back into the remaining soup. Substitute 1 bunch minced parsley for the watercress. Use 2 leeks in place of onions.

6 cups *Stock* (pages 175–76)
3 tablespoons butter
2 onions, chopped
3 carrots, thinly sliced
2 cups dried lentils
2 cups water
1 bunch watercress
1–2 tablespoons tamari

Preheat oven to 375°F

123

Makes 6 servings   # Potato Soup

3 cups diced, unpeeled
　　potatoes
2½ cups milk
⅔ cup water
¼ cup sour cream
1 small sweet onion
2 tablespoons minced fresh
　　dillweed or parsley
1 teaspoon ground coriander
dash of cayenne pepper
butter
parsley sprigs, garnish

Preheat oven to 350°F

1. Place the potatoes with the milk, water and sour cream in a large flameproof and ovenproof casserole. Place over medium to high heat.

2. Cut the onion in quarters lengthwise, then slice thin. Add to the potatoes, along with the dill or parsley, coriander and cayenne.

3. When the potatoes come to a boil, dot them with butter and place them in a 350°F oven, uncovered, for 40 minutes. Serve hot in individual bowls, garnished with parsley sprigs.

As-You-Like-It Lentil Soup

Makes 6 servings

4 cups water
4 cups chopped vegetables
　　(onions, peppers, celery,
　　carrots, tomatoes, potatoes,
　　broccoli or white cabbage)
1 cup tightly packed spinach,
　　kale, Swiss chard or endive,
　　chopped
1 garlic clove
1 cup dried red lentils
2 tablespoons tamari

Preheat oven to 400°F

1. Place the water in a large flameproof and ovenproof casserole dish, and bring to a boil over high heat.

2. Meanwhile, prepare the vegetables. For best flavor, use a mixture of several vegetables.

3. Place the chopped vegetables in the water, push the garlic through a garlic press into the mixture, and stir in the lentils and the tamari.

4. When the soup comes to a boil, cover the casserole, and bake in a 400°F oven for 40 minutes.

Note: *As-You-Like-It Lentil Soup* is a good base for pasta sauce. Just add tomato paste, some oregano, thyme and basil to taste, and serve hot over cooked whole wheat spaghetti or shells.

Gazpacho *Makes 4 servings*

A traditional Spanish soup to serve chilled.

1. Place the onion, tomato, pepper, water, tomato paste, oil, lemon juice, garlic and cayenne in a blender. Process on medium speed until smooth, scraping down the sides of the container when necessary. Pour mixture into four serving bowls.

2. Trim off the stems of the mushrooms. Finely chop the mushroom caps and the celery. Peel and seed the cucumber; chop fine.

3. Divide the mushrooms, celery, cucumber, parsley and chives and stir into the bowls of soup. Chill; serve cold.

1 small onion, quartered
1 large, ripe tomato, quartered
1 sweet red pepper, seeded and quartered
1½ cups water
¼ cup tomato paste
2 tablespoons olive oil
2 tablespoons lemon juice
1 garlic clove
⅛ teaspoon cayenne pepper
1 cup mushrooms
1 stalk celery
1 small cucumber
1 tablespoon minced fresh parsley
1 teaspoon minced fresh chives

Onion Soup *Makes 4 servings*

1. Cook the onions in oil in a large flameproof and ovenproof casserole dish over low to medium heat. When they are translucent, after about 10 to 15 minutes, add the garlic (pushed through a garlic press), stock, tamari, molasses and bay leaf.

2. Place the soup, covered, in a 350°F oven for 40 minutes.

3. Serve from casserole dish, or, if desired, pour soup into individual ovenproof dishes, then top with the bread slices, Gruyère and Parmesan. Place under a broiler until the cheese begins to brown.

2 Spanish onions, thinly sliced
2 tablespoons olive oil
2 garlic cloves
4 cups *Stock* (pages 175–76)
2 tablespoons tamari
1 teaspoon blackstrap molasses
1 bay leaf
4 thin slices whole wheat bread
4 small, thin slices Gruyère cheese
2 tablespoons grated Parmesan cheese

Preheat oven to 350°F

Eggs

Cheese Souffle *Makes 4 servings*

Perfect for luncheon with a green salad. It's light and fluffy with an excellent flavor.

1. Butter a 2-quart souffle dish. Dust with some of the Parmesan.

2. Melt the remaining butter in a large skillet or saucepan. Add the flour and stir for a minute or two over medium heat.

3. Add nutmeg and milk. Simmer over low heat, stirring occasionally, for about 3 minutes. As the cream sauce simmers, shred the longhorn, Swiss or Cheddar cheese.

4. Turn off the heat under the cream sauce when it has thickened slightly. Separate the eggs, placing the whites in a medium bowl and the yolks in a small bowl. Lightly beat the yolks and add them to the sauce along with the shredded cheese and the remaining Parmesan.

5. Beat the egg whites with the cream of tartar until stiff peaks form. Stir one-quarter of the whites into the cream sauce, then gently fold in the remaining whites.

6. Pour the batter into the prepared souffle dish. Place in a preheated 400°F oven, then turn heat down immediately to 325°F and bake for 35 minutes. Serve at once.

2½ tablespoons butter
½ cup grated Parmesan cheese
2 tablespoons whole wheat flour
dash of grated nutmeg
1 cup milk
½ cup shredded longhorn, Swiss or Cheddar cheese
4 eggs
¼ teaspoon cream of tartar

Preheat oven to 400°F

Cheese and Mushroom Quiche

A classic.

Makes 8 servings

½ cup sliced scallions
1 cup sliced mushrooms
3 tablespoons butter
1 tablespoon fresh parsley
2 eggs
2 egg yolks
1 cup heavy cream
1 cup milk
¼ teaspoon grated nutmeg
⅓ cup wheat germ
⅔ cup whole wheat flour
¼ cup sunflower or olive oil
¾ cup shredded Gruyère
    cheese

Preheat oven to 350°F

1. Cook the scallions and mushrooms in the butter in a large skillet over medium heat until the scallions are wilted. Mince the parsley and add it to the pan, stirring until the parsley is wilted. Remove from heat.

2. Beat the eggs with the additional yolks in a large bowl, then add the cream, milk and nutmeg.

3. Place the wheat germ and flour in the bottom of a 9-inch pie plate. Add the oil and toss with a fork until well combined. Press dough into the sides and bottom of the pie plate to make a crust.

4. Sprinkle the mushrooms, scallions and cheese over the bottom of the crust. Then gently pour the egg mixture over all.

5. Bake in a 350°F oven for 40 minutes, or until puffed and golden and set throughout. Serve hot or at room temperature.

Onion Pie with Cheese Crust

Makes 6 servings

4 scallions
2 tablespoons butter
1 cup Spanish (sweet) onion
2 teaspoons tamari
1 cup whole wheat pastry flour
2 tablespoons grated Parmesan
    cheese
¼ cup corn oil
3 eggs
1 cup milk
½ cup heavy cream
chopped parsley, garnish

Preheat oven to 375°F

1. Chop the scallions. Melt the butter in a medium skillet, and cook the onion and scallions over low heat until translucent.

2. Sprinkle the tamari over the onion and scallions, and cover. Stir occasionally to prevent sticking.

3. Place the flour and Parmesan in the bottom of a 9-inch pie plate. Add the oil, and toss together with a fork until well mixed. Press the dough into the bottom and up the sides of the pie plate.

4. When the onion and scallions are tender, in 10 to 15 minutes, place them in the unbaked pie shell. Beat the eggs in a medium bowl, add the milk and cream, and thoroughly combine. Pour mixture over the onion and scallions.

5. Bake in a 375°F oven for about 40 minutes, or until puffed and golden. Sprinkle with chopped parsley and serve.

Spinach-Cheese Pie

Makes 6 servings

"A great combination," I've been told.

1. Trim and chop the scallions. Melt the butter in a large skillet, and cook the scallions over low to medium heat.

2. Meanwhile, wash the spinach leaves and trim off the stems. Coarsely chop the leaves. Add the spinach to the scallions, dust with nutmeg, then cover the pan and steam until the spinach is wilted. Turn off heat.

3. Place the cottage cheese and milk in a blender. Process on low speed until smooth. Add the eggs and process on low speed just a few seconds until the eggs are combined with the cheese mixture.

4. Place the flour, oil and water in a 9-inch pie plate. Toss together with a fork until combined, then press dough along the bottom and up the sides of the pie plate.

5. Place the scallion and spinach mixture in the pie shell. Pour the egg and cheese mixture over top. Bake in a 375°F oven about 35 minutes, or until firm and browned on top.

2 scallions
2 teaspoons butter
4 cups tightly packed spinach
dash of grated nutmeg
1 cup cottage cheese
½ cup milk
3 eggs
1 cup whole wheat flour
¼ cup corn oil
2 tablespoons water

Preheat oven to 375°F

Parmesan Zucchini Bake

Makes 6 servings

A delectable dish for company. Serve with whole wheat rolls and salad.

1. Heat the oil in a large skillet, then add the scallions. Turn heat very low. While the scallions cook, trim the ends from the zucchini and slice about ⅛ inch thick. Add to the scallions.

2. Turn up heat under skillet to medium. When the zucchini begins to soften, add the garlic and herbs.

3. Beat the eggs, and add the Parmesan and tamari.

4. When the zucchini is tender, place the mixture in a lightly oiled 9-inch pie plate or quiche form. Pour the egg mixture over top.

5. Bake in a 350°F oven about 25 minutes, or until set.

2 tablespoons olive oil
4 scallions, chopped
3 small zucchini
1 garlic clove, crushed
1 tablespoon fresh basil or 1
    teaspoon dried basil
½ teaspoon dried marjoram
¼ teaspoon dried oregano
6 eggs
⅓ cup grated Parmesan cheese
1 teaspoon tamari

Preheat oven to 350°F

Vegetarian Main Dishes

Eggplant Lasagna

Makes 6 servings

A pleasing variation on a theme.

1. Place about 1 inch of water in the bottom of a large kettle. Set over high heat, cover pan, and bring water to a boil.

2. Quarter tomatoes, remove seeds, and place tomatoes in blender. Add the tomato paste, scallion, water, parsley, basil, oregano, marjoram and, if desired, garlic. Process on medium speed until smooth. Place the mixture in a saucepan over medium heat and cover.

3. When the water in the large pot is boiling, slice the eggplant into rounds about ½ inch thick. Place the rounds in a metal colander and set into the kettle. Steam the eggplant until tender but not mushy, about 5 minutes.

4. Stir the tomato sauce occasionally. Meanwhile, in a large mixing bowl, stir together the ricotta, eggs, wheat germ and Parmesan.

5. To assemble the lasagna, place a thin layer of the tomato sauce in the bottom of a 9 × 13-inch shallow baking dish. Place half of the eggplant slices in the bottom of the dish in one layer. Top with the ricotta mixture, followed by a layer of the remaining eggplant slices. Then pour the tomato sauce over all. Arrange mozzarella slices on top of casserole.

6. Bake in a 350°F oven for 40 minutes.

2 large, ripe tomatoes
⅔ cup tomato paste
1 scallion
1 cup water
1 tablespoon fresh parsley
2 teaspoons dried basil
1 teaspoon dried oregano
½ teaspoon dried marjoram
1 garlic clove (optional)
1 large eggplant
1½ cups ricotta cheese
2 eggs, beaten
½ cup wheat germ
⅓ cup grated Parmesan cheese
6 thin slices mozzarella cheese

Preheat oven to 350°F

Baked Macaroni and Cheese

Makes 4 servings

1¼ cups whole wheat elbow
    macaroni
1 cup shredded sharp Cheddar
    cheese
2 eggs
½ cup cottage cheese
½ cup milk
⅛ teaspoon paprika
wheat germ
butter (optional)
parsley sprigs, garnish

Preheat oven to 350°F

1. Nearly fill a large saucepan with water, and bring it to a boil. Add macaroni and boil, uncovered, just until firm-tender. Do not overcook.

2. Meanwhile, shred the Cheddar cheese.

3. Place the eggs, cottage cheese, milk and paprika in a blender, and process on medium speed until smooth.

4. When the macaroni is done, drain. Place about one-third of the macaroni in the bottom of a lightly oiled 1-quart baking dish. Sprinkle with one-third of the Cheddar cheese. Repeat with another two layers of pasta and cheese.

5. Pour the blended mixture over the macaroni and cheese. Top with wheat germ and, if desired, dot with butter. Bake at 350°F for 40 minutes. Serve in casserole dish, garnished with parsley sprigs.

Almond Noodle Casserole

Makes 6 servings

An elegant dish suitable for entertaining!

2 cups whole wheat or sesame
    pasta spirals
2 eggs
1½ cups cottage cheese
½ cup yogurt
½ cup slivered blanched
    almonds
½ cup raisins
1 tablespoon honey
wheat germ
butter

Preheat oven to 375°F

1. Place a large saucepan nearly filled with water over high heat. When it comes to a boil, add the pasta. When the water returns to a boil, turn down the heat and simmer the pasta, uncovered, just until firm-tender.

2. Meanwhile, separate the eggs, placing the whites in a small bowl. In a large bowl, combine the yolks, cottage cheese, almonds, raisins and honey.

3. Whip the egg whites until stiff. When the pasta is done, drain. Add to the cottage cheese mixture. Fold in the beaten egg whites.

4. Place the mixture in a lightly oiled 1¾-quart casserole dish. Sprinkle with wheat germ and dot with butter. Bake at 375°F for 40 minutes.

Note: This casserole can also be baked in a large, shallow baking dish, which is even more elegant. Reduce baking time to about 30 minutes, until the topping is golden brown.

Cheese and Spinach Bake

Makes 4 servings

Everyone rated this one tops.

1. In a very large bowl beat together the eggs and flour. Remove stems from the spinach leaves and discard. Tear the spinach into small pieces and add to the eggs.

2. Add the cheeses, and push the garlic through a garlic press into the bowl. Toss everything together until blended.

3. Place the spinach mixture in a lightly oiled shallow baking dish, about 9 × 13 inches. Cover the dish loosely with a piece of aluminum foil.

4. Bake at 350°F for 40 minutes.

2 eggs, beaten
¼ cup whole wheat flour
10 ounces spinach
1 cup cottage cheese
1 cup crumbled feta cheese
1 garlic clove

Preheat oven to 350°F

Baked Enchiladas

Makes 2 servings

Very, very good—and easy to do.

1. Place half of the tomatoes along with the tomato paste, garlic, peppers, tamari and molasses in a blender. Process on medium speed until smooth. Add the remaining chopped tomatoes and continue to process until thoroughly combined.

2. Place the tomato mixture in a medium pan and heat over a low to medium flame. Meanwhile, prepare the onions and cheese.

3. To assemble the casserole, bring a medium skillet with 1 inch of water to a boil. Lightly oil an 8 × 8-inch shallow casserole dish. Place a tortilla in the boiling water for about 30 seconds, just until soft. Place tortilla in the casserole dish, and sprinkle with some of the chopped onions, cheese and a little of the sauce. Cook and layer remaining tortillas with onions, cheese and sauce, ending with a tortilla.

4. Pour the remaining sauce over top of the stack of tortillas. Place casserole in a 350°F oven until the cheese is melted, about 25 to 30 minutes.

3 cups chopped tomatoes or cherry tomatoes
2 tablespoons tomato paste
2 garlic cloves
2 fresh hot peppers, seeds removed
2 teaspoons tamari
1 teaspoon blackstrap molasses
1 cup chopped onions
1 cup grated sharp Cheddar cheese
4 corn tortillas

Preheat oven to 350°F

Cheese-Stuffed Tortillas

Makes 4 servings

4 scallions, chopped
2 tablespoons corn oil
3 cups cooked tomatoes with juice
2–3 fresh hot peppers
12 corn tortillas
¾ pound Cheddar cheese
½ cup sour cream
¼ cup buttermilk
alfalfa sprouts, garnish
parsley sprigs, garnish

Preheat oven to 400°F

1. In a large skillet, cook the scallions over low heat in the oil until wilted, about 3 minutes.

2. Meanwhile, place the tomatoes and peppers in a blender, and process on medium speed until smooth. When the scallions are done, add the chili sauce, removing the skillet from the heat to prevent spattering. Continue to cook over low to medium heat.

3. Meanwhile, heat a skillet big enough to hold a tortilla flat on the bottom with about ½ inch of water. Dip each tortilla into the boiling water just until it is soft enough to roll up, about 15 seconds. Set aside to cool until remaining tortillas are softened.

4. Cut the Cheddar cheese into 12 long fingers, about 1 ounce of cheese each, and place a piece on the edge of each tortilla. Then roll up each tortilla tightly. Place the tortillas in a row in the bottom of a lightly oiled casserole dish that will accommodate the tortillas in one layer.

5. Pour the tomato sauce over the tortillas, covering well. Bake in a 400°F oven for 15 minutes.

6. While the tortillas are baking, mix together the sour cream and buttermilk. When the tortillas are ready, remove them from the oven, and pour the sour cream mixture down the centers of the tortillas.

7. Garnish on each side of the sour cream topping with the alfalfa sprouts and parsley sprigs. Serve immediately.

Variations: Use cooked, diced chicken in place of the cheese to stuff the tortillas. Or stuff with cooked, flaked fish or cooked, mashed beans.

Vegetarian Chili *Makes 6 servings*

Hearty fare with a spicy flair.

1. Place the water, brown rice and lentils in a deep, 2½-quart flameproof and ovenproof casserole dish. Stir and set over high heat until mixture boils, then reduce heat.

2. Meanwhile, chop the onion and the peppers, removing the seeds from the peppers. Add to the casserole.

3. Add the parsley, tamari, chili, cumin and molasses. Push the garlic through a garlic press into the casserole. Stir thoroughly to combine the ingredients.

4. Simmer atop the stove for about 5 minutes, then cover and place the casserole in a 400°F oven for 35 to 40 minutes. Stir and serve hot.

4 cups water
1 cup brown rice
⅔ cup dried split red lentils
1 large onion
1 sweet red pepper
1 fresh hot pepper
2 tablespoons minced fresh parsley
2 tablespoons tamari
2 tablespoons chili powder
2 teaspoons ground cumin
2 teaspoons blackstrap molasses
2 garlic cloves

Preheat oven to 400°F

Noodle and Cheese Casserole *Makes 4 servings*

1. Bring a large saucepan half filled with water to the boil. Add the noodles and cook until firm-tender. Do not overcook. Drain, rinse with cool water and set aside.

2. Meanwhile, heat a large skillet with the oil and add the scallions and broccoli. Stir over medium heat until the vegetables are coated with oil. Add ¼ cup water, and allow the vegetables to steam.

3. Push the garlic through a garlic press into the skillet, and add the basil while the broccoli is cooking.

4. Add the ricotta and 2 eggs when the broccoli is slightly tender, and turn off the heat. Add the nutmeg.

5. Stir the cooked noodles into the ricotta mixture, and pour all into a deep casserole dish. Beat the remaining egg with the milk and pour over the casserole. Top with wheat germ and bake for 30 minutes in a 350°F oven.

1½ cups whole wheat noodles
2 tablespoons safflower oil
3 scallions, chopped
1 cup broccoli florets, chopped
¼ cup water
1 garlic clove
1 teaspoon dried basil
2 cups ricotta cheese
3 eggs
dash of grated nutmeg
¼ cup milk
wheat germ

Preheat oven to 350°F

Makes 4 servings **Feta Cheese Souffle**

Feta cheese offers an interesting flavor for a cheese souffle.

2 tablespoons butter
1 tablespoon grated Parmesan
    cheese
2 tablespoons whole wheat flour
1 cup milk
⅔ cup finely crumbled feta cheese
3 eggs
2 additional egg whites

Preheat oven to 400° F

1. Butter a 2-quart souffle dish, then sprinkle with the Parmesan cheese, coating the bottom and sides of the souffle dish.

2. Melt the remaining butter in a large saucepan. Stir in the whole wheat flour and continue to stir over low heat for a minute or two.

3. Add the milk, stir and simmer for about 3 minutes, until the sauce begins to thicken. Add feta and stir an additional minute. Remove from the heat.

4. Separate the eggs, putting the whites in a medium bowl and the yolks in a small bowl.

5. Beat the whites until they stand in stiff peaks, using a whisk or hand beater, or use an electric mixer on low, then medium speed.

6. Stir the egg yolks into the cream sauce in the saucepan after it has cooled slightly. Stir in a quarter of the beaten whites, then gently fold in the rest.

7. Pour the souffle mixture into the prepared souffle dish. Place in a preheated 400°F oven, then immediately turn the heat down to 325°F. Bake for 35 minutes, undisturbed. Serve immediately upon removing from the oven, while the souffle is puffed and golden.

Cauliflower Curry *Makes 4 servings*

If you like Indian foods, or would like to become acquainted with them, this is a delicious start. Serve with Fried Bananas *(page 70).*

1. Separate the cauliflower into florets. Melt the butter in a large saucepan and saute the cauliflower florets for about 2 to 3 minutes, then remove from pan and place in a large ovenproof casserole.

2. Place the chopped onion in the saucepan and cook over low to medium heat until translucent.

3. Add the ginger and rice and stir together. Push the garlic through a press into the saucepan and add the remaining spices. Stir in the yogurt and water.

4. Bring the rice mixture to a boil. Turn down the heat and cover the pan. Simmer for 10 minutes.

5. Meanwhile, cook the peas in a small amount of water, just until firm-tender. Drain, cover and set aside.

6. Add the rice mixture to the cauliflower in the casserole dish and stir together. Cover the casserole dish and bake at 350°F for 40 minutes.

7. Stir in the peas just before serving.

1 head cauliflower
2 tablespoons butter
1 onion, chopped
1 tablespoon minced fresh
    ginger root
1½ cups brown rice
6 garlic cloves
½ teaspoon cumin seeds
½ teaspoon ground cinnamon
½ teaspoon chili powder
½ teaspoon curry powder
¼ teaspoon ground cardamom
dash of ground cloves
1 cup yogurt
2½ cups water
1 cup peas

Preheat oven to 350°F

Makes 6 servings   **Leek Tart**

Leeks always have a special flavor. Here they enhance a tart made with cottage cheese.

3 medium leeks
3 scallions
2 teaspoons olive oil
dash of nutmeg
1 cup cottage cheese
½ cup milk
3 eggs
2 teaspoons tamari
1 cup whole wheat flour
¼ cup corn oil
2 tablespoons water
1 tablespoon chopped parsley,
    garnish

Preheat oven to 375°F

1. Chop the leeks and scallions. Place them in a medium skillet with the olive oil and dust with a little nutmeg. Cook over low to medium heat until the leeks are soft.

2. Place the cottage cheese, milk, eggs and tamari in a blender. Process on low speed until smooth.

3. Place the flour, oil and water in a 9-inch pie plate. Toss the ingredients together with a fork, then press along the bottom and sides of the pie plate.

4. Scatter the cooked leeks and scallions over the bottom of the pie shell. Carefully pour in the cheese and egg mixture.

5. Bake in a preheated 375°F oven for 35 to 40 minutes or until puffed and golden. Let cool slightly before cutting. Sprinkle with chopped parsley and serve.

Fish

Italian Fish and Pasta Salad
Makes 4 servings

A delicious cold salad hearty enough for a meal!

1. Place a large saucepan half filled with water over high heat. Place water in a large skillet to a depth of 1 inch, and set the skillet over high heat.

2. Meanwhile, cut the haddock into bite-size pieces. When the water in the large skillet is just below boiling, add the haddock. Poach about 5 minutes.

3. When the water in the large saucepan is boiling, stir in the pasta. Let the water return to a boil, then stir and turn down the heat. Boil pasta until firm-tender, about 7 to 9 minutes.

4. When the haddock is poached, remove it to a large plate where it can be spread out to cool. Drain the cooked pasta and run under cold water to cool.

5. Halve the cherry tomatoes and place them in a serving bowl with the dill, parsley and onion rings. Push the garlic through a garlic press into the bowl.

6. Add the cooled fish cubes and pasta shells. Toss all together with the oil and lemon juice, and chill before serving.

1 pound haddock fillets
¾ cup whole wheat pasta shells
1 cup cherry tomatoes
¼ cup minced fresh dillweed
¼ cup minced fresh parsley
½ small red onion, thinly sliced into rings
1 garlic clove
2 tablespoons olive oil
2 tablespoons lemon juice

139

Baked Porgies with Scallions

Makes 2 servings

Whole fish make an easy, impressive main dish. Serve with brown rice and a green salad.

2 whole porgies, about
    ¾ pound each
1 tablespoon butter
4–5 scallions
    parsley sprigs, garnish
    cherry tomatoes, garnish

Preheat oven to 325°F

1. Lightly butter a shallow baking dish that will hold the fish flat, in one layer. Place the fish in the baking dish and dot with the remaining butter.

2. Chop the scallions and sprinkle them over the fish. Cover the dish with foil. Bake at 325°F for 20 to 25 minutes, or until the fish is done throughout. Garnish with parsley sprigs and cherry tomatoes.

Note: Have the fish seller remove the heads and tails if you wish, but the dish is more attractive if the fish remain intact.

Oven-Baked Flounder with Herbed Topping

Makes 4 servings

First you'll enjoy the way this dish looks, then you'll discover its flavor—double delight!

2 teaspoons olive oil
¼ cup minced celery
4 scallions, chopped
1 small zucchini, shredded
2 tablespoons minced fresh
    parsley
½ teaspoon dried thyme
¼ teaspoon dried basil
1½ cups soft whole grain bread
    crumbs
1½ pounds flounder fillets
1 large tomato, sliced

Preheat oven to 350°F

1. In a large skillet, heat the oil, then add the celery, scallions, zucchini and parsley. Cook a few minutes, until the vegetables are slightly tender.

2. Stir in the thyme, basil and bread crumbs.

3. Place the flounder in a shallow baking dish, and cover it with the bread crumb mixture. Top with tomato slices.

4. Place the fish in the oven and bake for about 35 minutes, until done.

Baked Fish with Spinach and Cheese Sauce *Makes 4 servings*

A lovely dish with fine flavor.

1. Chop the spinach and steam until wilted, then set it aside.

2. Heat the oil in a large skillet and cook the onion in it until translucent. Add the flour, paprika and cayenne, stirring until the onions are coated. Then add the milk slowly, and stir over low heat until the sauce is thickened. Stir in the spinach, tamari and cheese. When the cheese melts, remove from the heat.

3. Place the fish fillets in a shallow baking dish. Pour the spinach and cheese sauce over top. Place in the oven for 25 to 30 minutes, until the fish is done.

10 ounces spinach
2 tablespoons corn oil
1 small onion, finely chopped
2 tablespoons whole wheat flour
½ teaspoon paprika
dash of cayenne pepper
1½ cups milk
2 teaspoons tamari
½ cup shredded Cheddar cheese
1½ pounds cod or flounder fillets

Preheat oven to 350°F

Salmon Loaf *Makes 4 servings*

1. In a medium skillet, stir the onion and celery in the oil. Cook over low heat until firm-tender, about 5 to 10 minutes.

2. Meanwhile, flake the drained salmon into a large bowl, and crush the bones well. Break up the bread cubes and add to the salmon.

3. Just before removing the onion and celery from the heat, stir in the garlic (pushed through a garlic press), parsley and basil.

4. Stir the eggs, lemon juice and cottage cheese into the salmon along with the onion mixture.

5. Pack the salmon into a lightly oiled 8½ × 4½-inch bread pan. Bake at 350°F for 40 minutes, until firm. Serve garnished with lemon wedges and parsley sprigs.

1 medium onion, chopped
1 stalk celery, chopped
2 tablespoons corn oil
15½ ounces water-packed red salmon, drained
1½ cups whole wheat bread cubes
1 garlic clove
2 tablespoons minced fresh parsley
2 teaspoons dried basil
3 eggs
2 tablespoons lemon juice
½ cup cottage cheese
lemon wedges, garnish
parsley sprigs, garnish

Preheat oven to 350°F

Poultry

Turkey Stroganoff
Makes 4 servings

This was an instant favorite at my house.

1. Cut the uncooked turkey breast into 1-inch cubes. Pat dry, then dredge in the flour.

2. Place the oil in a large skillet over medium heat, then add the butter. As soon as the butter is melted, add the turkey cubes and begin browning. Turn heat to low.

3. As the turkey browns, slice the mushrooms thin. Mince the parsley.

4. Add the mushrooms, parsley and basil to the turkey when it has been lightly cooked on all sides. Push the garlic through a garlic press into the skillet. Cook together for 5 minutes.

5. Cut the tomato in half across and squeeze out seeds and juice. Chop the tomato and add it to the skillet. Stir in the water and tamari.

6. When the ingredients have come to a simmer in the skillet, transfer them to a deep casserole dish. Cover, and place in a 350°F oven for 40 minutes.

7. Remove from oven, stir in the sour cream and serve.

Variation: Substitute 1½ pounds boneless and skinless chicken breasts for the turkey.

1½ pounds boneless turkey breast fillets
2 tablespoons whole wheat flour
1 tablespoon olive oil
2 teaspoons butter
1 pound mushrooms
2 tablespoons fresh parsley, preferably flat-leaf parsley
2 teaspoons dried basil
1 garlic clove
1 large, ripe tomato
½ cup water
1 tablespoon tamari
⅓ cup sour cream

Preheat oven to 350°F

143

Makes 2 servings   # Cornish Game Hens

This special dish is lovely served with Ginger Rice *(page 201) and a green salad.*

2 Cornish game hens
2 tablespoons butter
1 teaspoon honey
2 teaspoons dried tarragon or 2 tablespoons minced fresh tarragon
2 scallions
parsley sprigs, garnish

Preheat oven to 450°F

1. Clean and dry the Cornish hens. Place half of the butter in a large skillet and melt. Add the honey and half of the tarragon. Quickly brown the poultry over medium-high heat.

2. Cut each of the scallions into three pieces. Place three pieces inside each bird, along with the remaining tarragon.

3. Arrange the Cornish hens on a baking rack set on a pan. Tie the legs together at the feet with string. Fold the wings back under the body of the Cornish hens. Cover both with a piece of cheesecloth, and place dabs of the remaining butter on top.

4. Place in a 450°F oven, then turn down heat immediately to 375°F. Bake 45 minutes. Serve on a platter garnished with parsley sprigs.

Makes 6 servings   # Chicken and Rice Casserole

4 cups chopped Italian plum tomatoes, with juice
1 cup brown rice
4 chicken breast halves, boneless and skinless
4 scallions
1 stalk celery
2 tablespoons olive oil
2 tablespoons fresh parsley
2 teaspoons dried basil
1 teaspoon dried oregano
½ teaspoon chili powder
½ teaspoon paprika
2 garlic cloves

Preheat oven to 375°F

1. Place the tomatoes with juice and the rice in a large saucepan. Cover and set over high heat until the mixture boils, then reduce heat and simmer.

2. Meanwhile, cut the chicken into bite-size pieces. Chop the scallions and the celery rather fine.

3. In a 2½-quart flameproof and ovenproof casserole dish, heat the oil, then quickly saute the chicken. When the chicken is golden, add the scallions and celery. Stir together until the scallions are slightly softened. Coarsely chop the parsley and add to the chicken along with the basil, oregano, chili and paprika. Push the garlic through a garlic press into the casserole dish.

4. When the tomatoes and rice have simmered about 15 minutes, add them to the chicken in the casserole dish and stir. Bake in a 375°F oven for 40 minutes.

Turkey with Peppers and Tomatoes

Makes 4 servings

Serve with boiled potatoes or brown rice.

1. Pound the turkey breast fillets to a little more than ¼ inch thick using a rubber mallet or the bottom of a small heavy-bottom skillet. Cut the turkey breast fillets into halves or quarters. There should be two pieces per serving. Pat the turkey dry, then dredge in the flour.

2. In a large skillet over medium heat, warm half of the oil. Cook the turkey, in one layer, in the skillet. Place in a shallow baking dish.

3. Chop the onion and dice the green pepper. Cut the tomatoes in half across, and squeeze out the seeds. Coarsely chop the tomatoes.

4. Place the remaining tablespoon of oil in the skillet. Cook the onion and pepper just until the onion is translucent, then add the tomatoes. Then add the parsley, tamari and oregano. Push the garlic clove through a garlic press into the pan, and add the red pepper flakes.

5. Stir the mixture over medium heat until heated through and well blended. Spread over the turkey in the shallow baking dish, cover with foil, and place in a 350°F oven for 40 minutes.

Variation: Substitute 1½ pounds boneless and skinless chicken breasts for the turkey.

1½ pounds boneless turkey breast fillets
2 tablespoons whole wheat flour
2 tablespoons olive oil
1 medium onion
1 small green pepper
2 large, ripe tomatoes
2 tablespoons minced fresh parsley
2 teaspoons tamari
1 teaspoon dried oregano
1 garlic clove
¼–½ teaspoon hot red pepper flakes

Preheat oven to 350°F

Side Dishes

Carrot Souffle *Makes 4 servings*

1. Place a large saucepan one-third filled with water over high heat and bring to a boil. Meanwhile, clean and slice the carrots; there should be approximately three cups. Place the carrots in the boiling water, reduce heat, cover and simmer.

2. Place the onion, wheat germ, parsley, coriander and eggs in a blender, and process on medium speed until smooth. Lightly oil a 2-quart souffle dish or a straight-sided casserole dish. Place the egg mixture in the dish.

3. After about 10 minutes of cooking, drain the carrots. Place them, along with the milk, oil, honey and tamari, in the blender, and process on medium speed until smooth. Scrape down the sides of the container as necessary.

4. Pour the carrot mixture into the souffle dish, and gently fold it together with the egg mixture using a rubber spatula.

5. Bake at 375°F for 30 minutes, or just until firm. Serve immediately while the dish is still puffed and golden.

4–5 medium carrots
1 small onion, chopped
¼ cup wheat germ
3 tablespoons fresh parsley
1 teaspoon ground coriander
4 eggs
⅓ cup milk
2 tablespoons sunflower oil
1 tablespoon honey
2 teaspoons tamari

Preheat oven to 375°F

147

Makes 2 servings   # Glazed Acorn Squash

Very moist and tasty—great for holiday meals.

1 small acorn squash
1 teaspoon butter
2 teaspoons medium unsulfured
   molasses

Preheat oven to 350°F

1. Cut the squash in half. Remove seeds and fibers from cavity. Place cut side up in a shallow baking dish.

2. Place ½ teaspoon of butter in each squash half. Drizzle a teaspoon of molasses over each half.

3. Place in a 350°F oven for about 50 minutes, or until tender.

Makes 6 servings   # Scalloped Potatoes

3 cups diced, unpeeled potatoes
2 cups milk
¼ cup sour cream
1 small sweet onion
2 tablespoons minced fresh
   dillweed or parsley
1 teaspoon ground coriander
dash of cayenne pepper
butter
parsley sprigs, garnish

Preheat oven to 350°F

1. Place the diced potatoes with the milk and sour cream in a 2-quart flameproof and ovenproof casserole dish. Place over medium to high heat.

2. Cut the onion in quarters lengthwise, then slice thin. Add to the potatoes, along with dill or parsley, coriander and cayenne.

3. When the potatoes come to a boil, dot them with butter and place them in a 350°F oven, uncovered, for 40 minutes. Serve hot, garnished with parsley sprigs.

Cinnamon-Sesame
Makes 2 servings   # Sweet Potatoes

2 medium sweet potatoes
2 teaspoons sesame tahini
dash of cinnamon

Preheat oven to 375°F

1. Scrub sweet potatoes, then pat them dry.

2. Coat the sweet potatoes with a thin layer of tahini. Sprinkle with cinnamon.

3. Place on aluminum foil and bake in a 375°F oven for about 50 minutes, until sweet potatoes are soft.

Note: For a quick vegetable at another meal, add extra plain sweet potatoes to the oven to bake. Cube and reheat later with a little orange juice in a saucepan, and serve with a light dusting of grated nutmeg.

Holiday Fruit Compote *Makes 8 servings*

A colorful and tasty addition to any winter holiday table. Try it accompanying a meal or as a dessert.

1. Place the pineapple, pears and apples in a large ovenproof casserole dish with cover.

2. Cut the orange in half. Peel one half and chop the flesh, removing any seeds. Place the chopped orange in the casserole dish with the pineapple, pears and apples.

3. Coarsely chop the remaining orange half, including the peel, removing any seeds. Place this, along with the cranberries, cider and spices, in a blender. Process on medium speed until the mixture is smooth.

4. Stir the blended mixture with the fruits in the casserole dish. Cover and bake in a 400°F oven for 40 minutes. Serve hot.

Variation: Allow the compote to cool, then chill thoroughly. Serve the compote cold with a small dollop of yogurt in each bowl.

½ pineapple, peeled and chopped
4 pears, seeded and chopped
2 apples, seeded and chopped
1 orange, preferably seedless navel
1 cup cranberries
2 cups apple cider
½ teaspoon cinnamon
¼ teaspoon grated nutmeg

Preheat oven to 400°F

Roasted Onions *Makes 4 servings*

An effortless side dish for less-than-formal dinners; it's especially appropriate in winter. Make the onions when baking a casserole to take advantage of a hot oven. Serve onions home-style, letting everyone cut into his or her own at the table.

1. Wash off the unpeeled onions and remove only loose pieces of the onion skin.

2. Put the onions in a baking pan, and place them in a 350°F oven. The onions will be soft enough to eat in about 35 to 40 minutes.

Note: If you are adding onions to an oven set higher or lower for other baking, vary time accordingly.

4 large yellow onions

Preheat oven to 350°F

Makes 4 servings **Braised Fennel**

An unusual vegetable that takes next to no time to prepare and wins approval for a unique hint-of-anise flavor.

1 large fennel bulb
½ cup *Stock* (pages 175–76) or
   water
1 tablespoon butter

Preheat oven to 350°F

1. Remove the coarse outer layer from the fennel. Cut off stems from the top, leaving just the bulb.

2. Cut bulb into quarters lengthwise. Arrange quarters in the bottom of a casserole dish in one layer. Pour on the stock and add butter.

3. Bake in a 350°F oven about 40 minutes, until tender.

Easiest-Ever
Makes 4 servings **Corn on the Cob**

Corn is so much easier to husk after the baking—so there's virtually no preparation time! To save energy, bake the corn while something else is in the oven.

4 ears corn with husks

Preheat oven to 350°F

1. Place corn with husks intact in oven, directly on oven racks.

2. Bake 30 minutes at 350°F.

3. Either husk before serving, or let each person husk his or her own.

Breads & Muffins

Date Nut Bread

Makes 2 loaves

Have fresh, delicious bread in an hour!

1. Combine the flour and baking soda in a large mixing bowl. Add the walnuts and dates and toss to combine.

2. Add the yogurt or buttermilk and the molasses, and stir until combined.

3. Pour into two lightly oiled metal bread pans, each 8½ × 4½ inches. Place in a 375°F oven and bake for about 50 minutes, until done.

5 cups whole wheat flour
4 teaspoons baking soda
1 cup chopped walnuts
1 cup chopped dates
3½ cups yogurt or buttermilk
1 cup medium unsulfered molasses

Preheat oven to 375°F

Sour Cream Corn Bread

Makes 16 servings

Moist and flavorful.

1. Mix the cornmeal, flour and baking soda in a medium mixing bowl.

2. In a small bowl, beat the egg and add the sour cream and honey. Beat together until thoroughly blended.

3. Add the egg mixture, the buttermilk and the oil to the dry ingredients. Beat together until blended.

4. Lightly oil an 8 × 8-inch baking dish. Fill with batter and bake 20 to 25 minutes at 375°F. Cut into squares and serve.

1½ cups cornmeal
½ cup whole wheat flour
1½ teaspoons baking soda
1 egg
1 cup sour cream
1 tablespoon honey
¾ cup buttermilk
2 tablespoons corn or sunflower oil

Preheat oven to 375°F

Cheddar Corn Bread

Makes 12 servings

2 cups whole grain cornmeal
1 cup shredded Cheddar cheese
1½ cups buttermilk
2 tablespoons melted butter or corn oil
2 eggs
1 teaspoon medium unsulfured molasses
1 teaspoon baking soda

Preheat oven to 375°F

1. Place the cornmeal in a large bowl and toss with the Cheddar cheese. Place an 8 × 8-inch lightly oiled glass baking dish or cast-iron pan in the oven to heat up.

2. Place the buttermilk, melted butter or oil, eggs, molasses and baking soda in a blender, processing on low to medium speed until combined.

3. Stir the buttermilk mixture into the dry ingredients until smooth. Take the preheated baking pan out of the oven and pour in the corn bread batter.

4. Bake at 375°F for 20 to 25 minutes, until golden brown.

Blueberry Corn Bread

Makes 9 servings

2 cups whole grain cornmeal
2 tablespoons wheat germ
1 teaspoon baking soda
2 cups yogurt or buttermilk
2 eggs, separated
2 tablespoons honey
2 tablespoons corn oil
1½ cups blueberries

Preheat oven to 350°F

1. Combine cornmeal, wheat germ and baking soda in a large bowl. Place a lightly oiled 8 × 8-inch baking dish in the oven to heat up.

2. Combine the yogurt or buttermilk with the egg yolks, honey and oil. Stir in 1 cup of the blueberries. Beat the egg whites until they form stiff peaks.

3. Stir the liquid ingredients into the cornmeal mixture, then carefully fold in the beaten egg whites.

4. Pour the batter into a preheated baking dish. Sprinkle on remaining blueberries and press into the batter slightly.

5. Bake in a preheated 350°F oven for 45 to 50 minutes or until a knife inserted in the center comes out clean. Serve immediately or toast in a broiler to reheat.

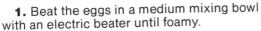

Cheddar Cheese Popovers *Makes 1 dozen*

If you like, substitute feta, Parmesan, Swiss or an herb cheese for the Cheddar, or make the popovers plain.

1. Beat the eggs in a medium mixing bowl with an electric beater until foamy.

2. Add the milk and continue beating. Add the butter and flour and continue to beat until smooth.

3. Place 1 tablespoon of the popover batter in the bottom of each of 12 oiled muffin or custard cups.

4. Sprinkle a teaspoon of the grated cheese into each cup. Top with the remaining batter, but do not fill the cups more than two-thirds full.

5. Bake at 375°F for 40 to 45 minutes, until puffed and golden brown. Do not open the oven sooner than 5 minutes before the popovers are finished baking, or they may fail to puff.

3 eggs
1 cup milk
3 tablespoons melted butter
1 cup whole wheat pastry flour
¼ cup grated Cheddar cheese

Preheat oven to 375°F

Sour Cream and Wheat Germ Biscuits *Makes 1 dozen*

Very easy to make, with good flavor. Try them with soup.

1. In a medium bowl, combine the flour, wheat germ and baking powder. Add the milk and sour cream, and stir together until combined.

2. Allow the biscuit batter to set for 5 minutes. Lightly oil two baking sheets.

3. Drop the biscuits (about ¼ cup for each) onto the baking sheets. Bake about 12 to 15 minutes in a 450°F oven.

2 cups whole wheat flour
½ cup wheat germ
1 tablespoon baking powder
1¼ cups milk
½ cup sour cream

Preheat oven to 450°F

Makes 1 dozen   # Cornmeal Muffins

1⅔ cups cornmeal
⅓ cup whole wheat flour
2 teaspoons baking powder
1 egg
¼ cup butter
1 teaspoon honey
1 cup milk

Preheat oven to 425°F

1. Place the cornmeal, flour and baking powder in a medium mixing bowl.

2. Beat the egg in a small bowl.

3. Melt the butter in a small saucepan, and stir in the honey. Add the milk and stir over low heat just until warm.

4. Add the egg and milk mixture to the dry ingredients. Stir together until well combined.

5. Lightly oil a dozen muffin cups, and divide the batter between them. Bake the muffins about 20 minutes, or until golden brown, in a 425°F oven. Serve warm.

Makes 1 dozen   # Banana-Nut Muffins

What a nice way to start another special day.

1 egg
¾ cup very ripe mashed
   bananas (about 2 medium)
⅓ cup corn oil
¼ cup medium unsulfured
   molasses
¼ cup yogurt
1 cup whole wheat pastry flour
1 cup wheat germ
½ cup finely chopped walnuts
½ teaspoon baking soda
½ teaspoon baking powder
½ teaspoon cinnamon

Preheat oven to 375°F

1. Beat the egg in a large mixing bowl, then add the bananas, oil, molasses and yogurt.

2. In a separate bowl, thoroughly mix together the flour, wheat germ, walnuts, baking soda, baking powder and cinnamon.

3. Lightly oil 12 muffin cups.

4. Add the flour mixture to the wet ingredients in the large bowl, and stir until combined. Divide the batter between the 12 muffin cups.

5. Bake the muffins at 375°F for about 20 minutes, until baked through.

Sunflower Raisin Muffins   *Makes 1 dozen*

1. Place sunflower seeds in a blender. Process in short bursts at high speed until ground to a mealy consistency.

2. In a large bowl, combine the seed meal, flour and baking powder. Stir to combine. Add raisins.

3. Beat the eggs in a small bowl. Then add the oil, milk and honey to the eggs, and stir to combine. Add to the dry ingredients and stir together thoroughly.

4. Divide the batter between 12 lightly oiled muffin cups, and bake about 20 minutes in a 375°F oven, until the muffins are golden.

1¼ cups sunflower seeds
1½ cups whole wheat pastry flour
1 tablespoon baking powder
½ cup raisins
2 eggs, beaten
⅓ cup sunflower oil
¾ cup milk
¼ cup honey

Preheat oven to 375°F

Banana Bran Muffins   *Makes 1 dozen*

These are wonderful muffins!

1. Add the bananas, buttermilk, honey and oil to the egg.

2. In a separate bowl, combine the flour, wheat germ, bran, cinnamon, baking soda and baking powder. Add the dry ingredients to the banana mixture, stirring just until combined.

3. Lightly oil 12 muffin cups. Divide the batter between them.

4. Bake at 375°F for 20 minutes.

¾ cup mashed, ripe bananas
½ cup buttermilk
3 tablespoons honey
2 tablespoons corn oil
1 egg, beaten
1¼ cups whole wheat pastry flour
½ cup wheat germ
¼ cup bran
1 teaspoon cinnamon
½ teaspoon baking soda
½ teaspoon baking powder

Preheat oven to 375°F

Desserts & Snacks

Date Souffle

Makes 6 servings

1. Place the dates and milk in a small saucepan over medium heat. Simmer until the dates are softened and the milk absorbed, about 5 to 7 minutes.

2. Meanwhile, separate the eggs, placing the whites in a large bowl and setting them aside. Place the yolks in a medium bowl and add the heavy cream, honey and vanilla.

3. As soon as the dates are soft, remove them from the heat, mash them to a paste with a fork, and allow them to cool slightly. Beat the egg whites with an electric mixer, beginning on low speed and then medium. They should hold stiff peaks.

4. Fold a little of the date mixture into the egg yolks to warm up the yolks. Then add the remaining dates and stir together well.

5. Butter a medium souffle dish well.

6. Fold one-fourth of the beaten egg whites into the yolk mixture. Gently pour the yolk mixture into the large bowl with the remaining egg whites, and fold together with a spatula.

7. Gently pour the souffle into the baking dish. Bake in a 350°F oven for 35 to 40 minutes, until puffed and golden brown.

1 cup pitted dates
½ cup milk
4 eggs
2 tablespoons heavy cream
2 tablespoons honey
1 teaspoon vanilla extract
butter

Preheat oven to 350°F

Makes 16 servings **Peanut Butter Brownies**

There's no excusing these brownies: They're sinfully rich and terribly delicious!

½ cup melted butter or corn oil
½ cup carob powder
½ cup peanut butter
½ cup honey
1 tablespoon blackstrap molasses
4 eggs
¾ cup whole wheat pastry flour
1 cup chopped walnuts

Preheat oven to 350°F

1. If the butter is not soft, melt it in a small saucepan. Place in a medium bowl and add the carob powder. Stir together.

2. Add the remaining ingredients in the order given, stirring thoroughly after each addition, including after adding each of the eggs.

3. Pour the batter into a lightly oiled 8 × 8-inch baking dish. Bake at 350°F for about 25 minutes. Cut into squares.

Makes 1 dozen **Sunflower-Nut Delights**

1 egg
½ cup honey
1 teaspoon vanilla extract
¾ cup whole wheat flour
½ teaspoon baking soda
½ teaspoon cinnamon
1 cup chopped walnuts
½ cup sunflower seeds

Preheat oven to 375°F

1. In a medium mixing bowl, beat the egg, adding the honey and the vanilla. Stir to combine. Add the remaining ingredients, and stir together all at once.

2. Lightly oil an 8 × 8-inch baking pan. Smooth the batter over the bottom of the pan. Bake at 375°F for 15 minutes. Allow to cool in the pan before cutting into bars.

Variations: Try adding a few dates, raisins or chopped prunes.

Makes 18 bars **Date Bars**

Excellent in texture and flavor—a snack or dessert to make a hit with all ages.

1 cup whole wheat flour
½ cup wheat germ
1 teaspoon baking powder
2 teaspoons cinnamon
¼ teaspoon ground allspice
1 cup dates, chopped
½ cup chopped walnuts
3 eggs, beaten
⅓ cup honey
1 teaspoon vanilla extract

Preheat oven to 350°F

1. Combine the flour, wheat germ, baking powder, cinnamon, allspice, dates and walnuts in a medium mixing bowl.

2. Mix the eggs, honey and vanilla together in a medium bowl, and then fold into the dry ingredients.

3. Spread the batter in a lightly oiled 9 × 13-inch baking pan. Bake at 350°F for about 20 minutes, until golden brown.

Cinnamon-Apple Coffee Cake

Makes 9 servings

Mixes in 15 minutes!

1. In a large mixing bowl, combine the flour, wheat germ, sunflower seeds, cinnamon, baking powder and nutmeg.

2. Core the apples and chop fine. There should be about 2¼ cups of chopped apples.

3. Beat the eggs in a small bowl, and add the buttermilk. Pour into the flour mixture with the apples, and add the honey and oil. Stir to combine smoothly.

4. Place the batter in a lightly oiled 8 × 8-inch baking dish. Place in a 400°F oven for 25 to 30 minutes, until done.

Note: Use Jonathan, Stayman Winesap or other good baking apples. McIntosh apples are too watery to work well here.

2 cups whole wheat pastry flour
½ cup wheat germ
¾ cup sunflower seeds
1 tablespoon cinnamon
2½ teaspoons baking powder
  dash of grated nutmeg
3 tart apples
3 eggs
½ cup buttermilk or yogurt
½ cup honey
2 tablespoons corn oil

Preheat oven to 400°F

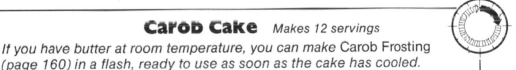

Carob Cake *Makes 12 servings*

If you have butter at room temperature, you can make Carob Frosting (page 160) in a flash, ready to use as soon as the cake has cooled.

1. Beat together the oil and molasses in a large bowl. Add the eggs one at a time, beating well after each addition. Add the yogurt and vanilla and beat together.

2. In a medium bowl, combine the flour, carob powder, wheat germ and baking soda.

3. Stir the dry ingredients into the wet ingredients. When thoroughly combined, pour the batter into a lightly oiled 9 × 13-inch baking pan.

4. Bake in a 350°F oven for 40 to 45 minutes, until a toothpick comes out clean. Make frosting.

5. Cool cake slightly before spreading with frosting.

¾ cup corn oil
¾ cup medium unsulfured
  molasses
3 eggs
1 cup yogurt
2 teaspoons vanilla extract
3 cups whole wheat pastry
  flour
½ cup carob powder
½ cup wheat germ
1½ teaspoons baking soda
Carob Frosting

Preheat oven to 350°F

Makes about ½ cup **Carob Frosting**

2 tablespoons soft butter
¼ cup honey
1 teaspoon vanilla extract
⅓ cup carob powder

1. Combine the butter (at room temperature), honey and vanilla. Stir in the carob powder.

2. Frost *Carob Cake* (page 159) or any other confection.

Makes 8 servings **Banana Cream Pie**

Very flavorful and light.

2–4 very ripe bananas
½ cup ricotta cheese
1 cup whole milk
3 eggs
¼ cup honey
1 tablespoon lemon juice
½ teaspoon vanilla extract
1 cup wheat germ
3 tablespoons corn oil
Whipped Dessert Topping
    (page 112)
8 walnut halves, garnish

Preheat oven to 350°F

1. Mash enough banana to make ½ cup. Place in a blender with the ricotta, milk, eggs, honey, lemon juice and vanilla. Process on medium speed until smooth.

2. Place the wheat germ in a 9-inch pie plate. Stir in the oil with a fork until blended. Press along the bottom and sides of the pie plate.

3. Slice enough bananas to completely cover the bottom of the pie shell. Pour the blended mixture over the bananas.

4. Bake in a 350°F oven about 35 minutes, or until slightly puffed and golden. Let cool slightly, then add *Whipped Dessert Topping,* and garnish with walnut halves.

Makes 4 servings **Baked Stuffed Pears**

An attractive dessert that's easy on the time budget.

4 firm pears
2 tablespoons raisins
3 tablespoons chopped walnuts
1 tablespoon lemon juice
1 teaspoon honey
¼ cup apple cider
dash of grated nutmeg
Whipped Dessert Topping
    (page 112)

Preheat oven to 350°F

1. Halve the pears, remove seeds and core. Combine the raisins and walnuts and place in the hollowed-out pear halves.

2. Mix together the lemon juice, honey and cider in a cup, and drizzle the mixture over the stuffed pear halves.

3. Dust with nutmeg and bake at 350°F for 30 minutes. Serve hot or cold with mounds of *Whipped Dessert Topping.*

Apple Crisp   *Makes 6 servings*

1. Place the unpeeled, chopped apples in a large saucepan with the water, honey and butter. Bring to a boil, reduce heat, cover and simmer for 10 minutes.

2. While the apples are cooking, grate the lemon peel and squeeze out 1 tablespoon of juice. Beat the egg in a measuring cup. Lightly oil a medium souffle dish.

3. When the apples are soft, set the pan in cold water. (Do not let water run into the apple mixture.) When the apples have cooled slightly, add the lemon peel, lemon juice and egg, stirring constantly.

4. Add the rolled oats and stir until combined. Pour the apple mixture into the souffle dish. Bake at 350°F for 30 minutes.

Note: Use a firm baking apple, such as Stayman Winesap or Jonathan. Do not use a watery apple, such as McIntosh.

4 cups chopped tart apples
¼ cup water
¼ cup honey
2 tablespoons butter
1 lemon
1 egg
1 cup rolled oats

Preheat oven to 350°F

Creamy Vanilla Pudding   *Makes 4 servings*
Yummy.

1. Gently heat 2 cups of the milk with the cream in a heavy-bottom saucepan. Meanwhile, stir the cornstarch until dissolved into the remaining ½ cup of milk in a small bowl.

2. Add the honey and vanilla to the cornstarch mixture.

3. When the milk in the saucepan is hot but not boiling, after about 5 minutes, add the cornstarch mixture. Continue heating gently for an additional 5 to 8 minutes, until the pudding is thick.

4. Remove the pudding from the heat. Beat the egg and the extra yolks in a medium bowl. Remove ¼ cup of the pudding from the saucepan and stir briskly into the beaten eggs to warm them slightly. Add the eggs to the cooked pudding in the saucepan, beating briskly.

5. Cool, then chill. To serve, top with fresh fruit, such as sliced strawberries, cherries or kiwi fruit.

2½ cups whole milk
½ cup heavy cream
3 tablespoons cornstarch
3 tablespoons honey
1 teaspoon vanilla extract
1 egg
2 egg yolks
fresh fruit, garnish

Makes 6 servings   # Maple Vanilla Custard
With old-fashioned flecks of real vanilla bean...

3 cups milk
3 eggs
⅓ cup maple syrup
½ teaspoon vanilla extract
1-inch piece vanilla bean or an
    additional ½ teaspoon
    vanilla extract
dash of grated nutmeg

Preheat oven to 400°F

1. Place the milk in a small saucepan over medium heat and scald. Fill another small pan with water and set it over medium heat to boil.

2. Beat the eggs in a medium mixing bowl. Beat in the maple syrup and ½ teaspoon of vanilla extract. Cut the vanilla bean section in half and scrape the seeds into the egg mixture (or stir in the additional ½ teaspoon of vanilla extract).

3. When the milk is scalded, stir a small amount into the eggs. Then add the remaining milk and stir together.

4. Place a paper towel in the bottom of a 9 × 13-inch baking pan. Set six custard cups on the paper towel, and fill them with the custard mixture. Dust with nutmeg. Pour the boiling water around the custard cups in the pan until it reaches a depth of 1 inch.

5. Bake the custard at 400°F for 20 to 25 minutes. If it is to be served cold, insert a knife at the edge of a custard near the end of the baking time. If the knife comes out clean, the custard will set as it cools. If the custard is to be served warm, bake an additional 5 minutes, until a knife inserted in the center of the custard comes out clean.

Makes 3 servings   # Whipped Apricot Dessert
Smooth.

¼ cup dried apricots
1¼ cups water
½ cup yogurt
½ cup heavy cream
1 egg
2 teaspoons honey
¼ teaspoon vanilla extract
2 ice cubes
mint sprigs, garnish

1. Place the apricots and the water in a small saucepan, and bring them quickly to a boil over high heat. Turn down heat and simmer 10 minutes. Remove from stove to cool.

2. Meanwhile, place the yogurt, cream, egg, honey and vanilla in a blender.

3. When the apricots have cooled for 5 minutes, stir in the ice cubes. Once the apricots are thoroughly cooled, pour them into the blender.

4. Process on medium speed until the apricot mixture is smooth. Garnish with mint sprigs. Serve at once, or chill.

Lemon Whip *Makes 4 servings*

1. Place about an inch or two of water in the bottom of a double boiler set over high heat, and bring the water to a boil.

2. Separate the eggs, placing the whites in a large bowl.

3. Place the yolks in the top of the double boiler. Juice the lemons, and add the juice to the yolks. The lemons should yield ⅓ to ½ cup of lemon juice.

4. Add 2 tablespoons of the honey and the tablespoon of water to the yolks. Set the top of the double boiler over the boiling water, and stir until the mixture thickens, about 10 to 12 minutes. Take off the heat and set aside to cool slightly.

5. Beat the egg whites with an electric mixer, beginning on low speed. When they just begin to get foamy, add the remaining honey, and beat on medium speed. Continue beating until the whites stand in stiff peaks.

6. Fold about one-fourth of the beaten egg whites into the yolk mixture. Then gently pour the yolk mixture into the bowl with the remaining whites. Fold together gently but thoroughly.

7. Place the mixture in four parfait glasses, or pile it gently in four small dessert dishes, and chill before serving. Garnish with mint sprigs.

Note: Serve the same day or the mixture will separate.

3 eggs
1½ lemons
2½ tablespoons honey
1 tablespoon water
mint sprigs, garnish

Makes 12 servings **Walnut and Raisin Pie**

A "special occasion" dessert—very rich, quite delicious!

½ cup melted butter
¾ cup wheat germ
½ cup whole wheat flour
2 tablespoons carob powder
½ teaspoon cinnamon
1 cup honey
3 eggs
1 cup chopped walnuts
1 cup raisins
1 teaspoon vanilla extract
Sweetened Whipped Cream
    (page 112; optional)
cinnamon, garnish (optional)

Preheat oven to 350°F

1. While the butter is melting, combine the wheat germ, flour, carob powder and cinnamon in a 9-inch pie dish. Add ¼ cup of the melted butter and toss together with a fork until the butter is evenly distributed.

2. Press the wheat germ mixture evenly across the bottom and sides of the pie plate.

3. In a large bowl, stir the honey into the remaining ¼ cup of melted butter. Beat in the eggs, one at a time, then stir in the walnuts, raisins and vanilla.

4. Pour the filling into the pie shell. Bake 35 to 40 minutes in a preheated 350°F oven.

5. Allow to cool to room temperature before serving. If desired, top with dabs of whipped cream and dust with a little cinnamon.

Makes 4 servings **Grapes Fantasia**

A cooling summertime dessert . . .

1 cup yogurt
1 small banana
1 teaspoon lemon juice
1 teaspoon honey
dash of grated nutmeg
3 cups white seedless grapes
mint sprigs, garnish

1. Place the yogurt, banana, lemon juice, honey and nutmeg in a blender and process on low speed until smooth.

2. Place the grapes in a serving bowl or divide between individual serving dishes. Pour the yogurt mixture over top and garnish with mint sprigs. Serve chilled.

Apricot Squares *Makes 16 bars*

"Great!" said a panel of taste testers.

1. In a medium bowl, blend the ingredients for the crust. Press into the bottom of a lightly oiled 8 × 8-inch baking pan and bake at 350°F for 5 to 7 minutes.

2. For the topping, place the water over high heat, and bring it to a boil. Cut the apricots in small pieces into the medium mixing bowl. Add the butter, and pour the boiling water over all. Let the mixture set for 5 minutes.

3. Add the remaining ingredients. Smooth the topping over the prebaked crust.

4. Bake at 350°F for 25 to 30 minutes. Cut into squares.

Crust:
2 tablespoons safflower or corn oil
¼ cup honey
1 cup rolled oats
¼ cup whole wheat flour

Topping:
½ cup water
⅔ cup dried apricots
1 tablespoon butter
1 egg, lightly beaten
¼ cup honey
¼ cup whole wheat flour
¼ cup wheat germ
1 teaspoon cinnamon
¼ teaspoon ground cloves
½ cup sunflower seeds

Preheat oven to 350°F

Lemon Squares *Makes 16 squares*

Who could count the happy hours I've spent adapting this recipe over the years since it was shared by a friend in college? Perhaps it will be one of your favorites, too.

1. Place the pastry flour in the bottom of an 8 × 8-inch baking dish. Stir the tablespoon of honey into the melted butter. Grind the walnuts in a blender in short bursts at high speed. Add the butter mixture and walnuts to the flour, stir together, and press into the bottom of the dish for a crust.

2. Place the crust in a 350°F oven for 15 minutes.

3. While the crust is baking, place the eggs, honey, lemon juice, lemon peel, whole wheat flour and baking powder in the blender and process on medium speed until smooth.

4. As soon as the crust is removed from the oven, pour the egg mixture over it, and bake 20 minutes. The lemon mixture must remain soft. Allow to cool before cutting into squares.

Crust:
¾ cup whole wheat flour
1 tablespoon honey
½ cup melted butter
¼ cup walnuts

Topping:
2 eggs
⅓ cup honey
2 tablespoons lemon juice
1 teaspoon grated lemon peel
1 tablespoon whole wheat flour
½ teaspoon baking powder

Preheat oven to 350°F

Golden Melon Cake

At harvest time—or anytime—this makes a delicious, unique use of melons.

1 cup cubed cantaloupe
1 cup buttermilk
3 eggs
½ cup honey
⅓ cup safflower oil
1 tablespoon lemon juice
1 teaspoon vanilla extract
3 cups whole wheat pastry flour
¼ cup raisins
¼ cup sunflower seeds
2 tablespoons cinnamon
1½ teaspoons baking soda

1. Place the cantaloupe, buttermilk, eggs, honey, oil, lemon juice and vanilla in a blender. Process on low to medium speed until smooth.

2. In a large bowl, combine the flour, raisins, sunflower seeds, cinnamon and baking soda. Stir in the liquid ingredients until combined.

3. Place the batter in a lightly oiled 8 × 8-inch baking pan. Bake in a preheated 350°F oven for 45 minutes, until golden.

Preheat oven to 350°F

Make It Ahead

By spending a few hours (I mean 2 or 3—not an entire afternoon by any means) once a month, you can have hearty, nutritious basic foods on hand for your meals, ready to be assembled and served in minutes.

Included in this section are some simple (and delicious!) whole grain yeast breads and specialty breads. Spread these with a little peanut butter or ricotta cheese, and you'll have a perfect protein-rich breakfast in no time at all.

The easy-to-prepare stocks in this section can be used in recipes throughout the book. (But even if you don't have time to make stock, the recipes are so good that you can also use just water.)

You'll save money as well as time when you follow my easy directions for making yogurt and sprouts. And if you prepare some crepes and set them aside for a timely (or time-less) occasion, you'll get high marks for elegance, too.

Cook brown rice by the potful, then refrigerate or freeze it for future servings. I'll tell you how to vary the flavors while you reheat the rice, too. I find that brown rice's nutritional superiority to white rice and its delicious nutty flavor make it worth the extra few minutes of cooking it requires.

Perhaps you never expected to find beans in fast company. But depending on how you handle them, beans can outpace many of their less nutritious fast-food buddies.

I've worked out a system here so that the beans all but cook themselves. You'll have no long hours stirring a bubbling pot of beans over a hot stove.

Here's how it works. One night you'll place a pound of beans in a large bowl with about 2 or 3 quarts of water. You'll need enough water to cover the beans as they expand.

Next day, you'll drain the beans and put them into a very large casserole dish or small roasting pan (especially recommended for soybeans, which tend to foam). You then re-cover the beans with a generous amount of water, cover the pan and bake until tender.

There's no tending, stirring, or raising or lowering heat. You're free to do chores, or just to relax and watch a movie on television. By the time you know "who did it," the beans are done!

168

I recommend cooking a pound of beans at a time so that the cooked beans can be frozen in pint or quart containers for later use. On the day before you plan to use them, allow the beans to thaw in the refrigerator.

Some folks swear by a pressure cooker for preparing beans. I feel it requires more attention than my method, so I don't use it. If you have a pressure cooker, check the directions carefully for cooking beans. You'll want to be sure that if there are any loose skins, or if the beans foam, that they do not clog the steam vent.

This book's "bean basics" will allow you to explore several variations on an international theme. Add chili powder and ground cumin, and you've got a Mexican meal in minutes. Oregano and basil bring an Italian flair to another batch of beans. Curry a little flavor with beans, and they'll shine up to rice!

Dried beans come to you straight from nature. The only processing that dried beans are likely to encounter is a short ride through a mechanical sorter. That's why it is wise to pick over the beans before cooking. Tiny stones or moldy, discolored beans may have slipped through; they should be removed. Also, the beans should be well rinsed before soaking.

You will find that my recipes give approximate times for cooking beans. Slight variations in cooking times are due to the climates in which the beans were grown and the length of their storage time. Never use baking soda to shorten the cooking time of beans since the leavening agent depletes thiamine, an essential B vitamin.

One cup of dried beans equals about 2 to 2½ cups after cooking. To reduce the amount of flatulence commonly associated with beans, they must be soaked and then cooked until tender. It helps to discard the water in which the beans were soaked. Though it means a small loss of vitamins, the increased digestibility of the beans enhances their acceptance.

There are two basic methods of soaking beans. The one I recommend is the overnight or all-day soak, since this method requires the least amount of attention. (Never soak beans longer than 12 hours, however, or they may lose their characteristic texture and flavor by absorbing too much water. If you cannot cook the beans soon after soaking, drain them and refrigerate or freeze them until you are ready to use them.)

A quick-soak method is to place the beans and water in a large kettle and bring them to a boil. After boiling, the beans must be left to soak for an hour before continuing with cooking.

For those who choose to make them ahead, I have kept the quick recipes calling for cooked beans and cooked rice in this section. These recipes are accompanied by the easy-to-read clocks, which tell how long the recipes take to prepare (black line) and to bake or chill (gray line.)

Basics: Beans, Rice, Stock, Sprouts & Yogurt

Oven-Cooked Baby Lima Beans
Makes about 6 cups

1. Rinse and pick over the beans. Place in a very large bowl. Cover with sufficient water to allow the beans to expand. Soak overnight.

2. Drain the beans, and place them in a very large ovenproof casserole dish or roasting pan. Add enough water (about 1 quart) to top the beans by about an inch. Cover casserole dish or roasting pan tightly with a lid or with aluminum foil.

3. Bake in a 350°F oven for 1½ to 2 hours, until the beans are tender.

2½ cups dried baby lima beans (1 pound)
water

Oven-Cooked Pinto Beans
Makes 5 to 6 cups

Delicious in South-of-the-Border specialties.

1. Place the beans in a large bowl with enough water to cover them as they expand. Soak overnight.

2. Drain the beans and place in a very large ovenproof casserole dish. Cover well with water, place a lid or aluminum foil over the dish, and bake at 350°F for 2½ to 3 hours, until tender.

2½ cups dried pinto beans (1 pound)
water

171

Oven-Cooked Lima Beans

Makes about 14 cups

5 cups dried large lima beans
    (2 pounds)
water

1. Place the limas in a very large ovenproof casserole dish or roasting pan. Cover with enough water so that the beans will stay submerged even after expanding. Soak overnight.

2. Next day, drain the beans, then cover again with water. Cover the pan with a lid or with aluminum foil. Place in a 350°F oven and bake for 1½ to 2 hours, until the beans are soft.

Oven-Cooked Navy Beans

Makes 5 to 6 cups

2½ cups dried navy beans
    (1 pound)
    water

1. Soak the beans overnight in sufficient water to cover them as they expand.

2. Drain the beans and place them in a very large ovenproof casserole dish. Cover well with water. Cover the casserole dish and bake the beans at 350°F for 1½ to 2 hours, until tender.

Oven-Cooked Chick-Peas

Makes about 6 cups

2½ cups dried chick-peas
    (1 pound)
    water

1. Rinse the chick-peas. Soak them overnight in enough water to cover them; use a very large bowl to allow the chick-peas to expand.

2. Drain and place the chick-peas in a large ovenproof casserole dish. Again cover them generously with water, and cover the casserole tightly.

3. Bake in a 350°F oven for about 3 hours, or until tender.

Note: *Oven-Cooked Chick-Peas,* as well as cooked red kidney beans, can be a tasty addition to tomato sauce for a vegetarian-style spaghetti.

Oven-Cooked
Red Kidney Beans
Makes about 6 cups

1. Rinse and pick over the beans. Place in a very large ovenproof casserole dish or roasting pan. Add sufficient water to cover the beans as they expand. Soak overnight.

2. Drain the beans and add enough water (about 1 quart) to cover well. Cover the casserole dish or roasting pan tightly with a lid or aluminum foil.

3. Bake in a 350°F oven about 2½ hours, or until the beans are tender.

Note: Cooked kidney beans have an excellent flavor in a vegetarian spaghetti sauce. Just add to your favorite tomato sauce and serve over whole wheat pasta for a complementary protein main dish.

2½ cups dried red kidney beans (1 pound)
water

Oven-Cooked Lentils
Makes about 6 cups

1. Rinse the lentils and place them in a large ovenproof casserole dish. Add the water and onion and stir. Cover.

2. Place the casserole dish in a preheated 350°F oven for about 1 hour.

2½ cups dried lentils (1 pound)
4 cups water
1 onion, finely chopped

Oven-Cooked Azuki Beans
Makes about 6 cups

1. Soak the beans overnight in enough water to cover, allowing for expansion of the beans.

2. Next day, drain the beans and place in a large ovenproof casserole or two medium baking dishes. Cover again with a generous amount of water.

3. Cover the beans tightly and bake at 350°F for 2½ to 3 hours, until the beans are soft.

2½ cups dried azuki beans (1 pound)
water

Makes about 6 cups   # Oven-Cooked Soybeans

2½ cups dried soybeans
     (1 pound)
water

1. Rinse and pick over the soybeans, and place them in a large bowl. Soak overnight in sufficient water to cover the beans as they expand.

2. Drain the beans and place them in the bottom of a small roasting pan. (This will provide ample space for the soybeans to cook without boiling over, as soybeans have a tendency to foam.) Cover generously with water.

3. Cover the pan and bake the beans in a 350°F oven for 3 to 3½ hours, until tender.

Note: The cooking liquid from soybeans is especially tasty and can be used in recipes calling for stock or wherever you wish to substitute it for water.

Makes 8 servings   # Brown Rice

Unless you are serving a group, you'll have enough rice here to serve some later in the week. Just refrigerate or freeze extras in pint containers.

2 cups brown rice
4–4½ cups water

1. Place the rice in a large saucepan.

2. Add 4 cups of water to the pan. (Use 4½ cups if you like rice that is quite soft.) Bring to a boil for 5 minutes, uncovered.

3. Cover the pan and turn heat very low. Allow the rice to cook, undisturbed, for 45 minutes. Remove the pan from the heat and keep covered 10 minutes more. Serve hot. Cool extra rice before storing.

Stock I (Vegetable Stock) *Makes 4 cups*

Keep a plastic bag in the freezer to collect vegetable trimmings that can be used in stock.

1. In a large saucepan or stockpot, saute the chopped onion in the melted butter until it becomes translucent.

2. Add the remaining ingredients, bring to a boil, then reduce heat and simmer about 1 hour.

3. Strain the stock into a bowl by lining a colander with a double layer of cheesecloth. Discard vegetables. Cool stock, then chill or freeze. Stock can be frozen in an ice cube tray, and then the cubes can be stored in a plastic bag to be used in small quantities.

Note: Vary the proportions of carrots and turnips or celery and trimmings according to what is available. Carrot tops, potato skins, scallion tops, mushroom stems, lettuce leaves and tomato skins can be stored in a plastic bag in the freezer until enough have accumulated to enrich a stock. Avoid cabbage, broccoli, cauliflower or brussels sprouts, since these have a strong flavor that will overpower the stock.

1 small onion, chopped
2 tablespoons butter, melted
6 cups water
2 cups chopped celery and vegetable trimmings
1 cup cubed carrots and turnips
1 bay leaf
¼ teaspoon dried thyme
dash of cayenne pepper

Stock II (Chicken Stock) *Makes 4 cups*

1. Cut up the chicken into serving-size pieces. Add all ingredients but the breast halves to a large kettle or stockpot.

2. Bring slowly to a boil, then add the breast halves. Reduce heat, cover, and simmer until the breast meat is tender, about 1½ hours.

3. Remove the chicken from the kettle or stockpot. Strain the stock into a large bowl by lining a colander with a double layer of cheesecloth. Cool uncovered, then refrigerate or freeze tightly covered. Stock can be frozen in an ice cube tray, and then the cubes can be stored in a plastic bag to be used in small quantities.

Note: Use meat in crepes and soups, substitute it for tuna in salads, or serve it as is.

1 4-pound chicken
6 cups water
1 carrot, sliced
2 celery stalks, chopped
1 onion, chopped
1 bay leaf
¼ teaspoon dried thyme

Stock III (Miscellaneous Stock)

bean cooking liquid or liquid drained from cooked vegetables

1. To have this stock on hand, reserve and either refrigerate or freeze liquids drained from cooking dried beans or many fresh vegetables.

Note: The stock from cooking soybeans and chick-peas is especially delicious, I think. Avoid adding a darker bean stock, such as liquid from cooked kidney beans, to a delicately colored or flavored dish. Liquid drained from cooking such strongly flavored vegetables as cabbage, brussels sprouts, broccoli or cauliflower can overpower many dishes and generally should not be used.

Yogurt

Makes 1 quart

It's easy—and inexpensive—to make your own yogurt at home. There's no need for special equipment.

1 quart milk
½ cup yogurt

1. Heat the milk to just under the boiling point in a stainless steel, enameled or flameproof glassware pan. Small bubbles will appear around the edge of the liquid when it reaches this point. Remove the pan from the heat and set aside to cool somewhat.

2. When the milk is just reaching lukewarm temperature, about 100°F, stir in the yogurt. (If the milk is too hot, the hard-working yogurt bacteria will be killed.) You can test the temperature with your finger: if the milk feels quite warm, but not too hot to the touch, the yogurt will survive. Have meticulously clean fingers if there is no thermometer handy.

3. Cover the pan and wrap in terry towels, or set it in a warm spot, such as a gas oven with a pilot light, by a sunny window, or on a countertop near the stove if you are baking.

4. Allow yogurt to rest, undisturbed, for about 8 hours. Do not move the pan while the bacteria are at work or the yogurt may not set. Store yogurt in the refrigerator.

Alfalfa Sprouts   *Makes 2 cups*

There's no mystery in having fresh sprouts on hand anytime: all you do is rinse them. With some simple equipment that you probably have on hand right now, you can spend just 3 to 5 minutes a day, and in no time you'll harvest a delicious, vitamin-rich crop!

¼ cup alfalfa seeds
water

1. You will need a widemouthed glass quart jar, a piece of cheesecloth to fit over the top and a rubber band. Place the alfalfa seeds in the jar and cover with water. Let them soak several hours or overnight.

2. Place the cheesecloth over the mouth of the jar and secure with the rubber band. Drain the water off the seeds, then shake the jar so that the seeds are spread out inside the jar. Rest the jar on its side on the kitchen counter. (Some folks prefer to grow sprouts in the dark, but we find this method best—and a good reminder to rinse them when they are in clear sight!)

3. Rinse the seeds 2 to 3 times a day, draining them thoroughly and shaking the jar to distribute the seeds each time.

4. Sprouts will be ready in about 3 or 4 days. The last day you might place the jar in full sunlight, and chlorophyll will develop in the seeds.

Variations: Use mustard, radish or sunflower seeds, mung beans, soybeans, lentils or chick-peas, wheat or other grains in place of the alfalfa seeds. Larger seeds and beans will not increase as greatly in bulk when they are sprouted, and you may want to begin with more than ¼ cup. For a greater quantity of sprouts, use a gallon jar and ½ cup of beans or seeds. Mix beans and seeds for a delicious, nutritious combination! Use the following table as a guide.

Sprouting:
Everything You Need to Know

	Rinses per day	Length at harvest (inches)	Sprout time (days)	Approximate yield	Characteristics	Stays fresh in refrig. (days)
Alfalfa	2	1–2	3–5	3 tablespoons =4 cups	Easy to sprout. Pleasant, light taste.	10
Lentil	2–4	¼–1	3	1 cup =6 cups	Chewy bean texture. Can be eaten raw or steamed lightly.	10
Mung bean	3–4	1½–2	3–5	1 cup =6–8 cups	Easy to sprout. Poplar in oriental dishes. Sprouts begin to lose their crispness after 7 days of storage.	7
Radish	2	¼–1	2–4	1 tablespoon =1 cup	Sprouts taste just like the vegetable.	9
Soybean	4–6	1–2	4–6	1 cup =4–6 cups	Difficult to sprout because they ferment easily. Need frequent, thorough rinses. Should be cooked before eating for optimum protein availability.	7
Sunflower	2	Sprout is length of seed	1–3	½ cup =1½ cups	Good snacks, especially if lightly roasted. Become bitter if grown too long.	11
Wheat	2–3	Sprout is length of seed	2–4	1 cup =3½–4 cups	Simple to sprout. Very sweet taste.	9

Breakfasts

Buttermilk Rice Waffles *Makes 4 servings*

Serve with chopped fresh fruit and maple syrup.

1. Combine the flour and baking soda in a medium bowl.

2. Beat the egg in a small bowl. Melt the butter.

3. Combine the egg, butter, buttermilk, rice and honey with the dry ingredients, and stir together until combined.

4. Pour half the batter onto a four-waffle iron. When cooked, repeat with remaining batter.

1 cup whole wheat flour
2 teaspoons baking soda
1 egg
2 tablespoons butter
1¼ cups buttermilk
½ cup cooked brown rice
1 tablespoon honey

Preheat waffle iron

Cooked Rice Breakfast *Makes 2 servings*

1. Place the rice, milk and honey in a small saucepan.

2. Heat through, stirring occasionally, over low heat. Serve hot.

Variations: Serve cold, without heating the cooked rice, tossed with cubed fresh fruit. Add raisins or chopped dates to the rice while cooking. Substitute maple syrup or medium unsulfured molasses for the honey.

1 cup cooked brown rice
¾ cup milk
2 teaspoons honey

Makes 2 servings **Apricot-Rice Cereal**

Creamy and sweet, without being sweetened.

1 cup cooked brown rice
1 cup water
¼ cup dried apricots
milk (optional)

1. Place the cooked rice and water in a small saucepan over medium heat. Chop the apricots and add to the pan.

2. Bring to a boil, then reduce heat and simmer about 8 minutes, until most of the water is absorbed and the rice is soft.

3. Serve hot, with milk, if desired.

Makes 2 servings **Honey-Rice Pancakes**

Light and fluffy.

1 cup whole wheat flour
1½ teaspoons baking powder
2 eggs
½ cup cooked brown rice
1 cup milk
2 tablespoons honey

1. Place the flour and baking powder in a medium bowl.

2. In a small bowl, beat the eggs and stir in the brown rice. Add with the milk and honey to the dry ingredients, stirring until combined.

3. Cook the pancakes on a large, lightly oiled griddle. Serve hot.

Makes 2 servings **Banana Rice Cereal**

1 cup cooked brown rice
¾ cup water
1 large, ripe banana, sliced
1 tablespoon wheat germ
dash of cinnamon
milk

1. Place all the ingredients except the milk in a small saucepan over medium heat and bring to a boil.

2. Reduce heat and simmer, uncovered, about 8 minutes, until rice is soft and water is absorbed. Serve hot, with milk.

Rice Porridge Deluxe   *Makes 2 servings*

A melange of healthful additions to a morning's meal.

1. Place all the ingredients except the milk in a small saucepan and bring to a boil.

2. Reduce heat and simmer, uncovered, about 8 minutes, until the water is absorbed and the rice is quite soft. Serve immediately, with milk.

1 cup cooked brown rice
1 cup water
2 tablespoons chopped dried figs
1 tablespoon chopped walnuts
1 tablespoon sunflower seeds
1 tablespoon wheat germ
2 teaspoons honey
milk

Maple Date-Nut Porridge   *Makes 2 servings*

Share a nutritious, ever-so-tasty breakfast with someone you love. For big appetites, double the recipe.

1. Place all the ingredients except the milk in a small saucepan over medium heat and bring to a boil.

2. Reduce heat and simmer, uncovered, about 8 minutes, until the water is absorbed and the rice is quite soft. Serve hot, with milk.

1 cup cooked brown rice
¾ cup water
2 tablespoons chopped dates
2 tablespoons slivered blanched
   almonds
1 tablespoon maple syrup
milk

Appetizers & Hors d'Oeuvres

Lentil Pâté
Makes 8 to 12 servings

1. Place lentils in a bowl and mash with a potato masher or a fork.

2. Add the mayonnaise, tamari, basil, allspice, mace and cayenne until smooth.

3. Lightly oil an 8½ × 4½-inch bread pan. Line the pan with a piece of aluminum foil, with the ends of foil extending up over the sides. Put a light coating of oil on the aluminum foil.

4. Press the pâté into the bottom of the foil-lined bread pan. Fold the ends of the foil over the pâté to cover, then chill pâté 40 minutes or more.

5. To serve, use the foil to lift the pâté out of the bread pan. Invert the pâté onto a serving plate.

6. To garnish, cut the cherry tomatoes in half and place on top of the pâté in a line down the center. Add sprigs of parsley to the top and around the sides of the pâté. Serve with whole grain crackers.

4 cups cooked lentils, well drained
⅓ cup *Blender Mayonnaise* (page 91)
1 tablespoon tamari
1 teaspoon dried basil
¼ teaspoon ground allspice
¼ teaspoon mace
⅛ teaspoon cayenne pepper
3 cherry tomatoes, garnish
parsley sprigs, garnish
whole grain crackers

Makes 2 cups **Soybean Spread**

This protein-rich spread can be used in sandwiches, as a dip with whole wheat pita bread or as a filling for crisp celery stalks.

2 cups cooked soybeans
¼ cup water
1 tablespoon lemon juice
1½ tablespoons tamari
1 teaspoon ground coriander
½ teaspoon ground cumin
⅛ teaspoon cayenne pepper
2 garlic cloves

1. Place the soybeans with the remaining ingredients in a blender, pushing the garlic cloves through a garlic press before adding.

2. Process on medium speed until smooth, scraping down the sides of the container and stirring ingredients together as necessary. Cover tightly and store in the refrigerator.

Makes 2 cups **Marinated Mushrooms**

1 pound mushrooms
3 tablespoons lemon juice
1 tablespoon cider vinegar
¼ cup olive oil
¼ cup water
½ teaspoon dried marjoram
½ teaspoon ground coriander
¼ teaspoon celery seeds
1 garlic clove

1. Clean the mushrooms gently with a soft nylon brush. Cut large mushrooms in halves or quarters.

2. Place the mushrooms, lemon juice, vinegar, oil, water, marjoram, coriander and celery seeds in a medium saucepan over medium heat. Push the garlic through a garlic press into the saucepan. Stir everything together.

3. When the mushrooms come to a boil, reduce heat and simmer, stirring occasionally, for 8 minutes. Allow to cool, then chill. Let mushrooms marinate for a day before serving.

Note: After serving mushrooms, save marinade to use as a salad dressing.

Makes 2 cups **Chili Bean Dip**

1 large, ripe tomato, coarsely
  chopped
1 medium onion, coarsely
  chopped
1 fresh hot pepper, halved
2 garlic cloves
2 tablespoons tamari
4 teaspoons chili powder
2 teaspoons ground cumin
2 cups cooked kidney beans

1. Place the tomato, onion, pepper, garlic, tamari, chili and cumin in a blender. Process on medium speed until smooth.

2. Add 1 cup of the beans and process on medium speed until blended. Add the remaining cup of beans and repeat.

Note: Serve dip with natural corn chips, or break up corn tacos into bite-size pieces after heating them for 5 minutes in a 350°F oven.

Hummus Tahini *Makes 3 cups*

To serve as a dip, provide whole wheat pita bread cut in sections or raw vegetables for dipping. For sandwiches, spread the inside of pita bread with Hummus Tahini, *then fill the "pocket" with lettuce, chopped scallions and tomatoes, alfalfa sprouts and minced fresh mint leaves. Even kids like this kind of sandwich.*

1. In the order listed, place the first five ingredients in a blender. Process on medium speed until smooth, scraping down the sides of the container as necessary.

2. To serve, spread about 1 cup of dip in a shallow bowl, swirling a design in the top with a spatula or spoon. Drizzle about 2 teaspoons of olive oil over the hummus, dust with a few grains of cayenne pepper for color, and garnish with parsley sprigs.

Note: Store any leftovers tightly covered in the refrigerator.

2 tablespoons fresh parsley
⅓ cup sesame tahini
½ cup lemon juice
2 garlic cloves
2 cups cooked chick-peas
olive oil, garnish
cayenne pepper, garnish
parsley sprigs, garnish

Soups

Bean and Cheddar Chowder
Makes 6 servings

Rich and delicious, a soup for cold seasons.

1. Pour the water in a kettle, place over high heat and bring to a boil. Melt the butter in a large saucepan over medium heat. Cut the pepper half into large dice and add to the melting butter.

2. Coarsely chop the onion and add to the pepper, stirring over medium heat. Allow to cook a few minutes.

3. Meanwhile, chop the parsley and cut the zucchini into large dice. Add the parsley and zucchini, with the basil, to the pepper mixture in the saucepan.

4. Add the 3 cups of boiling water and the macaroni to the saucepan. Stir, and when boiling, turn down heat. Allow the soup to simmer partially covered, stirring occasionally.

5. Measure out the remaining ingredients. When the macaroni is firm-tender, after about 10 minutes of cooking, add the remaining ingredients and quickly heat through before serving.

Variation: Substitute a celery stalk for the pepper half.

3 cups water
3 tablespoons butter
½ sweet red pepper
1 medium onion
¼ cup fresh parsley
1 small zucchini
1 teaspoon dried basil
¾ cup whole wheat macaroni
1 cup grated sharp Cheddar cheese
1 cup milk
1 cup cooked navy beans
¼ teaspoon turmeric
1 tablespoon tamari

Makes 8 servings # Golden Chili Soup

3 medium sweet potatoes
1 small onion, chopped
3 tablespoons corn oil
2 tablespoons whole wheat flour
3 cups milk
1 cup cooked chick-peas or
    soybeans
1 tablespoon tomato paste
2 teaspoons tamari
2 teaspoons chili powder
½ teaspoon ground cumin
dash of cayenne pepper

1. Fill a medium saucepan halfway with water. Place over high heat. Cube the sweet potatoes and place them in the saucepan. Bring to a boil, reduce heat and simmer, covered, for 15 minutes.

2. Place the onion in a large saucepan with the oil. Cook over medium heat until the onion is translucent and slightly tender. Sprinkle with the flour and stir a minute or two.

3. Add 2 cups of the milk all at once, and stir to eliminate lumps. Add the chick-peas or soybeans, tomato paste, tamari, chili, cumin and cayenne. Bring to a boil over medium to high heat.

4. Place the remaining cup of milk in a blender, and when the sweet potatoes are cooked, drain them and add them to the milk in the blender. Process on low, then medium speed until smooth.

5. Stir the sweet potato mixture into the soup. Serve hot.

Makes 6 servings # Vegetarian Split Pea Soup

Let this simmer away in the oven while you attend to other chores.

1 cup dried split peas
4 cups water
2 stalks celery
2 medium carrots
6 scallions
6 large mushrooms
3–4 large, ripe tomatoes
1 tablespoon tamari
½ teaspoon ground cumin

Preheat oven to 375°F

1. Place the split peas and water in a large flameproof and ovenproof casserole dish. Set over high heat.

2. Chop the celery, dice the carrots, chop the scallions and slice the mushrooms. Cut the tomatoes in half across, squeeze out seeds, and chop the tomatoes. You should have about 2 cups of tomato pulp.

3. Puree the tomatoes in a blender on low speed. Add the tomatoes along with the celery, carrots, scallions, mushrooms, tamari and cumin to the split peas and water.

4. Bring the soup to a boil, stirring occasionally, then place the covered casserole dish in a 375°F oven for about 45 minutes, until the split peas are tender. Serve hot.

Bean and Macaroni Soup *Makes 6 servings*

A hearty soup with complementary proteins of beans and whole grain. Serve with a salad and bread.

1. Heat the oil in a large skillet or saucepan. Cook the onion and pepper until the onion is translucent, about 5 minutes. Then chop the parsley and add.

2. Push the garlic through a garlic press into the skillet or saucepan, then add the bay leaves, basil, oregano and pepper flakes. Add the stock.

3. When the stock is boiling, add the macaroni and cook about 8 minutes, until the macaroni is firm-tender.

4. Stir in the tamari, molasses and beans or chick-peas and cook just until heated through. Remove bay leaves before serving.

3 tablespoons olive oil
¾ cup chopped onions
½ cup chopped green pepper
2 tablespoons fresh parsley
2 garlic cloves
2 bay leaves
2 teaspoons dried basil
1 teaspoon dried oregano
¼ teaspoon hot red pepper flakes
4½ cups *Stock* (pages 175–76)
1 cup whole wheat macaroni
1 tablespoon tamari
1 teaspoon blackstrap molasses
2 cups cooked kidney beans, navy beans or chick-peas

Vegetable Bean Soup *Makes 8 servings*

1. Place a large saucepan with the stock or water over high heat. Dice the potatoes, add them to the pan and cover.

2. Trim the tough outer skin from the broccoli stalks. Coarsely chop the broccoli and add to the pan. When the water boils, turn down heat so soup simmers.

3. Chop pepper, removing and discarding seeds. Add the pepper to the saucepan. Chop scallions and add, along with tamari, basil, oregano, marjoram and tomato paste. Stir to combine.

4. Simmer until the vegetables are firm-tender, about 15 minutes. Stir in the cooked beans, heat through, and serve.

Note: This soup is even tastier when reheated. Just refrigerate or freeze leftovers.

5 cups *Stock* (pages 175–76) or water
2 medium potatoes
1 bunch broccoli
1 sweet red pepper
4 scallions
2 tablespoons tamari
2 teaspoons dried basil
1 teaspoon dried oregano
½ teaspoon dried marjoram
¼ cup tomato paste
2 cups cooked navy or baby lima beans

Curried Chicken and Rice Soup

Makes 8 servings

This is a thick and hearty main-course soup, served with whole grain rolls or crackers and a salad. As an appetizer, it will serve 12. Make it for entertaining or freeze some for later use.

4 chicken breast halves, boneless and skinless
3 tablespoons butter
2 large sweet onions, chopped
2 celery stalks, chopped
3 leeks, chopped
7 cups *Stock* (page 175)
2 tart apples, chopped
3 tablespoons curry powder
3 cups cooked brown rice
1 tablespoon tamari
1 tablespoon lemon juice
2 teaspoons blackstrap molasses
1 garlic clove

Preheat oven to 350°F

1. Cut the chicken breasts into bite-size pieces. In a large heavy-bottom saucepan, saute the chicken in 1 tablespoon of the butter. Remove the chicken and set aside.

2. Add the remaining butter to the saucepan. Cook the onions, celery and leeks over low to medium heat until they are soft and lightly browned.

3. Stir 3 cups of the stock and the apples into the vegetables and add the curry powder. Place the vegetable and apple mixture in a blender, a few cups at a time, and process on low speed until smooth. Place in a large ovenproof casserole dish as mixture is blended.

4. Add the remaining stock and the chicken, rice, tamari, lemon juice, molasses and garlic (pushed through a garlic press) to the vegetable mixture in the ovenproof casserole and stir.

5. Bake at 350°F for 30 minutes, covered. Serve hot.

Vegetarian Main Dishes

Falafel Patties *Makes 6 patties*

The ethnic gourmet's answer to ground chuck. For an appetizer, prepare smaller patties and provide yogurt for dipping.

1. Place the egg, oil, parsley, garlic, tamari, lemon juice and tahini in a blender, and process on medium speed until smooth. Add the chick-peas, cumin, coriander and chili, and process again until smooth, stopping and scraping down the sides of the container as necessary.

2. Using a rubber spatula, stir in the wheat germ by hand, getting well down in the blended mixture to combine thoroughly.

3. Form the chick-pea mixture into six patties, and saute until golden on both sides in a lightly oiled large skillet.

Variations: To serve as a Middle Eastern sandwich, cut whole wheat pita bread in half, open the "pocket," and place one patty in each half. Garnish with chopped scallions, alfalfa sprouts, tomatoes and a spoonful of yogurt.

To serve as a dinner main course, provide two patties per serving. Sprinkle with chopped scallions, tomatoes and sprouts, top with yogurt and garnish with parsley sprigs.

1 egg
2 tablespoons olive oil
2 tablespoons fresh parsley
2 garlic cloves
1 tablespoon tamari
1 teaspoon lemon juice
¼ cup sesame tahini
2 cups cooked chick-peas
1 teaspoon ground cumin
1 teaspoon ground coriander
½ teaspoon chili powder
½ cup wheat germ

191

Makes 4 servings   **Cabbage and Tofu Stir-Fry**

A hearty, delicious meal from very plain ingredients.

½ small head cabbage, thinly
   sliced
1 teaspoon minced fresh ginger
   root
2 garlic cloves, minced
2 tablespoons corn oil
6 ounces cubed tofu
2 tablespoons tamari
2 cups cooked brown rice

1. After slicing the cabbage and mincing the ginger and garlic, heat the oil in a large skillet or wok. Add the cabbage and stir quickly to coat with oil. Add the ginger and garlic and continue stirring.

2. When the cabbage is crisp-tender, after about 3 to 5 minutes, add the tofu and tamari. Stir.

3. When the tofu is heated through, add the rice and continue stirring. When all ingredients are hot, serve promptly.

Makes 4 servings   **Beans Stroganoff**

Use any beans you have on hand in this combination. Serve with Bulgur Pilaf (page 64) or brown rice.

1½ cups chopped onions
 ½ cup chopped green pepper
 3 tablespoons olive oil
 ¾ cup chopped walnuts
 2 cups cooked pinto beans,
    navy beans or soybeans
 1 cup cooked chick-peas,
    kidney beans or lima beans
 1 tablespoon tamari
 1 tablespoon whole wheat flour
 1 teaspoon ground coriander
 ¼ teaspoon paprika
dash of cayenne pepper
 ⅔ cup milk
 ⅓ cup sour cream
 1 tablespoon minced fresh
    parsley
 ¼ cup wheat germ

Preheat oven to 350°F

1. Saute the onion and green pepper in a medium skillet in 1 tablespoon of the oil. When the vegetables are slightly softened, stir in the walnuts. Cook another 2 to 3 minutes.

2. Place the beans in a medium casserole dish. Stir in the onion mixture and tamari.

3. In the pan where the onions were cooked, place the remaining 2 tablespoons of oil. Stir in the flour, coriander, paprika and cayenne. Continue stirring the mixture over medium heat 1 or 2 minutes. Add the milk slowly to prevent lumping.

4. Cook the sauce over low heat just until blended and thickened. Remove from heat, and stir in the sour cream.

5. Stir the cream sauce and parsley into the bean mixture. Sprinkle with wheat germ.

6. Cover casserole and place in a 350°F oven about 30 minutes. Serve hot.

Kidney Bean Pie *Makes 6 servings*

A tasty and different way to serve kidney beans.

1. In a large skillet, heat the oil and melt the butter over low heat. Meanwhile, chop the onion, then add to the skillet. Cook over low to medium heat until translucent.

2. While the onion is sauteing, mash the kidney beans in a medium bowl.

3. Push the garlic through a garlic press into the onion. Stir together, then add the flour. Stir over medium heat for a minute or two before adding the milk.

4. When the onion and white sauce mixture begins to thicken, add the mashed beans, parsley, marjoram or thyme, oregano, tamari and ¼ cup of wheat germ. Stir together.

5. Place the bean mixture in a lightly oiled 9-inch pie plate. Beat the eggs and pour over top of the beans. Garnish with additional wheat germ, then bake at 400°F about 25 minutes, or until golden brown.

1 tablespoon corn oil
2 tablespoons butter
1 medium onion
2 cups cooked kidney beans
2 garlic cloves
3 tablespoons whole wheat flour
¾ cup milk
1 tablespoon minced fresh parsley
1 teaspoon dried marjoram or thyme
½ teaspoon dried oregano
1 tablespoon tamari
¼ cup wheat germ
2 eggs
wheat germ, garnish

Preheat oven to 400°F

Quick Chili Non Carne *Makes 6 servings*

Serve with corn bread and a salad. You will enjoy a spicy treat!

1. Heat a large skillet with the oil and cook the onion and green pepper about 5 minutes, until slightly tender.

2. Meanwhile, bring the stock or water to a boil in a small pan.

3. Add the onion, pepper and the remaining ingredients to the skillet and simmer about 10 minutes.

2 tablespoons corn oil
1 small onion, chopped
½ green pepper, chopped
2½ cups *Stock* (pages 175–76) or water
4 cups cooked kidney beans
⅔ cup tomato paste
2 tablespoons chili powder
1 tablespoon tamari
2 teaspoons blackstrap molasses
1 teaspoon ground cumin
½ teaspoon dried hot red pepper flakes

Makes about 4 quarts **Basic Lentil Stew**

Spend 45 minutes one Saturday morning, and you will have about 4 quarts of a versatile lentil stew that can be used for a range of entrees. With this basic recipe you can plan weeks in advance, freezing portions for terrific tacos, enchanting enchiladas and stupendous spaghetti sauce!

1 pound dried lentils
6½ cups water
2 cups thinly sliced carrots
2 large yellow onions, coarsely chopped
2 green or sweet red peppers, coarsely chopped
3 garlic cloves, minced
3 tablespoons corn oil
3 large, ripe tomatoes, chopped
1½ cups tomato paste
2 tablespoons tamari
2 tablespoons blackstrap molasses
1 tablespoon dried basil
1 tablespoon dried oregano
1 tablespoon chili powder
1 tablespoon ground cumin

1. If desired, place the lentils and water in a large bowl, and soak 2 hours or overnight. (This will hasten cooking time.)

2. Place the lentils, water and carrots in a large pot or kettle and bring to a boil.

3. Place the onions, peppers and garlic in a large saucepan with the oil. Saute until the onions and peppers are firm-tender, then stir them into the lentils.

4. Place the tomatoes in a blender and process until fairly smooth. Add the tomatoes and the tomato paste to the lentils as soon as the lentils are tender.

5. Stir the tamari, molasses, basil, oregano, chili and cumin into the lentil mixture.

Note: For Mexican meals, stir in some extra chili powder, ground cumin and a dash of hot red pepper flakes. For Italian-style dishes, sprinkle with grated Parmesan cheese.

South-of-the-Border Lentils

Makes 3½ cups

Stuff them into tacos, roll them in tortillas, or serve with corn bread and a salad.

3 cups cooked lentils
¾ cup water
1–2 garlic cloves
½ cup raisins
⅓ cup tomato paste
1 tablespoon blackstrap molasses
1 tablespoon chili powder
1 teaspoon ground cumin

1. Combine lentils and water in a large saucepan. Push garlic through a garlic press into the pan. Place over medium heat.

2. Add the remaining ingredients and bring to a boil. Reduce heat and simmer about 15 minutes, stirring occasionally, until the flavors are combined.

Pureed Lentils *Makes 1 quart*

Delicious as a sandwich spread, stuffed into tacos or rolled in tortillas.

1. Cook the onion in the oil in a large skillet over medium heat, stirring occasionally. Slice the celery and carrot very thin and add it to the onion.

2. Stir the mixture, then add the water and raisins and bring to a boil. Reduce heat and simmer.

3. Mince the parsley and add it to the mixture along with the chili and cumin. Simmer until the vegetables are tender, about 5 minutes.

4. Add the lentils and heat through over medium heat, stirring occasionally. Add additional water, if necessary, to prevent sticking.

5. Place small amounts in a blender, and process on medium speed until smooth.

Variation: To serve as a vegetable side dish, omit the chili and cumin, and add ½ cup yogurt to thin the puree. Serve hot.

1 medium onion, chopped
1 tablespoon sunflower oil
1 small stalk celery
1 small carrot
½ cup water
1 tablespoon raisins
1 tablespoon fresh parsley
1 tablespoon chili powder
½ teaspoon ground cumin
3 cups cooked lentils

Lentil Pasta Sauce *Makes 8 to 10 servings*

1. In a very large skillet, heat the oil, and add the onion and green pepper. Cook until the onion is translucent and is slightly tender.

2. Crush the garlic through a garlic press into the skillet. Stir in the lentils, then the tomatoes, water, tomato paste and herbs.

3. Cover and cook over low to medium heat until the lentils are tender, about 40 minutes. Stir occasionally. Serve over whole grain pasta.

Note: For a more liquid consistency, add additional tomato paste and water as desired. Freeze or refrigerate leftovers for future meals. Simply reheat and serve!

3 tablespoons corn oil
1 large onion, chopped
1 green pepper, chopped
2 garlic cloves
1½ cups dried lentils
4 cups Italian plum tomatoes, with juice
2½ cups water
3 tablespoons tomato paste
3 tablespoons minced fresh parsley
2 tablespoons dried basil
1 tablespoon dried oregano
2 teaspoons dried marjoram

Makes 2 servings **Pronto Tortillas**

3 tablespoons tomato paste
2 tablespoons yogurt or water
2 tablespoons chopped fresh
    hot peppers
2 teaspoons chili powder
1 teaspoon ground cumin
2 teaspoons tamari
½ garlic clove
2 cups cooked kidney beans
4 corn tortillas
½ cup shredded Cheddar cheese
chopped tomatoes
chopped onions
alfalfa sprouts

1. Place the tomato paste, yogurt or water, hot peppers, chili, cumin, tamari and garlic in a blender. Process on medium speed until smooth. Gradually add the kidney beans, blending on low or medium speed and scraping down the sides of the container with a spatula when necessary. Continue until all beans have been blended smooth. Place bean mixture in a medium saucepan over low heat.

2. Bring about half an inch of water to a boil in a medium skillet. Heat the tortillas in the boiling water about 30 seconds, or just until softened slightly.

3. Place the tortillas on a baking sheet. Spread the warmed bean mixture over the tortillas in a thick layer to the edges. Sprinkle with the shredded cheese.

4. Place the tortillas under a broiler until the cheese is melted.

5. Serve the tortillas hot, topped with tomatoes, onions and sprouts.

Makes 2 servings **A Tiempo Tacos**

These timely tacos will get you out of the kitchen "pronto."

1½ cups cooked kidney or
    pinto beans
1-2 fresh hot peppers, seeded
3 medium, ripe tomatoes,
    seeded and chopped
2 teaspoons whole wheat
    flour
1 tablespoon chili powder
2 teaspoons ground cumin
1 tablespoon tamari
2 garlic cloves, crushed
    or minced
6 taco shells
¾ cup grated sharp Cheddar
    cheese
1-1½ cups alfalfa sprouts

1. Place the beans with the pepper, ½ cup of the chopped tomatoes, the flour, spices, tamari and garlic in a blender. Process on medium speed until smooth. Place the bean mixture in a medium skillet, and heat over a medium flame until thickened.

2. Meanwhile, place the tacos in a hot oven or under a broiler (not too close) just for a moment or two, turning them before they begin to brown.

3. When the bean mixture and tacos are hot, assemble by placing some of the bean mixture in each taco shell, topping with grated cheese. Add the remaining chopped tomatoes and sprouts. Serve with plenty of napkins!

Tostadas *Makes 2 servings*

"Excellent in every way!" So who's going to argue with success?

1. Place the tomatoes, pepper, scallions, tamari and garlic in a blender. Process on medium speed until smooth.

2. Warm the oil in a heavy-bottom skillet. Add the beans all at once to minimize spattering. Heat the beans through while stirring and crushing them with a wooden spoon.

3. Put about an inch of water in a skillet just large enough to hold a tortilla. Heat the water, bringing it to a boil. Place tortillas in the boiling water one at a time, just long enough to soften each of them slightly, then remove to a baking sheet. Place the four tortillas close together on the baking sheet.

4. Spread the tortillas with the beans, then top with the blended tomato sauce. Sprinkle with cheese and place under a broiler until the cheese is melted.

5. Serve hot, garnished with alfalfa sprouts and avocado slices.

1 cup chopped tomatoes
1 fresh hot pepper, seeded
2 scallions, chopped
2 teaspoons tamari
1 garlic clove, crushed
1 tablespoon corn oil
2 cups cooked pinto beans
4 corn tortillas
½ cup grated sharp Cheddar cheese
½ cup alfalfa sprouts, garnish
½ avocado, thinly sliced, garnish

Chick-Peas with Spinach *Makes 2 servings*

Make a meal by adding whole wheat bread and salad, or serve with Bulgur Pilaf (page 64). This dish has fabulous flavor!

1. Heat the oil in a medium skillet. Stir the onion in the oil over medium heat until it becomes translucent and nearly soft.

2. Stir in the tomato paste, tamari and chick-peas. Add the water and cover, lowering the heat so the mixture simmers.

3. Chop the spinach, mince the parsley, and stir both into the chick-peas. Push the garlic through a garlic press directly into the chick-pea mixture. Stir until the spinach is wilted.

4. Cover and simmer for about 5 minutes, until the spinach is tender and the flavors are well blended. Serve hot.

1 tablespoon olive oil
1 small onion, chopped
1 tablespoon tomato paste
2 teaspoons tamari
2 cups cooked chick-peas
2 tablespoons water
2 cups packed spinach, stems removed
1 tablespoon fresh parsley
1 garlic clove

Crunchy Broccoli Casserole

Makes 4 servings

2 teaspoons safflower oil
2 teaspoons butter
1 medium onion, chopped
1 bunch broccoli
2 cups cooked brown rice
1 cup chopped walnuts
2 teaspoons dried basil
½ teaspoon ground coriander
½ cup ricotta or cottage cheese
4 eggs, beaten
½ cup wheat germ
2 tablespoons grated Parmesan
   cheese

Preheat oven to 350°F

1. Heat the oil and butter in a large skillet. Add the onion and cook briefly over low to medium heat, just until the onion is translucent. Turn off heat.

2. Remove the tough green skin from the broccoli stalks, and cut the stems into ½-inch pieces. Separate the tops into bite-size pieces. Add the stems first to the skillet, over medium heat. After 2 to 3 minutes, add the tops and stir until coated with the oil. Add a few drops of water to prevent scorching, and cover the pan, turning heat low.

3. Stirring the broccoli occasionally, cook about 8 minutes, then add the rice, walnuts, basil and coriander. When heated through, add the ricotta or cottage cheese. Place in a lightly oiled casserole dish.

4. Pour the eggs over the broccoli, and top with wheat germ and Parmesan. Bake 35 to 40 minutes at 350°F, until broccoli is crisp-tender.

Side Dishes

Saffron Rice Pilaf   *Makes 6 servings*

An exotic pilaf with Moroccan flavor, rich with dates and almonds. This recipe yields enough for entertaining so you can share this dish, ready in minutes, since you've cooked the rice ahead.

1. Heat a large skillet with the oil. Add the butter. Turn off heat while slicing onion. Cut onion in half lengthwise, then slice in thin, lengthwise slivers.

2. Turn the heat low to medium under the skillet. Add the onion and saffron. Stir occasionally until the onion is translucent and slightly soft.

3. Meanwhile, cut the dates into small pieces, roughly quartering each of them.

4. When the onions are softened, remove them to the serving dish. Place the almonds in the pan over medium heat, and stir until they begin to turn slightly golden. Add the honey and stir until the almond slivers are coated.

5. Return the onions to the pan and combine with the almonds. Add the dates or raisins, rice, coriander and cinnamon. Stir all together until heated through. Serve hot.

Variation: Substitute 1 cup raisins for dates.

2 teaspoons corn oil
2 tablespoons butter
1 medium onion
¼ teaspoon saffron
1 cup pitted dates
½ cup slivered blanched almonds
1 teaspoon honey
4 cups cooked brown rice
1 teaspoon ground coriander
¼ teaspoon cinnamon

Makes 4 servings # Rice and Peas

1½ tablespoons butter
1 medium onion, chopped
⅓ cup water
1 cup peas
1 tablespoon minced fresh
   parsley
1½ teaspoons ground coriander
2 cups cooked brown rice
parsley sprigs, garnish

1. Melt the butter in a medium skillet and add the onion. Stir and cook until the onion is translucent, adding a little of the water, if necessary, to prevent scorching.

2. Add the remaining water, peas, parsley and coriander, and cover the pan. Over low to medium heat, cook for about 5 minutes, or until the peas are tender, but not too soft.

3. Stir in the cooked rice and heat through. Turn into a serving dish and garnish with parsley sprigs. Serve hot.

Makes 4 servings # Tomato Rice

A rosy rice with Mediterranean flavor.

1½ tablespoons olive oil
2 scallions
1 cup chopped tomatoes or
   halved cherry tomatoes
2 tablespoons minced fresh
   parsley
1 teaspoon dried basil
2 teaspoons tamari
1 garlic clove
2 cups cooked brown rice

1. Heat a medium skillet with the oil. Chop the scallions and add to the heated oil, stirring until slightly softened, about 1 or 2 minutes.

2. Add the tomatoes, parsley, basil and tamari. Push the garlic through a garlic press and add. Over low to medium heat, simmer the mixture until the liquid from the tomatoes has nearly evaporated and the vegetables are soft.

3. Add the rice and stir until heated through. Serve hot.

Makes 3 servings # Orange Rice

A slightly sweet, exotic edition. Wonderful with fish.

1 tablespoon corn oil
2 scallions
1 stalk celery, leaves removed
½ cup chopped walnuts
1 teaspoon finely grated
   orange peel
3 tablespoons orange juice
1 teaspoon honey
⅛ teaspoon ground coriander
dash of turmeric
2 cups cooked brown rice

1. Place a medium skillet with the oil over low heat. Chop the scallions and add, then chop and add celery. Stir, then cook over medium heat until the scallions begin to soften.

2. Add the walnuts and continue to saute for 3 to 4 minutes. The celery should retain some crispness.

3. Remove skillet from heat. Stir in orange peel, orange juice, honey, coriander, and turmeric. Add rice, then place skillet over medium heat until warmed through. Serve hot.

Ginger Rice   *Makes 6 servings*

An aromatic offering, perfect when served with curried dishes but deliciously fragrant anytime.

1. Place rice, stock or water and ginger in a large saucepan over high heat.

2. Bring rice to a boil, then reduce heat and simmer, uncovered, for 5 minutes. Cover the pan, turn the heat very low, and steam the rice 45 minutes. (No peeking or stirring.)

3. Remove pan from heat, still covered, and set aside about 10 more minutes.

4. Toss rice with the butter, then pour rice into a serving dish and sprinkle with parsley.

Note: Store leftovers, tightly covered, in the refrigerator or freezer.

2 cups brown rice
4 cups *Stock* (pages 175–76) or water
2 tablespoons minced fresh ginger root
2 tablespoons butter
chopped parsley, garnish

Parmesan Rice   *Makes 6 servings*

1. In a medium saucepan, melt the butter and stir in the rice. Continue stirring until the rice is coated.

2. Add the stock and the bay leaf and bring to a boil. Boil 5 minutes, then turn heat very low, cover pan and let rice steam undisturbed for 45 minutes.

3. Remove rice from heat and let stand another 5 to 10 minutes. Discard the bay leaf.

4. Toss the rice with the parsley and cheese. Serve hot.

2 tablespoons butter
2 cups brown rice
4¼ cups *Stock* (pages 175–76)
1 bay leaf
⅓ cup minced fresh parsley
⅔ cup grated Parmesan cheese

Brown Rice with Walnuts   *Makes 4 servings*

1. Saute the onion in the butter in a large skillet. When the onion is translucent and begins to soften, stir in the walnuts and toast over low to medium heat for 3 to 4 minutes.

2. Stir in the rice. Turn the heat to low, cover the pan, and heat through, stirring occasionally. Serve hot.

1 small onion, chopped
3 tablespoons butter
⅓ cup chopped walnuts
2 cups cooked brown rice

Makes 4 servings   # Fried Rice

A perfect place for a cup of leftover cooked chicken or turkey to make a hearty main-dish meal.

1 tablespoon corn oil
1 egg
1 stalk celery
4–6 scallions
1 green pepper
½ cup mung bean sprouts
1 tablespoon tamari
1 tablespoon water
2 cups cooked brown rice

1. Heat a large skillet with 2 teaspoons of the oil. Beat the egg, then scramble it in the skillet just until cooked but yet soft. Remove the egg to the serving dish.

2. Add the remaining teaspoon of oil to the pan. Chop the celery and begin to cook over low heat as you chop the scallions and pepper. Add these to the skillet.

3. Turn up heat to medium and continue to cook, stirring, until the vegetables are just beginning to soften, about 4 to 5 minutes. Add the sprouts and stir together.

4. To reduce the chance of spattering, remove the skillet from the heat momentarily while adding the tamari and water. Return skillet to the heat, and stir in the cooked rice.

5. Break up the scrambled egg and stir into the rice mixture. Heat through and serve.

Variation: Add 1 cup shredded, cooked chicken or turkey with scrambled egg and heat through. Makes four main-dish servings.

Makes 4 servings   # Mushrooms and Rice

You can also reheat rice with leftover cooked broccoli, zucchini, summer squash or other vegetables.

2 tablespoons butter
2 scallions, chopped
2 cups sliced mushrooms
2 teaspoons tamari
2 cups cooked brown rice

1. Melt the butter in a large skillet and add the scallions. Cook, stirring, over medium heat until the scallions are translucent.

2. Stir in the mushrooms and cook, stirring occasionally, until the mushrooms are nearly tender.

3. Stir in the tamari, then the brown rice, and heat through. Serve hot.

Marinated Eggplant
and Bean Salad *Makes 8 servings*

This salad keeps well under refrigeration, so serve it anytime during the week.

1. Dice the unpeeled eggplant and steam until soft, about 5 minutes.

2. Meanwhile, chop the pepper and half of the onion. Place in a large bowl. Add the cherry tomatoes, oil, lemon juice, garlic (pushed through a garlic press), basil and oregano.

3. When the eggplant is done, drain it and add to the salad. Then add beans. (Thin rings can be sliced from the remaining half of the red onion to be used as a garnish.)

4. Let the salad marinate in a cool place for at least 40 minutes before serving on lettuce leaves. Garnish with parsley and top with the onion rings, if desired.

Note: Salad is best served at room temperature.

1 large eggplant
1 small green pepper
1 medium red onion
1 cup cherry tomatoes
½ cup olive oil
¼ cup lemon juice
2 garlic cloves
2 teaspoons dried basil
1 teaspoon dried oregano
2 cups cooked kidney, azuki or
   pinto beans
lettuce leaves
parsley sprigs, garnish

203

Makes 4 servings **Soybean Salad Olé**

A colorful, tasty and nutritious dish, South-of-the-Border style.

2 cups cooked soybeans
8 cherry tomatoes, halved
½ cup chopped celery
¼ cup chopped scallions
¼ cup minced fresh parsley
2 fresh hot peppers, minced
¼ cup alfalfa sprouts
2 hard-cooked eggs, chopped
2 tablespoons vinegar
¼ teaspoon Dijon-style mustard
¼ teaspoon chili powder
⅓ cup corn oil
romaine lettuce leaves

1. Combine the soybeans, tomatoes, celery, scallions, parsley, peppers and alfalfa sprouts in a serving bowl. Toss to combine. Top with the eggs.

2. In a small bowl, whisk together the vinegar, mustard and chili. Add the oil very gradually to the mixture, whisking between each addition.

3. Pour the dressing over the salad, and toss gently just before serving. Serve on romaine lettuce leaves.

Salad Toss with
Makes 4 servings **White Beans**

Protein-rich, with beans, cheese and whole grain croutons, this salad scores high in taste, too.

1 small head romaine lettuce
1 large carrot
3 radishes
1 thin slice red onion
½ cup crumbled feta cheese
½ cup cooked navy beans
1 cup *Whole Wheat Croutons*
   (page 97)
Vinaigrette Dressing (page 89)

1. Tear the lettuce leaves into pieces, and place them in a serving bowl. Slice the carrot and radishes very thin, and separate the onion slice into rings.

2. Add the feta, beans and croutons. Add dressing and toss before serving.

Mixed Bean Salad *Makes 6 servings*

1. Place the beans, scallions, radishes, parsley, dill and mint in a serving bowl. Push the garlic through a garlic press and add.

2. Combine the remaining ingredients and pour over the bean mixture; toss to combine thoroughly. Chill to combine flavors.

2 cups cooked kidney, azuki or black beans
2 cups cooked soybeans, navy beans or baby lima beans
4 scallions, chopped
4 radishes, thinly sliced
¼ cup minced fresh parsley
2 tablespoons minced fresh dillweed
1 tablespoon minced fresh mint leaves
2 garlic cloves
2 teaspoons tamari
¼ cup olive oil
2 tablespoons lemon or lime juice
1 tablespoon cider vinegar
1 tablespoon tomato paste

Garlic Bean Salad *Makes 4 servings*

1. Combine the beans, celery and scallion in a serving bowl. Push the garlic through a garlic press and add it to the serving bowl along with the parsley.

2. In a small jar, combine the oil, lemon juice and mustard. Shake, then pour over the salad. Toss to combine.

3. Chill before serving.

2 cups cooked baby lima, navy or pinto beans (or a combination)
1 stalk celery, finely chopped
1 scallion, fincly chopped
1 garlic clove
2 tablespoons minced fresh parsley
2 tablespoons olive oil
2 tablespoons lemon juice
½ teaspoon Dijon-style mustard

Makes 4 servings # Tuna and Rice Salad

Complete a summer meal with a bowl of chilled soup and whole wheat rolls.

2 cups cooked brown rice
1 stalk celery, thinly sliced
2 scallions, thinly sliced
¼ cup minced fresh parsley
1 teaspoon dried basil
6½ ounces water-packed tuna, drained
¼ cup lemon juice
¼ cup olive oil
spinach or lettuce leaves
2 tomatoes, cut in thin wedges, garnish
lemon slices, garnish

1. Toss together the rice, celery, scallions, parsley, basil and tuna. Pour the lemon juice and oil over these ingredients and toss again, until juice and oil are thoroughly distributed.

2. Serve the salad on spinach or lettuce leaves, garnished with tomato wedges and lemon slices.

Breads & Muffins

High-Protein Wheat Bread   *Makes 2 loaves*

A good bread with a fine texture.

1. Scald the milk in a small saucepan over medium heat, and set it aside to cool. Dissolve the yeast in the lukewarm water.

2. Place the dissolved yeast in a very large mixing bowl. Add the oil and honey. When the milk has cooled to lukewarm, pour it into the mixing bowl.

3. Add 2¼ to 3 cups of the whole wheat flour. Beat together the contents of the bowl with an electric mixer for 5 minutes on medium to high speed.

4. Add the soy flour, the rice and enough of the remaining whole wheat flour to make a slightly stiff dough. Knead the dough until smooth and elastic.

5. Place the dough in a warm place, covered with a kitchen towel. Allow it to rise until doubled in bulk. Punch down the dough, and divide it in half. Knead each half into a ball, then press into 8½ × 4½-inch lightly oiled bread pans.

6. Let the dough rise again until not quite doubled in bulk. Cut a shallow slit down the middle of each loaf, and brush the loaves with melted butter.

7. Bake in a preheated 375°F oven for 45 minutes.

1⅔ cups milk
1 tablespoon active dry yeast
¼ cup lukewarm water
¼ cup olive or sunflower oil
¼ cup honey
4½–5½ cups whole wheat flour
½ cup soy flour
1 cup cooked brown rice
2 tablespoons melted butter

Makes 2 loaves **Oatmeal Bread**

A high-protein bread with lots of flavor.

2 cups milk
1 tablespoon active dry yeast
¼ cup lukewarm water
2 cups rolled oats
2 tablespoons butter
½ cup honey
3½–4 cups whole wheat flour
1/3 cup soy flour
2 tablespoons melted butter

1. Scald the milk in a small saucepan over medium heat. Dissolve the yeast in the lukewarm water.

2. Place the rolled oats in a large bowl, and add the butter and honey.

3. Pour the scalded milk over the oats, and stir until the butter is melted. When the milk mixture has cooled to lukewarm, stir in the dissolved yeast.

4. Add 2 cups of the whole wheat flour to the milk mixture, and beat with an electric mixer for 5 minutes. Stir in the soy flour and as much of the remaining wheat flour as is needed to form a slightly stiff dough.

5. Knead the dough until smooth, then set in a warm place to rise, covered with a kitchen towel.

6. When the dough has doubled in bulk, punch it down, divide in half, and knead each half into a ball. Place the two balls of dough on a lightly oiled baking sheet and set in a warm place to rise again.

7. Brush the loaves with melted butter and bake in a preheated 375°F oven for 45 minutes.

Makes 1 loaf **Carrot and Raisin Bread**

An unusually tasty loaf—good enough for dessert!

2 cups whole wheat flour
1 tablespoon baking powder
2 eggs
½ cup safflower oil
½ cup honey
1 cup shredded carrots
1 cup chopped walnuts
⅔ cup raisins
1 teaspoon finely grated
    lemon peel

Preheat oven to 350°F

1. In a large bowl, combine the flour and baking powder.

2. In a medium bowl, beat the eggs and add the oil, honey, carrots, walnuts and raisins. Add the lemon peel.

3. Fold the egg mixture into the dry ingredients. Transfer the batter to an 8½ × 4½-inch bread pan.

4. Bake at 350°F about 1 hour, or until a toothpick inserted in the center comes out clean.

Cinnamon Raisin Bread   *Makes 2 loaves*

For that occasional Saturday when you feel like baking bread, here's the loaf you'll definitely want to try—no tiresome kneading, naturally delicious ingredients and insured success. "Worth the effort!" said the panel of taste testers.

1. Dissolve the yeast in the lukewarm water, and stir in the honey. Warm the buttermilk over low heat, adding the tamari. (Don't worry if the buttermilk curdles.) When the buttermilk is heated to lukewarm, add it to the yeast.

2. Stir the wheat germ and 3 cups of the flour into the yeast mixture. Beat with an electric mixer on high speed for at least 5 minutes, until the mixture is "stretchy."

3. Stir in 1½ cups of the raisins and the cinnamon and oil. Then add the remaining flour, 1 cup at a time, stirring after each addition. As the dough becomes firmer, fold in the remaining flour by hand. Add only enough flour to make the dough smooth, not too stiff. Form the dough into a ball.

4. Lightly oil a large bowl or kettle. Turn the ball of dough around in the oiled container until it is lightly coated. Cover the container, and put it in a warm place until the dough has doubled in bulk. (The time will vary with the temperature and the yeast.) Punch the dough down, form again into a ball, and cover. Allow to rise again to double in bulk.

5. Lightly oil two 8½ × 4½-inch bread pans. Punch down the dough and divide in half. On a lightly floured surface, flatten each half of the dough into a rectangle as long as the bread pans. Sprinkle each with 1 tablespoon of the butter and ¼ cup of the raisins. Roll up and seal edges, placing seam side down in the bread pan.

6. Cover the bread with waxed paper and allow to rise in a warm place until nearly doubled in bulk. Place the bread in a cold oven, and then turn the heat to 400°F. After 15 minutes, turn the heat to 350°F, and bake the bread an additional 45 minutes, or until the bread pulls away from the sides of the pans and sounds hollow when tapped. Cool on racks before slicing.

Variation: For plain *Whole Wheat Bread,* eliminate the cinnamon, raisins and butter.

2 tablespoons active dry yeast
½ cup lukewarm water
½ cup honey
3 cups lukewarm buttermilk
1 tablespoon tamari
1 cup wheat germ
7–8 cups whole wheat flour
2 cups raisins
2 tablespoons cinnamon
¼ cup sunflower oil
2 tablespoons softened butter

Makes 2 loaves # Banana Bread

If you're going to take the time for baking your own specialty bread, it should be nothing less than fabulous. I think this one fits the bill.

1 cup honey
1 cup butter
3 cups mashed, ripe bananas
4 eggs, beaten
1 cup chopped walnuts
1 tablespoon cinnamon
1 teaspoon vanilla extract
3½ cups whole wheat flour
½ cup bran or wheat germ
2 teaspoons baking soda
¼ cup buttermilk

Preheat oven to 350°F

1. Place the honey and butter in a small saucepan over low heat until the butter is melted. Place the mashed bananas in a large mixing bowl. Add the honey and butter, eggs, walnuts, cinnamon and vanilla.

2. Place the flour and bran or wheat germ with the banana mixture. Dissolve the baking soda in the buttermilk and add, stirring all together.

3. Lightly oil two 8½ × 4½-inch bread pans, and divide the batter between them. Bake in a 350°F oven about 1¼ hours, or until a knife inserted in the bread comes out clean.

Note: This bread makes a high-protein breakfast treat when spread with peanut butter. Two loaves will make 20 servings, with two slices per serving. If desired, slice and freeze a loaf for later use.

Makes 1 dozen # Date-Nut Rice Muffins

Good in every way.

1¼ cups whole wheat flour
1½ teaspoons baking soda
½ cup pitted dates
½ cup chopped walnuts
2 eggs
2 tablespoons honey
1 cup buttermilk
2 tablespoons corn oil
1 cup cooked brown rice

Preheat oven to 350°F

1. Combine the flour and baking soda in a large mixing bowl. Cut up the dates and add them to the dry ingredients with the walnuts.

2. In a small bowl, beat the eggs and stir in the honey. Add these to the dry ingredients along with the buttermilk, oil and rice. Stir until combined.

3. Divide the batter among 12 lightly oiled muffin cups. Bake 25 minutes in a 350°F oven.

Honey and Spice Tea Bread   *Makes 1 loaf*
A moist, flavorful specialty bread.

1. In a small saucepan, place the butter and honey over low heat until the butter is melted.

2. Place the flour, baking powder, cinnamon, allspice, cardamom and nutmeg in a large bowl and stir together.

3. Combine the milk with the beaten eggs in a small bowl. Add the vanilla.

4. Add the butter and honey and the milk and egg mixtures to the dry ingredients in the large bowl and stir together just until combined.

5. Pour the batter into a lightly oiled 8½ × 4½-inch bread pan. Bake at 350°F for 1 hour or until a cake tester inserted in the center comes out clean.

½ cup butter
½ cup honey
2¼ cups whole wheat flour
2 teaspoons baking powder
2 teaspoons cinnamon
¼ teaspoon allspice
¼ teaspoon ground cardamom
⅛ teaspoon grated nutmeg
1 cup milk
2 eggs, beaten
1 teaspoon vanilla extract

Preheat oven to 350°F

Tarragon Zucchini Bread   *Makes 1 loaf*
You'll want to use fresh tarragon for this delicately flavored bread. Tarragon is an easy-to-grow perennial.

1. Place the eggs, buttermilk, oil, tarragon, maple syrup and lemon rind in a blender. Process on medium speed until well combined, about 1 minute.

2. In a large bowl, mix together the flour, wheat germ, baking soda and baking powder. Add the egg mixture and zucchini and stir until well combined.

3. Place the batter in a lightly oiled 8½ × 4½-inch bread pan. Bake in a preheated 350°F oven for 1 hour or until a cake tester inserted in the center comes out clean.

2 eggs
¾ cup buttermilk
¼ cup olive oil
3 tablespoons packed fresh tarragon leaves
2 tablespoons maple syrup
½ teaspoon finely grated lemon rind
2 cups whole wheat flour
¼ cup wheat germ
1 teaspoon baking soda
¼ teaspoon baking powder
1 cup shredded zucchini

Makes 1 loaf **Lemon Caraway Bread**

An unusual, slightly sweet loaf, studded with caraway and poppy seeds.

2¼ cups whole wheat pastry flour
1½ teaspoons baking soda
2 tablespoons poppy seeds
1 tablespoon caraway seeds
2 eggs
1 cup buttermilk
3 tablespoons honey
3 tablespoons corn oil
1 tablespoon lemon juice
2 teaspoons finely grated lemon rind
1 teaspoon vanilla extract

1. Combine the flour, baking soda, poppy seeds and caraway seeds in a large bowl.

2. In a medium bowl, beat the eggs and add the buttermilk, honey, oil, lemon juice, lemon rind and vanilla. Stir into the dry ingredients.

3. Pour the batter into a lightly oiled 8½ × 4½-inch bread pan. Bake in a preheated 350°F oven for 1 hour or until a cake tester inserted in the center comes out clean.

Crepes & Fillings

Crepes

If you're intimidated by the idea of making crepes, just think of them as thin pancakes. Glorified flapjacks. That should make them seem less imposing.

Crepes offer an elegant means of conveying leftovers to the table, affording a humble filling an air of mystique. For this reason alone they are worth learning about.

But crepes can also be the basis for the most splendid desserts or delicate main dishes. There is no limit to the number of filling and topping combinations. So give your fancy free flight, and follow up on my suggestions with a better one.

Keep these thoughts in mind when making crepes.

After placing about 3 tablespoons of batter in the pan, swirl the pan immediately to cover the bottom in a thin layer of batter. Swirl the pan gently, now; you're not trying out for the Red Sox. If you can't easily cover the bottom of the pan, try a little more batter next time. If the crepe is too thick, or if there is a lot of excess batter, use less.

About heat: you want the pan hot enough, but not too hot. The crepe should not brown too quickly. If the bottom scorches before the top of the crepe is dry, turn down the heat. If the crepe takes longer than 2 minutes to cook, turn up the heat slightly.

A little oil can be used in the pan, or a little oil followed by a little butter. However, if placed over heat that is too high, the butter used alone can burn. Lightly oil or butter the pan between each crepe.

To store, place a layer of waxed paper between each crepe and wrap well. Refrigerate or freeze. Be sure frozen crepes are completely thawed before using, or they will break.

Makes 12 crepes   # Whole Wheat Crepes

As quickly as you can wrap them, leftovers take on a sophisticated air when served in crepes.

1 cup whole wheat pastry flour
1 cup water
½ cup yogurt
2 eggs
¼ teaspoon vanilla extract

1. Place the ingredients in a blender and process on medium speed until smooth. Stop blender and scrape down the sides so batter is thoroughly mixed.

2. Heat a crepe pan and oil lightly. Pour 2 to 3 tablespoons of batter into the pan, and swirl the pan gently to distribute batter in a thin layer across the pan bottom.

3. Cook on one side until surface appears dry, about 1 minute. Remove to cool on a kitchen towel draped over cooling racks.

4. To serve, wrap crepes around desired filling (some suggestions are included on page 218). Add topping, if desired, and heat through in a preheated 350°F oven.

Makes 10 crepes   # Buckwheat Crepes

1 cup buckwheat flour
⅓ cup apple juice
1 cup yogurt
2 eggs

1. Combine ingredients in a medium bowl and beat until smooth, or place in a blender and process on medium speed until smooth, scraping down the sides as necessary.

2. To make crepes, place about 3 tablespoons of the batter on a hot, lightly oiled crepe or omelet pan. Quickly swirl the pan so that the batter coats the bottom in a thin layer.

3. Cook the crepe over medium heat until bubbles appear on top, and the surface is dry, about 2 minutes.

4. Turn crepe with a spatula or quickly with your fingers, and cook the remaining side about 30 seconds. Repeat for remaining crepes.

5. Cool the crepes on a kitchen towel draped over a cooling rack. Fill and serve immediately, or store.

Carob Crepes   *Makes 12 crepes*

You will never be at a loss for a stunning dessert with these on hand. Wrap them around any of the suggested sweet fillings, mentioned later in this section, or fill with all-natural ice cream or pudding. Top with Whipped Dessert Topping (page 112) or Sweetened Whipped Cream (page 112) for a real show-stopper.

1. Combine ingredients in the order given in a blender. Process on medium speed until smooth, scraping down the sides of the blender as necessary. Let set 5 minutes, then process on medium speed again for about 30 seconds.

2. Heat a lightly oiled or buttered crepe or omelet pan. Pour about 3 tablespoons of the batter into the pan, then tip and swirl the pan immediately to coat the bottom with a thin layer of batter.

3. Cook over medium heat about 1 minute, or until the surface of the crepe appears dry, then turn and cook the other side for 30 seconds.

4. Cool crepes on a kitchen towel draped over a cooling rack. Fill and serve, or store.

⅓ cup whole wheat pastry flour
¼ cup carob powder
3 eggs
½ cup milk
¼ cup safflower oil
1 tablespoon honey
¼ teaspoon vanilla extract

Savory Crepe Filling I   *Fills 10 crepes*

1. Remove stems from spinach. Steam spinach for 2 minutes, until wilted. Drain and chop.

2. Beat the ricotta with the eggs in a medium bowl until light. Add the remaining ingredients and beat again until combined.

3. Fill each crepe with about ¼ cup of the filling. Roll up and place seam side down in a lightly oiled shallow baking dish.

4. Top with tomato sauce, if desired. Bake at 325°F for 15 minutes, until heated through.

Note: Tomato sauce can also be served separately and added at the table.

10 ounces spinach
2 cups ricotta cheese
2 eggs
¼ cup grated Parmesan cheese
2 tablespoons minced fresh
    parsley
2 tablespoons wheat germ
⅛ teaspoon grated nutmeg
tomato sauce (optional)

Preheat oven to 325°F

Fills 10 crepes # Savory Crepe Filling II

Excellent flavor and consistency.

2 cups crumbled farmer cheese
2 eggs
2 egg yolks
¼ cup minced scallions
2 teaspoons lemon juice
1 teaspoon tamari
tomato sauce (optional)

Preheat oven to 325°F

1. In a medium bowl, beat the farmer cheese with the eggs and the additional yolks. Add the remaining ingredients and beat until combined.

2. Fill each crepe with a little less than ¼ cup of the filling. Roll up each crepe and place seam side down in a lightly oiled shallow baking dish.

3. Add a topping of tomato sauce, if desired. Bake at 325°F for 15 minutes, or until heated through.

Note: Tomato sauce can also be served separately and added at the table.

Fills 10 crepes # Savory Crepe Filling III

A quick alternative to manicotti.

2 cups ricotta cheese
¾ cup shredded or diced
    mozzarella cheese
¼ cup grated Parmesan cheese
1 teaspoon dried basil
tomato sauce (optional)

Preheat oven to 325°F

1. Beat the ricotta with the mozzarella, Parmesan and basil.

2. Fill each crepe with about ¼ cup of the filling. Roll up and place seam side down in a lightly oiled shallow baking dish.

3. If desired, top crepes with tomato sauce. Bake for 15 minutes, until heated through.

Sweet Crepe Filling I   *Fills 10 crepes*

Everyone loves the different fruits.

1. In a medium bowl, beat together the ricotta and honey.

2. Fold in ½ cup of the strawberries along with the grapes, bananas and vanilla.

3. To serve, divide the filling between crepes. Place a mound of the filling at one edge of the crepe, then roll up and place seam side down on serving plates. Top with the remaining strawberries.

1½ cups ricotta cheese
1 tablespoon honey
1 cup sliced strawberries
¾ cup seedless grapes, halved
2 ripe bananas, diced
½ teaspoon vanilla extract

Sweet Crepe Filling II   *Fills 10 crepes*

For those days when your sweet tooth yearns to bite into something satisfying.

1. Place the chopped apples and the cider in a blender and process on low speed until smooth.

2. Meanwhile, chop the dates. Add the dates and walnuts to the blender. Process on low to medium speed until smooth.

3. Spread the filling generously on crepes, then roll the crepes, placing each of them seam side down on a serving plate. Garnish with a little whipped cream, if desired, then sprinkle with chopped walnuts.

2 medium apples, chopped
¼ cup apple cider
½ cup pitted dates
¼ cup walnuts
whipped cream (optional)
chopped walnuts, garnish

Sweet Crepe Filling III   *Fills 10 crepes*

Easiest ever! Just blend, spread on crepes and roll.

1. Core and coarsely chop the apple. Place in a blender with the remaining ingredients.

2. Process first on low, then on medium speed until smooth.

3. Spread filling generously on crepes, then roll crepes and place seam side down on a serving plate. Top with a little whipped cream, if desired.

1 tart apple
1 cup blueberries
2 tablespoons apple juice
1 teaspoon lemon juice
drop of vanilla extract
whipped cream (optional)

Crepe Fillings

From dressing up leftovers to creating an original masterpiece—only your imagination dictates the limit to what you can do with crepes.

cooked vegetables (one vegetable or mixed)
cooked fish or poultry, boneless and flaked
creamed spinach
cream cheese mixed with ground nuts
ricotta cheese mixed with chopped dried fruits
stewed dried fruits
scrambled eggs with herbs or tomatoes
applesauce
grated or shredded cheeses
fresh berries mixed with whipped cream

Crepe Toppings

Cheddar Cheese Sauce (page 93)
Maple-Applesauce Topping (page 94)
Blueberry Sauce (page 94)
Whipped Dessert Topping (page 112)
Sweetened Whipped Cream (page 112)
creamed, cooked vegetables
tomato sauce
fresh fruit
grated or shredded cheeses
creamed cooked fish or poultry, boneless and flaked
chopped or ground nuts
finely grated lemon or orange rind
cream soups
sauteed mushrooms

Desserts & Snacks

Vanilla Rice Pudding
Creamy—the way you like it!

Makes 6 servings

1. Combine the cornstarch in a small bowl with ½ cup of the milk. Set aside.

2. Heat the remaining milk, rice, honey and vanilla in a large saucepan. Do not boil. Add the cornstarch mixture.

3. Stir the pudding over low to medium heat for about 8 to 10 minutes, or until the pudding begins to thicken. Again, it must not boil. Remove from heat.

4. Beat a few tablespoons of the pudding into the beaten eggs in a small bowl. Add additional tablespoons of hot pudding to the eggs slowly, until about ½ cup of pudding has been beaten in. (Do not add the pudding too quickly, or the eggs will curdle.)

5. Stir the egg mixture back into the pudding.

6. Pour pudding into individual serving dishes. Serve warm, or chill, if desired.

3 tablespoons cornstarch
3 cups milk
1 cup cooked brown rice
⅓ cup honey
1 teaspoon vanilla extract
2 eggs, well beaten

Baked Rice Pudding with Raisins

Makes 6 servings

1⅓ cups milk
¼ cup honey
1 teaspoon vanilla extract
¼ teaspoon cinnamon
3 eggs
2 cups cooked brown rice
⅓ cup raisins
1 tablespoon butter
dash of grated nutmeg

Preheat oven to 325°F

1. Place the milk, honey, vanilla, cinnamon, eggs and 1 cup of the rice in a blender, and process on medium speed until well combined.

2. Stir in the remaining rice and raisins by hand.

3. Butter a medium souffle dish and pour in the mixture. Dot with butter and add nutmeg.

4. Bake at 325°F for about 50 minutes, or until set.

Rich Rice Custard

Makes 6 servings

1½ cups milk
½ cup heavy cream
⅔ cup cooked brown rice
1–2 cups water
2 eggs
¼ cup honey
½ teaspoon vanilla extract
½ teaspoon finely grated lemon peel
butter
⅓ cup raisins (optional)

Preheat oven to 350°F

1. Place the milk, cream and rice in a medium saucepan over low to medium heat.

2. In a separate pan, bring the water to a boil.

3. Place the eggs, honey, vanilla and lemon peel in a blender. Process on low speed until combined.

4. When the milk and rice mixture is scalded, pour *slowly* into the blender with the egg mixture while the blender is running on low speed.

5. Butter six custard cups, and divide the custard mixture between them. Sprinkle a few raisins in each cup, if desired. Place the custard cups in a baking pan, and pour the boiling water into the pan around them to a depth of about 1 inch.

6. Bake the custard in a 350°F oven for 35 to 40 minutes, or until a knife inserted in the center of each custard comes out clean.

Frozen Grapes *Makes 2 cups*

It's all in the name, but just wait until you taste them! Stock up when grapes are in season, and enjoy them whenever you like. This is a terrific hot weather snack for kids, or anyone!

1. Wash grapes and remove stems.

2. Freeze the grapes in a single layer on cookie sheets. When frozen, store in covered plastic containers.

3. Serve frozen or slightly defrosted so they will be juicier. Eat them plain, or use them as a garnish for many desserts.

2 cups seedless grapes or seeded grapes

Frozen Oriental Persimmons *Makes 2 servings*

Replace high-calorie sherbet with a fresh fruit dessert.

1. If the persimmons are not yet ripe, allow them to stand on a kitchen shelf for a few days until very soft. Rinse the fruit, then freeze.

2. Serve in a bowl with a sprig of mint as garnish. Persimmons can be eaten by scooping out the pulp with a spoon or by cutting them into pieces.

2 persimmons
mint sprigs, garnish

Frozen Banana Pops *Makes 4 servings*

Wonderful in summer, and nothing can be easier. Just pop the bananas into the freezer for a cold, refreshing and nutritious snack.

1. Peel bananas and place on wooden sticks.

2. Wrap bananas in plastic wrap or foil. Place in the freezer until firm.

Variation: For *Carob Banana Pops,* dip the bananas in yogurt, then dust with carob powder. Freeze as above.

4 small, very ripe bananas

Makes 16 servings

Spiced Raisin Squares

1½ cups whole wheat flour
1 cup raisins
½ cup cooked brown rice
½ cup chopped walnuts
1½ teaspoons baking soda
1½ teaspoons cinnamon
½ teaspoon ground cardamom
or ginger
¼ teaspoon grated nutmeg
⅛ teaspoon ground allspice
2 eggs
¼ cup butter
3 tablespoons honey
1 cup buttermilk
1 teaspoon finely grated
orange peel

1. Combine the flour, raisins, rice, walnuts, baking soda, cinnamon, cardamom or ginger, nutmeg and allspice in a large mixing bowl.

2. In a small bowl, beat the eggs. Place the butter and honey over medium heat in a small pan, stirring occasionally until butter melts.

3. Add the eggs, melted butter and honey mixture, buttermilk and orange peel to the dry ingredients, and stir together until thoroughly combined.

4. Place the batter in a lightly oiled 8 × 8-inch baking dish. Bake in a 350°F oven for 30 to 35 minutes, or until a knife inserted in the center comes out clean.

Preheat oven to 350°F

Index

223